AF505838

A Handful of Stars

Concepts on Preaching

**by Maurice Berquist
and Gerald Marvel**

compiled and edited by
Maxine McCall

Church Ministries Division
Warner Press
Anderson, Indiana

All scripture passages, unless otherwise indicated,
are from the King James Version,
the Revised Standard Version, © 1972, Thomas Nelson,
Nashville,
The New King James Bible, © 1979, Thomas Nelson, Nashville,
    or the
HOLY BIBLE, NEW INTERNATIONAL VERSION®.
© 1973, 1978,1984 International Bible Society.
Used by permission of Zondervan Bible Publishers.
All rights reserved.

David C. Shultz, Editor in Chief
Dan Harman, Book Editor
Cover by Larry Lawson

Dedicated

To all the men and women influenced by
Maurice Berquist and Gerald Marvel
to answer God's call to ministry.

May they, like these two pulpit giants
Who have been their inspiration and example,
Ever stand with one hand reaching out to the people
and the other reaching into the heavens to grasp
"A handful of stars."

Table of Contents

Foreword

If a survey were taken within the Church of God (Anderson, Ind) to name the most popular speakers in recent years within that movement, two names would surely surface at or near the top of the list: Maurice "Berk" Berquist and Gerald Marvel.

In many ways these two pulpit giants are similar in their captivating style. Both preach without notes. Both are master storytellers. Both preach with a deep-seated passion for God's Word and a commitment to make it understandable to common people.

Both are skilled at making Scripture relevant to everyday life. And both are remarkably gifted in the art of painting memorable word pictures that nail home their ideas in ways hard to forget. It is not unusual to find people who can recite almost word for word some favorite illustration they heard one of these two men use in a sermon years before

In Berk's later years, his driving passion had been to share whatever he had learned in a lifetime of preaching with as many younger men and women as possible who were just starting out in their preaching careers.

All his life, Berk had been a great mentor for countless young men and women aspiring to serve God in ministry. One of the first of those was Gerald Marvel, who developed a close friendship with Berk. And the one topic, Gerald says, that invariably dominated their conversations was preaching.

In recent years the two were conducting classes on preaching for ministers' retreats and college seminars. Out of these experiences, Berk had proposed that they coauthor a book on preaching. And Berk had, in fact drafted some preliminary chapters, when God interrupted the project by calling Berk home while he was on an evangelistic mission to India in the winter of 1992.

From Berk's manuscript and a collection of audiotapes from Mid-America Bible College, where Berk and Gerald conducted a preaching seminar in 1988, we have been able to capture the secrets of their preaching success for anyone who would learn from these masters how to be more effective in the pulpit.

In keeping with the tone of the work Berk had begun, the book has been written in Berk's voice.

Talking enthusiastically to Marvel one day about the prospective book, Berk quoted a couple of lines from "Caliban in the Coal Mines" by Louis Untermeyer:

God, if You wish for our love,
Fling us a handful of stars!

"That's what we should call the book," he said, *a handful of stars.*

And so it is. For no other image conveys so well what these men through their preaching have tried to do—to touch heaven through God's Word and divine inspiration and grasp "a handful of stars" to bring hope to the people of their generation.

—Maxine McCall

Preface*

I first met Maurice Berquist in 1952, when I was a sophomore in high school. He had just returned from a trip around the world and was preaching at the Oklahoma Youth Convention. I went to hear this dynamic, totally captivating young man who preached on faith. And I remember going home from that convention thinking, "I'll never be a preacher, though I would love to be. And if I ever could be a preacher, I would want to be one like that man."

The next year he was married and returned to Oklahoma, this time to hold camp meeting. Having heard him the year before, I could hardly wait to go. I told my brother, "A preacher is coming to camp meeting that we've got to go hear. He's a preacher like I've never heard before."

My mother, my brother, and I went to that camp meeting. And the tall young preacher was there with his new bride. The campground was abuzz because the new evangelist had come and everybody was so enamored with him. But he was wearing, of all things, a gold wedding band! The church frowned on wearing jewelry in those days; yet we listened to him in spite of it! For he captured all our hearts as he preached the Gospel. I remember standing behind him in the cafeteria line, so captivated by this tall young evangelist and his new bride and wondering if I could ever be a preacher.

I have idolized Berk from day one to this very moment and will as long as I live.

In late summer of 1954 I was in Anderson, Indiana. I was eighteen years old, still trying to make up my mind whether I should try to go to college and study for the ministry or go on to the army. I made a long-distance call to Maurice Berquist in Southern California to ask his advice. Berk and Herb Joiner were at that time involved in starting Arlington College, a school for ministerial studies in Arlington, California.

Berk said, "Get here as soon as you can and give God a chance."

That night I hitchhiked from Anderson to Los Angeles. He met me there and got me a job. He gave about a half dozen of us an old car and said, "This will get you around." They took us in, and we started in studying for the ministry.

In 1956 he accepted the call to pastor White Chapel Church of God in South Daytona Beach, Florida. I saw him again shortly after he had taken that pastorate.

"I hear you are pastoring," I said.

"Yes," he said, "I've been pastorized!"

I recall that some ministers around Southern California said, "He won't make it a year in the pastorate. He is too unconventional; and he has preached so much across the country, he'll never make a pastor."

He pastored that church until 1977, a pretty fair start for a first pastorate—twenty-one years.

Over the years seldom was there a month of my ministry that I did not call Maurice Berquist, just to talk. I remember calling him as a young pastor in my first pastorate in Louisiana. I was so frustrated!

"And another thing, Berk," I said, "three of my church stalwarts sleep every time I preach."

His response: "Don't worry about that, Fats. They trust you!"

So the next Sunday when I rose to preach and they checked out, I said to myself, "Check!"

I've never forgotten that. Berk took care of those matters for me with a word of wisdom, often laced with humor. I always valued his advice.

When he and Berny moved to Vancouver, Washington, in 1987, they came to our church. He used to come to the first service at 8:30, and I would preach. During Sunday school, he would go home to get Berny and bring her back. And then he would listen to me preach again—the same sermon—at 11:00 o'clock. He did that Sunday after Sunday.

During those years while Berk was in our congregation, another preacher said to me, "With his being there, aren't you intimidated when you get up to preach?"

I said, "Honestly, no, I'm not; for there is no man on this earth who is pulling for me more than Maurice Berquist."

Berk prayed for me. And he always had helpful comments. Sometimes during Sunday school he would come and sit in my study, and we would go over the sermon I had just preached. He would, you might say, patch it up for the next service. It was a wonderful experience to be together. Berk was always at his best.

Into the task of preaching he poured all his diligence as a student. He had an extremely keen mind and was forever learning. His quest for knowledge was insatiable. In fact, he read all the time and read widely—in every field. Once, for example, we spent an entire afternoon talking about the engineering feats of Buckminster Fuller, creator of the geodesic dome. Berk saw in Fuller's engineering concepts applications for the ministry, particularly for preaching. In virtually everything he read, he found some application for preaching.

No matter what subject he and I ever started discussing, in any field, we always ... always ... always wound up talking about preaching. He loved to preach. He believed in preaching—the power to communicate the gospel.

His fertile mind brought to the pulpit probing and challenging insights that broke new ground in interpretation of Scripture, making it alive and relevant for everyone who ever heard him speak. He was a creative thinker. And his sermons sparkled with originality and freshness and humor.

Berk loved people. He was always a pastor, even after he left his pastorate in Florida to assume ministerial assignments at national and state levels. He never forgot people, and he always remembered them as individuals. He cared for people as a true pastor. He never grouped or blocked people, never bundled and labeled them, but took every person on his or her own worth. He believed in people and drew the best out of them.

Also an excellent writer, Berk wrote seventeen books and had many more books in mind to write. He was always after me to do a book with him on preaching. We had put down some ideas and had even come up with a title. It was taken from Louis Untermeyer's poem "Caliban in the Coal Mines," in which he said, "God, if you wish for our love, fling us a handful of stars."

Berk said, "That will be the title of our book, *A Handful of Stars*."

I said, "Well, you write the book, Berk; and I'll read it."

And he said, "No, you write the book; and I'll read it."

Berk had started the manuscript before he left for India. And what you now hold in your hands, thanks to our friend and colleague, Maxine McCall, is a compilation of those ideas we put together and shared in seminars at Mid-America Bible College and various other preaching clinics and ministers' meetings around the country.

On the Sunday before Berk died, I was at a meeting with a committee at a restaurant. One of the committee members lived in Berk's neighborhood, and we got to talking about Maurice Berquist. In that conversation I said, almost rhetorically, "Well, Maurice Berquist had one last remaining life's ambition."

They said, "What is that?"

And I said, "To die out on the road preaching."

Little did I realize that in less than fourteen hours that would be the case—that he would die as he wished, doing what he loved best. I really believe God granted him his life's wish—to live and to die preaching.

A Handful of Stars seems a fitting legacy. May you find in the book inspiration, challenge, and help that will be a blessing to your preaching ministry.

That was Berk's greatest wish—and mine.

—Gerald Marvel

* Excerpts from "Eulogy for Maurice Berquist" delivered at his Memorial Service on February 16, 1993, in Wichita, Kansas.

Introduction

God has called us to this ministry of preaching, and whether the world honors it or not, God still honors it.

For everyone reading this book, my earnest prayer is that God will give you a greater ministry. For if I had a thousand lives to live, I would want to live them as a preacher of the gospel.

With Paul I say, "I magnify my office."

I say that not to magnify Maurice Berquist or anyone else. To say that does not mean that I am smarter or better or work harder than anyone else. It is not that I am anything, but that God has called me—as he has called you—to a sacred ministry.

In the act of preaching, we do not glorify ourselves.

What I magnify is the calling God has given me.

It deserves the best I can give it.

If my work is effective, I thank God for it. I hope God will not be ashamed of his call to me—or to you.

The greatest words any of us can hear are these:

"Well done, thou good and faithful servant. Enter into the joy of your Lord."

And I don't interpret those words to mean just in heaven. We can experience joy in God's using us down here.

Over the years I have been blessed to receive help from many people; thus, I feel not only obligated, but also eager to help as many of you as I can to become better preachers. My goal at this point in life is to share anything I have learned that can help you.

Another reason for my wanting to help you preach better is that I care a great deal about what happens to the church. And revival of the church has always been preceded by a revival of preaching.

Twice in my life I have been privileged to hear Clovis Chapel. Considered in the old days to be a prince of preachers, this well-known Methodist minister was in great demand as a speaker. I first heard him preach in Louisville, Kentucky. I was attending seminary there.

As a ministerial student, I had certainly heard of Clovis Chapel. In those days, every preacher had several of Clovis Chapel's books. And many stole his sermons almost verbatim. I never did, but I had always heard that he was a great preacher.

In chapel one day Dr. Frank Caldwell, president of Louisville Presbyterian Seminary, sat on the platform with a guest speaker. I didn't know who the speaker was.

To appreciate fully the drama of the moment, you need to know that Dr. Caldwell was everybody's idea of what a preacher should look like: tall, handsome, impeccably dressed. He had dignity and a gift of speech and diction that made announcing a faculty ball game sound like the Twenty-third Psalm. I took homiletics from him. Or, more accurately, let's say I was exposed to homiletics by him. In any case, he did it correctly. His sermons were precise, very Presbyterian and Calvinistic, and highly effective.

The fellow sitting next to him made quite a contrast. He looked like a retired farmer, sitting there somewhat slouched down in the chair. I thought, "What is this today?"

In due course, Dr. Caldwell rose and said, "Now, gentlemen,"— no women graced the seminary in those days. "Now, gentlemen," he said, "we are honored today to have one of America's most beloved, most honored preachers to speak to us."

He went on to give some credits about all of the man's accomplishments. Then he said, "And so it is my great delight and honor to present to you Dr. Clovis Chapel."

Then this fellow in the rumpled suit got up—I'll never forget it—and he walked to the pulpit and leaned over it—in a way we had been told never to do—and looked around for a moment like a farmer counting his cows. Then he spoke:

> I take a text today—I always take a text—from the Book of Acts, the story of the early church. Now, our text takes us to a strange land where people dress in strange costumes and speak a strange language. And we are, as a matter of fact, in a strange service. And only one thing strikes us as familiar: there arose a murmur.
>
> In my years of pastoring, I have seen churches too dead to pay the debts, too dead to send missionaries, too dead to fight; but never

so dead they couldn't raise a murmur!

And the church was there. And they were murmuring because certain people were neglected in the daily potluck supper. So the apostles said, "We will appoint seven men full of the Holy Ghost and wisdom to handle this and wait the tables, and we will give ourselves to prayer and the ministry of the Word."

Good preaching may not save a church, but it certainly doesn't hurt. And many a church has been ruined by poor preaching, as foolish as it seems.

Now, you men are in seminary, and you will identify with a biblical seminarian—one of the few we read about—who, when the bishop sent him to his first pastorate, looked out over the congregation and behold they were very dead. So dead there was not even a murmur.

And he looked out, and with the critical eye of the scholar he observed their characteristics: they were all dead bones.

But our seminarian was not ill prepared for that, for he had studied pastoral methods and began immediately to organize those dead bones. He said, "I think I'll put all the ankle bones over here; shin bones over there. I'll make a committee of the head bones over here; trombones there—because we have this fantasy in our church—Methodist church, of course—that if you get the data on three-by-five cards, it always looks a little more powerful."

So he is organizing the church—but it's still a dead church—when God comes and says, "I didn't call you to organize. I called you to preach."

And Ezekiel began to preach.

Now, he didn't preach because he saw any results. He preached because he was called to preach. Prophesy to the wind!

And then, the thing began to happen. And those dead bones began to organize themselves. And they began to join, and finally to move, and to be clothed with flesh.

Gentlemen, that is God's call to you—to preach.

And that, my friends, is a major theme of this book. God has ordained preaching as a means to energize his church. Organization alone will not revive a dead or dying congregation. God-ordained and God-inspired preaching will.

Contrary to what some people think, preaching is important. Jesus himself said that he was anointed to preach:

> The Spirit of the Lord is upon Me,
> Because He has anointed Me to preach
>   the gospel to the poor.
> He has sent Me to heal the brokenhearted,
> To preach deliverance to the captives
> And recovery of sight to the blind,
> To set at liberty those who are oppressed,
> To preach the acceptable year of the Lord.
>
> (Luke 4:18, NKJV)

Note the sequence there:

Before he mentioned anything about healing or a social ministry to the poor, Jesus said, "He has anointed me to preach."

Preaching is not all there is to being a pastor, but it is way ahead of whatever is in second place. And I am covetous for the church that we have the best preaching possible in every pulpit to inspire and challenge people in the work of God's kingdom.

At this stage in my life, I view the privilege of talking to young men and women just entering the ministry, as well as to more seasoned pastors who may be discouraged or disillusioned about their work in ministry, as perhaps the most important work I do. And as Gerald Marvel and I spoke of writing this book, our prayer was that it would be a blessing to thousands of ministers who might read it and be strengthened and encouraged.

Through the ministry of this book, may we see souls saved, churches renewed, built, and revived. May the Spirit of God breathe upon us now as in the bone-yard of Ezekiel so that the body of Christ comes together and the whole church rises to praise God!

* * * * *

Our Father, we are thankful for those who will seek inspiration and help from the reading of this book, but more important, who shall in their lifetime share the precious treasure of preaching.

Although we meet with many people in many places in this world, we feel a strange and wonderful kinship with those who are called to preach. We are united by a particular bond, a certain camaraderie, a certain understanding, a certain interdependence.

We thank you for that spirit of kinship and for the open hearts and minds that have received what you have given us. We thank you, also, for the many people who have contributed to our lives—those who have been mentors by their personal input, those who have written things that have helped us, and those who have been models and examples for us.

We pray your blessings upon all who are called into this holy, rewarding ministry of preaching the Word of God.

And today for those who peruse the pages of this book, may they find enlightenment and relevance in what you have given us to share, that the thoughts included herein may be helpful to those who desire to create a better pattern and practice of preaching.

In Christ's name we pray this and believe. Amen.

—Maurice Berquist

Chapter 1

The Stubborn Pulpit

"The surest proof of the truth of Christianity is that it has survived the preaching of its friends."

That statement was handed to me in a note one night after I had spoken in a church service. It was folded like a check, and I welcomed it with restrained delight. Since it looked like a check, I did not unfold it until I was safely in my room.

There, to my utter disappointment, I unfolded not a check, but a bit of practical wisdom masquerading as humor … or criticism … or the naked, unwelcomed truth.

Well, having long ago recovered from that startling, though unforgotten, missive, I can tell you this glad truth today: not only has Christianity survived, but preaching as well!

Scorned by its enemies, ignored by millions, attacked by its friends—still, preaching has survived.

That says something for it.

My office boasts a collection of turtles, all kinds of turtles: brass turtles, ceramic turtles, wooden turtles, even a solid silver turtle. People who know I like turtles keep sending them.

Turtles teach us a lot about life. Note some of their admirable qualities:

1. Turtles are among the oldest creatures surviving.
2. Turtles make progress only when they stick their necks out.
3. Turtles know when to stick their necks out and when to pull in and be content within themselves.
4. Turtles win races by persistence.

In many ways these turtles adorning my office are miniature sermons, for they are the ultimate survivors.

Like the noble turtle, preaching survives.

It comes as no surprise that many obituaries have been written for preaching. Prophets of gloom point to declining audiences and discouraged preachers as they announce the death of preaching. But like Samuel Clemens' observation upon reading in the paper of his demise—"The news of my death is greatly exaggerated"—the same can be said for preaching.

Clyde Fant's observation speaks well to the point:

> Whatever virtues the pulpit may lack, stubbornness is not one of them. The vine over Jonah's head would have withered in less than a day if it had suffered the heated blasts directed at the pulpit across the centuries.

In every age, thoughtful and scholarly men have spoken last rites over the art of preaching. But preaching survives.

In 1923 Joseph Fort Newton quoted the *London Times* as saying, "For the present at least, the noble art of the pulpit must be considered as lost." He asked, "If the great sermons of Bishop Butler were preached today, would they fill the smallest church in London?" Newton pointed out that "in his own day, the Bishop sat in his castle brooding over the decay of religion, while the miners, touched by the wondrous evangelism of Wesley and Whitfield, were singing hymns of praise almost under his window."

Not long ago I walked with a professor across a seminary campus. Our conversation ranged over many subjects, but mainly we spoke of the changes taking place in the life of the church. We talked about new approaches to evangelism and service to humankind.

"One thing is certain," said my friend, "the day of preaching is over."

That from a professor of homiletics—a specialist in the art of preaching!

My friend and colleague in ministry, Gerald Marvel, had an unsettling experience when he was a beginning pastor in Louisiana. He attended the local Kiwanis Club, where on one occasion the dean of a nearby university addressed the group about the future. Backed by skilled research, he told of miracles awaiting them in the rest of this century, including massive telecommunications networks.

"Preaching as we know it," he said, "will be a thing of the past. Instead of local churches and local pastors, there will be only a few televised preachers who will speak to the masses."

As a young pastor sitting in that audience, Gerald was tempted to be overly impressed by the authoritative voice and the prestigious title of the guest speaker. His mind grappled with the man's disturbing words. Could it be true that he, a young man, was at the beginning of a doomed career?

Observe that years later that dean is no longer at the university. His career and circle of influence are gone. Yet Gerald is still preaching, and increasing numbers of people are responding.

If preaching is indeed dead, it is a strangely active corpse!

Today Gerald says of preaching and television:

> I don't watch television much … headline news is about all. But every year television networks come out with new programs. And people eagerly await the Nielsen ratings to see which programs capture top billing in the ratings race. These programs all have a bevy of script writers, top-name performers, fancy sets or on-location filming, elaborate plots, intrigue, and action! Oh, how we have to have action today—explosions, cars tumbling end over end! We've got to entertain the public!
>
> "Preaching is dead!" That's what the Neilson ratings tell us. Preaching is "out." TV is "in."
>
> Listen. Television programs come and go—with all the script writers, the paraphernalia, and everything else that goes with them. But every week I stand before my congregation—my material five thousand years old! I open the Script. Ninety percent of the people who hear it read have heard it all their lives. I read it. Then I close the Book and expound on it. And people come to listen Sunday after Sunday after Sunday. It has been going on in my personal life for more than thirty years. The Neilson ratings never touch it. And in recent years more and more people have been coming to hear it.
>
> Preaching is not dead!
>
> It is demanding. It is powerful. It will always have a place. Contrary to some popular opinions these days, I hold firm to the belief that it is the preaching of God's Word that builds the church.

Gerald is right. Recent statistics report that on any given Sunday morning in America, more people attend church than attend all professional athletic events combined for an entire year. And in almost all of these services, preaching is considered the main event.

Not a bad record for a dying art!

Through this book we hope to show that preaching the gospel is not only an important part of the past, but also a vital part of the future.

Without question, preaching and preachers deserve some of the bad press. One critic observed that he had listened to three kinds of sermons: "Dull, duller, and dullest."

But listen, my friend. Preachers may be trivial, but preaching is not. Sermons may be irrelevant, but the gospel is not. There have always been and will always be dead preachers droning dead sermons to dozing congregations. But this sad fact does not consign the future of preaching to the obituary columns. God has ordained preaching as a way to reach people in this world.

Preaching is not dead. Real preaching is very much alive.

To be sure, some kinds of preaching are dying—and none too soon. Mistaken ideas about preaching have only their antiquity to recommend them. They deserve to die.

That statement is not meant to dishonor any of God's servants who preached in the past. We honor both the people and their methods. God used them. Who is to say that the quill pen of the Apostle Paul was less effective than the typewriter or the word processor of a modern preacher? Who can say that the flowery language that adorned the oratory of a nineteenth-century preacher was not effective in its time?

Honoring such preaching is good; imitating it is deadly!

If preaching is living, it is constantly changing. Life is changing. One generation leaves; another comes. In the words of Thomas Carlyle: "The story of history is simply that of silken slippers going down the stairs and hobnailed boots coming up."

Put plainly, God still speaks through the voices of those God has called. Their message is not an echo of the past, but a fresh revelation. Its authority comes not from its antiquity, but its authenticity. God is still God, and his Word is still his Word. Such a message has vitality and power. It moves.

Without freshness, preaching is like Coleridge's ship in "The Rime of the Ancient Mariner," as idle "as a painted ship upon a painted ocean."

Picture perfect preaching pleases purists, but it is plastic and powerless. In it God becomes the Great "WAS" instead of the Great "I AM."

Preaching is an event. It lives!

We cannot sail today's boat on yesterday's wind, however strong it blew. Thus, we must venture into the present to rediscover God's authentic call. Both the successes and failures of the past have brought us to this present exciting moment—a step into the future.

Chapter 2

The Authority of the Pulpit

Gerald Marvel and I have arrived at an axiom about preaching. Simply stated, it goes like this: *Your preaching will be about as important to other people as it is to you.*

Amazingly, some of the strongest criticism of preaching has come from preachers. They shoot themselves in the foot, then wonder why they limp! Or, changing the metaphor, they make the question mark their coat of arms and then wonder why they cannot rally God's troops to battle.

Too many pastors have allowed their churches to minimize preaching. Sometimes out of frustration, sometimes out of discouragement, sometimes out of despondency—preachers have replaced preaching in their lives. They have found it more expedient to substitute other things—administrative duties or counseling or programs of various kinds—for preaching. And the church is suffering for it.

Have they never read the Scripture "if the trumpet makes an uncertain sound, who will prepare himself for battle?" (1 Corinthians 14:8, NKJV).

Unconvinced preachers are unconvincing preachers.

I remember the early years of our trying to build Arlington College—now part of Azusa University. The school occupied Army camp facilities—an officers' clubhouse and barracks—that had formerly been a part of Camp ANZA during World War II. In those early days the students took turns cooking breakfast. Since the "cooks" had to be the first ones out of bed, they had the job of not only preparing the food, but also sounding the alarm. We had, as I recall, a toy trumpet that could sound only a few notes. So each morning we were awakened by "Taps" because no one knew how to play "Reveille."

Now that I think of it, we should not have been surprised if students had pulled the covers over their heads and gone back to sleep!

Listen, pastor, if the trumpet we sound from our pulpits has an uncertain sound we should not be surprised when we fail to rally the troops!

If you are not sure that God has called you, that the words you speak are *God's words*, and that the spirit that motivates you is *God's Spirit*—it is doubtful that you will be received as *God's ambassador.*

In the preaching ministry, without God's call we have no authority, no capability, and no security.

We all have heard of the timid shadow of a preacher who crept into the pulpit and whined: "If you do not believe as it were and repent in a measure, you will be damned I fear to some extent."

The yawning silence that answered was kinder than he deserved.

Not that the raucous thundering of an empty mind and heart would have been any better. Nowhere is uncertainty and emptiness more visible than in the pulpit. If the preacher is to speak for God, it is imperative that God has called him or her to speak. A preacher unsure of God's call will also be unsure of what God has called him or her to say.

On the other hand, a preacher certain of God's call can walk with quiet confidence into the arena of the lions of criticism and challenge.

Sometimes the called preacher will be like the called Abraham, who journeyed *"not knowing wither he went,"* but that he was headed for a promised land that God would afterward give him. Every authentic minister knows the anxiety of searching for God's message, but that he or she is to be God's messenger should never be open to question. The call to preaching is the first assurance that God will effectively use the preacher. *"He is faithful who calls you, who also will do it"* (1 Thessalonians 5:24, NKJV).

The words that came to Jeremiah ought to be written large and legibly on every preacher's desk—and indelibly on the heart:

> The word of the Lord came to me, saying,
> "Before I formed you in the womb I knew you,

before you were born I set you apart;
I appointed you as a prophet to the nations."

"Ah, Sovereign Lord," I said, "I do not know
how to speak; I am only a child."

But the Lord said to me, "Do not say,
'I am only a child.' You must go
to everyone I send you to and say
whatever I command you. Do not
be afraid of them, for I am with you
and will rescue you," declares the Lord.

Then the Lord reached out his hand
and touched my mouth and said to me,
"Now, I have put my words in your mouth.
See, today I appoint you over nations
and kingdoms to uproot and tear down,
to destroy and overthrow, to build and to plant."
(Jeremiah 1:4–10, NIV)

The young prophet of Anathoth, known more for his tears than his triumphs, would have many occasions to remember this call. It was all that sustained him. Many were the times when he wished he had never been called, but he never doubted the reality of the call—its painful reality.

He would have understood the modern Jewish lad on his way to the synagogue. He let his hand rest lightly on the shiny Mercedes automobile of his wealthy Arab neighbor and commented: "Sometimes I wish we were not the chosen people."

Sometimes the call is a call to frustration before it is a call to fulfillment. Jeremiah experienced that truth:

O Lord, you deceived me, and I was deceived;
        you overpowered me and prevailed.
I am ridiculed all day long;
        everyone mocks me.
Whenever I speak, I cry out
        proclaiming violence and destruction.
So the word of the Lord has brought me
        insult and reproach all day long.

> But if I say, "I will not mention him
> or speak any more in his name,"
> His word is in my heart as a burning fire,
> a fire shut up in my bones.
> I am weary of holding it in; indeed I cannot.
> (Jeremiah 20:7–9, NEV)

In this lament of the weeping prophet, we can understand his anxiety. But we can only imagine the increased level of anxiety he would have felt had he not responded to the call to preach. While the way of obedience is sometimes difficult, the way of disobedience to the call is impossible.

Paul sensed this dilemma when he cried out: *"Woe is me if I do not preach the gospel"* (1 Corinthians 9:16, NKJV).

One of the greatest guarantees that God still uses preaching to reach people is that God continually calls people to be preachers. It is part of God's eternal plan.

At times every preacher may feel like one pastor who, having met with little obvious success in his ministry, said: "When I get to Heaven I am going to ask God why he called me to preach and didn't tell me *how*." An earthly answer will have to suffice for this frustrated minister until he reaches the Celestial City. The truth is that God may indeed have called him both to preach and to learn how to preach.

As long as we live, we preachers will be searching for the best way to preach. On numerous occasions we may find ourselves uncertain about what to preach. But somewhere, undergirding all our questions, must be the assurance that God has called us to preach.

One of the strongest assurances of our call to preach is the anxiety that assails when we disobey that call. Jonah could testify about that. Little did he relish the thought of carrying God's message to the pleasure-mad people of Nineveh; but while he was in the Seaweed Chapel of the fish's belly, the prospect of preaching surely seemed far more attractive.

God Speaks

Whether or not we honor preaching *God honors it.* God is revealed through speech. It has been so since the beginning of time. The formless darkness of Genesis was changed by what the Almighty spoke. Light, life, and finally humans came into being, because "God *said.*" And that was only the beginning of the creative speech of God.

Speech was and is creative.

Other religions in the world may have their personalities, their altars, and their sacrifices. But these lower-case gods do not "utter a sound with their throats" (Psalm 115:7, NEV).

Through the Old and New Testaments God *spoke* to people:

> In the past God spoke to our forefathers through the prophets at many times and in various ways, but in these last days he has spoken to us by His Son whom He appointed heir of all things.
>
> (Hebrews 1:1, 2, NEV)

Jesus himself saw his ministry as a fulfillment of the promise made in the Old Testament when he stood in the synagogue to read the ancient prophecy of Isaiah: "The Spirit of the Lord is upon me … to preach the acceptable year of the Lord" (Luke 4:18, 19, NKJV).

Jesus was not only to be the incarnate Word, but he was also to be the *preacher* of the Word. If God honored his Son by sending him to this wayward planet to *preach*, we should not take lightly our call to *preach*. In fact, the "Great Commission" as recorded by Mark says, "Go into all the world and *preach the gospel* to every creature" (Mark 16:15, NKJV).

We have not yet discussed what preaching is, but even the dullest spiritual ears know what it is *not*.

Jesus not only gave the call to preach, he gave the pattern of how to preach. His words fell like hammer blows on the encrusted religious traditions. He "taught them as one having authority, and not as the scribes" (Matthew 7:29, NKJV).

Then, as now, people recognize the difference between *proclaiming* and *disclaiming*.

Modern critics of preaching have pointed out that many sermons are like colorful travel folders describing exotic places to which the speaker has never gone. Such a "would-be preacher" is not a voice, but merely an echo of another's opinion.

Preaching has its roots in the soul of a man or woman called to preach. Mere speaking may have its roots only in the mind. It is not difficult to tell the difference.

If preaching is without friends, the rejection has most likely been aimed at pseudo-preaching. A mere recitation of sociological commentaries—or biblical texts, for that matter—is not preaching. Could it be, to paraphrase an often-quoted observation about Christianity, that preaching has not been tried and found wanting; true preaching has been found difficult and not tried?

Whatever the world's opinion of preaching, God's opinion is still high. The coming of the gospel age is heralded by God's calling preachers.

Those who listened to the newly empowered disciples who came down from the Upper Room on the day of Pentecost had no vocabulary to describe what they saw. Drunkenness seemed the most logical explanation.

Peter enlightened them:

> These men are not drunk, as you suppose …
> No, this is what was spoken by the prophet, Joel:
> "In the last days, God says,
> I will pour out my Spirit on all people.
> Your sons and your daughters will prophesy,
>   your young men will see visions,
>   your old men will dream dreams.
> Even on my servants, both men and women,
>   I will pour out my Spirit in those days,
>   and they will prophesy."
>
> (Acts 2:16–18, NEV)

We do not assume that the 120 persons who met in the Upper Room were the only ones who believed that Jesus was the Word made flesh. Certainly others believed. But not until Peter's inspired preaching on the day of Pentecost did the thousands respond. *The preaching was incarnational.* The Word, spoken with the authority of the Spirit, melted hearts. *Preaching made the words of God come alive to BE the Word of God.* That is the difference.

Small wonder that the authorities, frightened by this powerful minority of Spirit-filled preachers said, "Speak no more in his name."

Speak no more. If only these flaming evangelists could be kept quiet, the strange doctrines they believed could be kept in a corner. Preaching had power and its enemies knew it!

The disciples responded to these stern warnings with a standard answer: "We cannot help speaking the wondrous works of God" (Acts 5:20). Speak they did, with the threat of imprisonment, exile, and death. The Word of God was again clothed in flesh, often the lacerated flesh of believers chained to a whipping post.

When Paul listed the priorities of spiritual gifts, it is no coincidence that prophecy led the list. Not content with merely emphasizing prophecy on the list, Paul explains why he thinks the proclamation of the gospel is so important:

> Follow the way of love and eagerly desire spiritual gifts, especially the gift of prophecy ... everyone who prophecies speaks to men for their strengthening, encouragement, and comfort ... he who prophesies edifies the Church ... he who prophesies is greater than one who speaks in tongues ... if an unbeliever or someone who does not understand comes in while everybody is prophesying, he will be convinced by all that he is a sinner and will be judged by all, and the secrets of his heart will be laid bare. So he will fall down and worship God, exclaiming, "God is really among you!"
>
> (1 Corinthians 14:1–5; 24–25, NEV)

What is this strange magic of preaching that makes scoffers who come to laugh remain to pray? What brings the atheist or the agnostic into a sanctuary and there to fall on his or her face and declare that "God is in this place"? Is such power still possible?

Not long ago a businessman began to attend worship services in Vancouver, Washington. After several Sundays he asked to take the pastor to lunch.

"I have a question," he began. "Do you realize that while you are preaching something happens to you? You are changed. And," he added, "so am I."

How do you explain such a metamorphosis unless it is the authentic preaching event?

Recently I served as interim to a congregation seeking pastoral leadership. The Sunday before my arrival, the people responded to a survey designed to identify their expectations for a new spiritual leader. I read the results. On every form "inspirational preaching" was number one.

If listeners want it … if God ordains it … and Jesus exemplifies it, perhaps we who are called to preach should take a hard look at what preaching really is. If God has truly called us, God will help us do it.

Our Attitude Speaks

Consider again the axiom: *Your preaching will be about as important to the people who hear you as it is to you.*

Conviction is contagious. If we regard preaching as the necessary filler between the announcements, the songs, and the rush to beat neighboring churches to the cafeteria, little wonder that it has no power to inspire any emotion but sympathy. Note well—the sympathy will not always be for the preacher.

One day when I was pastoring in Daytona Beach, a salesman showed up at my office. His opening line after claiming a chair near my desk was, "Pastor, I'm here to solve your problem."

My unspoken reaction was, "Where have you been all my life?"

Unaware of my thoughts, he continued, "I have a guaranteed formula for getting a crowd out on Wednesday night to prayer service."

Then I spoke. "Well, I'm really not interested."

Stunned, he said, "You're not?"

"No, not really."

"You mean you don't have a problem with Wednesday night prayer service?"

"Not particularly. We're setting up chairs now in the back of the sanctuary. We're full up for prayer meeting."

With an incredulous, raised eyebrow, he said, "What program do you have on Wednesday nights?

Aware of his rising curiosity, I said, "Oh, it's fairly orthodox. We sing some songs; have prayer around the altar; I give a Bible study; and we go home. The church is full, and people are sitting in chairs behind the back row."

He was now leaning forward in his chair. "If you've got some secret, I'd sure like to know about it."

"Well, I do have a secret."

"What is it?"

"Something quite simple really: I think prayer meeting is important."

"That's no secret."

"Oh, but it is."

And then I told him this story:

When I first came to this church, we were experiencing the conventional pattern of church demise. Our biggest service was Sunday morning, with about half of that number on Sunday night and half of that on Wednesday night. That's the average ratio of attendance for church services. And I assumed that was normal. I lived with it for a couple of years. And then, one day, something happened.

One week a man in my church who was going to Atlanta on business invited me to go along.

"Ride with me up to Atlanta on Monday," he said. "We'll be back Tuesday night or Wednesday noon at the latest."

"Okay," I said, "I'll ride along. I'd like to spend some time with you."

So we drove up to Atlanta. He spent Monday and Tuesday out buying merchandise and what not. Then Tuesday night he said, "I'm not finished yet. I may have to stay a little longer."

And I said, "Well, okay."

On Wednesday morning he got up and said, "Based on the appointments I've got today, we probably won't get back to Daytona by tonight."

"Well, in that case," I said, "I'll fly home."

"Do you know what it will cost to fly home?" he asked.

"No, but I'll find out."

So, I called the airline. "I want a ticket one way from Atlanta to Daytona."

Airlines have special rates now, but back then there were no special rates. I remember exactly what it cost. It cost eighty-five dollars. This was during the 1950s. Eighty-five dollars was my total week's pay. Cash pay. I had a house to live in, but I mean that eighty-five dollars was my cash income for a week.

Nevertheless, I went out to the airport, and I bought a ticket for eighty-five dollars and flew one hour to Daytona.

When time for the evening service came, I was there with my usual half-of-the-half of the people who came regularly for prayer meeting. And I did the usual thing.

After service they said, "We thought you went to Atlanta this week with Buddy."

"I did."

"Is he back?"

"No, he's not back."

"How did you get back?"

"I flew."

"Well, how did you fly?"

Dumb question. They knew I didn't get home flapping my arms. Nevertheless, I gave the obvious answer: "I took an airplane."

Next question: "Wasn't that expensive?"

"Yes."

But they really probed: "How expensive was it?"

"Eighty-five dollars."

They knew what I got paid. And the next question was, "You mean you spent eighty-five dollars to come to prayer meeting?"

"That's right."

"Why?"

"Because I thought it was important."

From that moment on—I told the salesperson as I am now telling you—our prayer meeting crowds began to build. After that day nobody would ever say to my face, "Well, I was going to come tonight, pastor, but it started to rain at the last minute." Or "I had to attend the PTA." Or "Aunt Tilly came to see me, and I didn't want to leave her home alone." From that Wednesday on, there were very few excuses.

It didn't require a program; it didn't require a change. All it required was that I let them know I thought it was important.

Today, I fear, too many pastors are giving their congregations the impression that church services are not all that important. I see a growing trend to dismiss church on a whim—a dinner at the church, a ball game, some community function. Any excuse to get out of preaching is welcome. Listen, if we get in the habit of substituting other meetings or other agenda in the place of assembling together to hear the proclamation of God's Word, we should not then wonder why nobody comes.

Our Call Is Based on God's Authority

"Then Lord reached out his hand and touched my mouth and said to me, 'Now, I have put my words in your mouth' (Jeremiah 1:9, NIV).

Oh, what a challenge that is!

If we preachers are not into the Word, we are speaking our own opinions. And we have no more authority than our own opinions.

As I preach and lecture around the country, surprisingly I have found all too often that the biggest critics of what I teach are preachers, because I make some rather bold statements about healing and about God's guidance and other things. Preachers will say to me, "Berquist, you're far out. You're off the wall. How can you say these things?"

My standard response is this: "I don't say them. I'm just *reading* them! If you don't like the copy, talk to the Author. Is this what it *says?*"

"But we don't understand it that way."

"Forget what you understand. *This* is what Scripture *says*. If it requires explanation, let God explain it."

Our call—and our preaching—is contingent upon God's authority.

I often preach on healing. I say, "The Bible says God wants to heal everybody."

As sure as I say that in any church meeting, half a dozen people will confront me afterwards—not the least of which are pastors and teachers

"Well, now, Brother Berquist, I know the Bible says that; but I have a sister who's a saint if there ever was one, and she's been prayed for, and we've anointed her and tried to do all the Bible says. She's still sick. What do you do with that?"

Well, in the first place, I sympathize with her. My heart aches for her. But any time we take our theology from people's experience instead of coming out of God's Word, we're in trouble. I agree that not everybody gets well. Not everybody I pray for gets well. A lot of them do. The more I believe and the more I preach what I am convinced is God's unadulterated message, the more healings I see.

My reasoning is this: why not bring our experience up to the level of the Scripture, rather than bringing the Scripture down to the level of our experience?

"It is *my* Word," God says, "that I have put in your mouth. You didn't put it there; I put it there. Your job is to speak what I have told you to say, even if you do not fully understand the message yourself."

Friends, we can speak that Word *with confidence* and simply trust God for the results.

Our Confidence Is in the Call

Recently I was caught with the price of a free meal and found myself a reluctant listener to a speech about how to protect oneself from the attack of a rapist. That has not, I assure you, been a problem for me. Nonetheless, I listened. The principal target group for the speaker's words were women.

"Always appear to be going somewhere," she advised. "Never amble. Always look confident. Rarely will a rapist attack a bold, confident woman."

Not bad advice for a preacher. If the call is uncertain and convictions are uncertain and delivery is uncertain—one thing is certain: our preaching will be attacked.

This is not a plea for brashness in the pulpit, nor for arrogance. It is affirmation for an attitude of conviction and confidence. In my life I have met many great preachers. They may have been humble about their abilities, but never about their call.

Look again at the authority God gave to Jeremiah—and to us who are called by him today:

> See, today I appoint you over nations
> and kingdoms to uproot and tear down,
> to destroy and overthrow, to build and to plant.
> (Jeremiah 1:10, NIV)

"I appoint you over...." God says. "I put you in charge."

By God's authority the called pastor is commissioned and charged with certain responsibilities: to pull down and build up; to root out and plant; to balance negative with positive; to attack what is evil and confirm what is good. All these things should be included in our preaching ministry.

Several years ago the religion editor of the *Los Angeles Times* wrote an article stating that in his twenty-five years with the paper, he had seen some of America's greatest preachers come to that city. Their personalities, their methods, and their messages were often different; but four things characterized them all:

1. They actually believed that what they were preaching was true, and their confidence in that belief permeated the message.

2. Not only did they themselves believe in the truth of their message, but they also believed they could convince others to believe it. That confidence came through in their delivery.

3. They all exhibited a trace of the actor or actress, in a seemingly unconscious way. Though it seemed effortless and natural, all had a "stage presence" and a bit of dramatic flair in their preaching that made them captivating.

4. They all were accompanied by a power not their own. Something took over during the preaching act, taking it beyond the realm of merely human wisdom and merely human skill. The message became more than a human act; it became supernatural in its power and effect.

Does not this testimony underscore what we have been saying? If we do not recognize the greatness of the divine calling and the divine command, it is not likely that our hearers will!

Too many pastors today are suffering from a paralyzing inferiority complex. Notice that I didn't say they were inferior. I said they have a complex. Pastoring in a small church someplace—the average sized church in America, by the way, is seventy-five members—the pastor grows accustomed to smallness and falls into the pattern of making excuses for not being able to have a more dynamic ministry.

I hear it all the time:

"Reverend Berquist, I'd like to do more; but we're just a little church, and I'm just a poor struggling preacher; I don't know how we could meet expenses if we were to...." On and on it goes.

Listen, friend. The God who called you "owns the cattle on a thousand hills"(Psalm 50:10). The problem is not money. The problem is *you*. There are no little places. There are only little people. But if we feel that way about ourselves—if we have no vision, no confidence in our call to change the way things are—it is no surprise that those who listen to us feel the same way.

A well-known story tells of a preacher who had his car repaired; and when he went to get it, the bill was more than he expected it to be. Trying to get a little discount, he said to the mechanic, "Sir, I don't know if you know it or not, but I'm just a poor preacher."

The man said, "Yes, I know. I've heard you."

The point is this: You must be confident of your call to preach, and you must put a priority on it if you want anybody else to see it as important. Preaching is not a second-rate occupation!

Gerald Marvel told me of a man in his church who, when his son felt called to become a missionary, said, "I hoped he could do better."

Sometimes when I am in a place where I am particularly well received, some businessman will say to me, "Brother Berquist, you're an intelligent man. You know, if you were in business, you could make a million dollars."

My reply is, "Of course. I believe that, if that were a priority. But I'd rather have a million souls. I may not pay as much for my clothes as you do, or drive a car like yours; but I am in big stakes! I'm doing God's work. I am called of God. I thought it was important."

In his book *Preaching for Today*, Clyde Fant quotes many widely recognized theologians, each in his own way affirming the importance of preaching. It might be highly profitable for the aspiring (or even perspiring) preacher to copy these and paste them on the flyleaf of his or her study Bible. Even better would be to memorize them and hang them on the walls of the mind, to be instantly aware of them whenever facing the challenge of being God's prophet.

> *Dietrich Bonhoeffer*: The proclaimed word is the incarnate Christ himself … the preached Christ is the historical Christ and the present Christ … He is the entrance to the historical Jesus. Therefore the proclaimed Word is not a medium of expression for something else, something which lies behind it, but it is Christ Himself, walking through His congregation as the Word.
>
> *Gustaf Wingre:* The task the preacher faces is that of bringing about a meeting of the Word and men…. The Word exists to be

made known; only when it is preached is its objective content fully disclosed.

P.T. Forsyth: [Preaching is] the most distinctive institution in Christianity.... With its preaching, Christianity either stands or falls.

Emil Bruner: ... wherever there is true preaching and the Word of God is genuinely proclaimed, in spite of all appearances to the contrary, the the most important thing that ever happens upon this earth takes place.

I am not suggesting that anyone print these in Sunday's worship folder. But I am suggesting that those who are called to preach tuck these statements away in their hearts. Read them. Believe them! Make them a part of the preparation process. In time, they will filter though your preaching until their truth is echoed by all.

If the preacher is not certain of them, others are not likely to be certain of them either. As the scripture says, "If the trumpet makes an uncertain sound, who will prepare himself for battle?" (1 Corinthians 14:8, NKJV).

Perhaps we have been playing "Taps" long enough.

Sound "Reveille"!

Chapter 3

The Preaching Event

Having answered God's call to preach, you no doubt remember in vivid detail your first major preaching experience. Gerald Marvel recalls what it was like for him:

It was the first time I had ever preached on Sunday morning. It was a big thing in my life—a big thing! I had my only suit dry cleaned. I borrowed my friend's Pontiac—an old torpedo type. Had it washed and cleaned.

And the sermon … I had that sermon all written out … pages of it. I had really labored over that manuscript. Even had notes in the margin: "Move back" … "clap hands" … "put emphasis!" I had practiced in front of the mirror and everything.

That Sunday morning, I rolled up in that black "torpedo" Pontiac wearing my freshly dry-cleaned suit. Sunlight was streaming through the stained-glass windows, and the people were all there. I had practiced. I was ready.

When my moment in the service came, I stepped up to the pulpit —the preacher of the hour. That's when I realized that I had forgotten one thing: there were people there!

It scared the wits out of me. The pulpit had two little hooks in back there, and resting on those hooks was a rod with a curtain to hide all the stuff that accumulates in pulpits.

Anyway, I started preaching, following my manuscript down the page line for line, the way I'd been taught. I looked like a chicken drinking water, bobbing my head up and down as I glanced up from the manuscript and back again. My mouth was bone dry, because I was painfully conscious of the people in front of me and that they were seeing mostly the top of my head (albeit it was covered with hair in those days).

I was so nervous I kept rigidly glued to that manuscript and those all-important marginal notes. I followed the notes religiously the way I'd rehearsed them: "look up": "clap hands": "put emphasis"; "move back."

I guess I was concentrating so much on my feet when I "moved back" that my hands got away from me, because when I moved back I pulled those curtains off in the floor!

Well, I got all tangled up in that curtain, fiddling with that thing. And the congregation just cracked up.

Finally I rolled that rod up in that curtain, and I threw it across that sermon, and I said, "I've unveiled the temple for you people!"

"Now," I said, "I want to tell you something that's on my heart."

And, friends, for the first time in my life, I started preaching. From that moment on, I totally lost my place in time and space and was caught up in the power of that message.

I will always be grateful that I couldn't move further back on that platform ... that I got tangled up in that curtain and ruined my well-rehearsed speech. God was merciful; for in that moment, he taught me how to preach.

The Divine Act of Preaching

Prophecy is not *declaring the end of the world.* Prophecy is *declaring, through inspiration of the Holy Spirit, the eternal Word of God.*

Some people come to church with the attitude of "coming to hear a sermon." A sermon to them is nothing more than "just a person up there talking."

But if that sermon is prophecy, those same people will be saying, "Wait a minute, pastor. Something powerful is happening here. Tell me, what is going on?"

A very distraught young man approached Gerald Marvel after a worship service.

"What is it when I come to this place?" he asked. "Have you noticed I've moved from the floor of the sanctuary to the balcony? I don't stay on the floor any more. It's safer in the balcony. Got an iron railing up there. I want to know, pastor. What is going on?"

This troubled young man had no church background, knew nothing about God or the Holy Spirit. He pressed for answers.

"I come with my wife, and I want to know what is happening

here when the service has come to a close and we stand to sing and you're down there talking to people around the altar? Something is pushing and pushing on me to go down there. What is it?"

Gerald answered him in a word: "God."

Next Sunday the young husband was at the altar. Once he realized that the power he felt was God pushing him to come down and get saved, he came.

Gerald Marvel and I have each pastored in one location for more than twenty years. I served a congregation in Daytona Beach, Florida. Gerald Marvel continues to pastor in Vancouver, Washington. As pastors we have been called upon to do a lot of counseling, and over the years we have counseled hundreds of people.

While we were leading a preaching conference in Oklahoma a few years back, Gerald made this interesting observation:

> In twenty years, I have never had anyone say to me, "Years ago, pastor, when I was sitting in your office in a counseling session, you said this and this and this."
>
> But it is utterly amazing how often people will say to me, "I remember when I was in high school, pastor, one Sunday when you were preaching, you said thus and so."
>
> People don't remember words of wisdom from my office. They remember what was said from the pulpit.
>
> You know why?
>
> The divine is mixed in with what happens in the pulpit. The divine is not always mixed in with the counseling sessions in my office.
>
> Don't misunderstand. Much prayer goes into those counseling sessions. But many times, right or wrong, counseling involves batting around opinions and ideas.
>
> Preaching, however, must always involve more than personal opinion and human wisdom.

Henry Brant, who operates a counseling center in Florida, spoke at a ministers' meeting in Oregon. He said, "I've been running a counseling center for nearly thirty years, and I must tell you, counseling does very little. It's what you people do in the pulpit that makes a difference in the churches."

I believe that.

People remember the Word of God spoken in sermons because it is mixed with the Holy Spirit in an element different from any other. It is different from reading sermons in print or hearing them on tape. God can use taped messages, but hearing a sermon presented live is different from listening to a recording.

Preaching is a divine action: a human agent presenting to other human beings the eternal Word of God mixed with the powerful presence of the Holy Spirit. That divine act of preaching people crave, because they need it.

If you come to the pulpit thinking, "I've got to fill up so much time here because it is customary"—you're in trouble. You are not killing time when you are truly preaching.

Even on occasions when I have been ill prepared—and I confess to some of those times—God has been faithful to honor the divine act of preaching.

Gerald Marvel has a similar testimony.

One Saturday night his phone rang at 3:00 AM. Two high school students had been killed in a head-on collision, and their grief-stricken parents were in shock. He spent the rest of the night at their home, and by early morning—Sunday morning—in his words, "I was shot."

The weight of the tragedy pressed in, right down to thirty minutes before the first worship service. Gerald had not had a moment's time to think about his message.

He describes what happened:

> In a total state of upheaval, I walked into my study, closed the door, got on my knees, and said, "God, you know. You know my life. You know my patterns. You know what I have done this week. You know. God, deliver this disposition of mine to preach your Word." God was faithful. I was amazed at how well the sermon came together. But that experience made me more keenly aware than ever that preaching is a "God-happening."

A *God-happening*. That is truly what preaching is and we who profess to be preachers must think of it as a *God-happening*.

Many people in your congregation won't share that view.

Granted, many people do come to church prepared to worship. Like saints of old in the Book of Acts, they can say, "We have come to hear the Word of God. It's the most exciting thing in our life."

But you have other people in those pews—sleepers out there—who won't see your sermon as a *God-happening*. You have husbands out there biding their time until the final hymn and benediction. They are there only because of promises made to their wives. You have teenagers writing notes. Precious little infants trying to out-scream you. Everything in the world is going on out there while you are trying to deliver a message from God.

Preacher, you had better believe it's a *God-happening*—whether anyone else believes it or not. If it doesn't happen with you, it will not happen with them.

Why Not Angels?

Since preaching is a *God-happening*—a divine event—why on earth does God rely on mere mortals to be his spokespersons?

I don't know.

God could bring in an angel every Sunday at 11:00 AM if he chose to. He doesn't. God doesn't use angels to prophesy—to proclaim the Word of God.

Take note in the tenth chapter of Acts, regarding the redemption of a Roman centurion. Cornelius prayed to God always. He gave alms. He was spiritually seeking God. An angel came. Did the angel instruct him in the way of salvation? No!

The angel brought a message from God, but it was not the Gospel. The message was this: "Send for a preacher down in Joppa."

God knew that the preacher in question would experience considerable uncertainty about going up to Caesarea. Still the order was, "Send for him."

God knew that the preacher being summoned was, right at that moment, confused. He was bigoted. Certainly the preacher was not perfect. Even so, God planned to use him.

It distresses me that so many preachers are always down on themselves—bemoaning the fact that they are not "Class A perfect" in everything. Look at the people God used. Peter was far from being perfect. Still God said, "Send for him."

So Peter came down off the housetop. He had seen a strange vision. He did not understand it. He disagreed with it. Even so, he said to the man at the door, "I'll go."

By the time he got to Caesarea and came into the home of Cornelius, what did he say? "The Lord has shown me ..."

Where did God give him that revelation? In the process of obedience.

Whether we understand completely or not, if we follow God, God will reveal the way. God will reveal the truth. Peter left Joppa still confused, but on the way to Caesarea—in the process of being obedient—God got through to him, and he saw the light: Jesus died for Gentiles, too. Thus, Peter instructed a Roman centurian in the way of salvation, and opened a new road for the spread of Christianity.

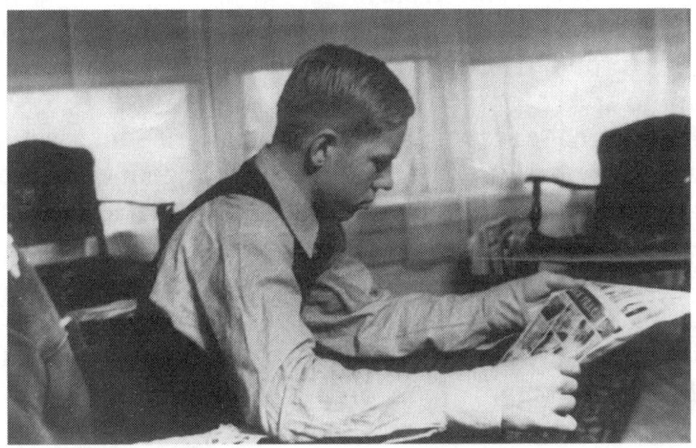

Maurice Berquist as a teenager

God uses people—always has.

When God wanted a nation, he found a person. God didn't send an angel. He found a person who was obedient—Abraham.

When God wanted a deliverer, he found another person. He sought out a washed-up fugitive of the law with an inferiority complex, hiding in the desert, and brought him back to Egypt. Moses had bungled the job once, forty years before; but God called him back into service to deliver God's message.

Trace it through the Bible. Whenever God wants to speak, he speaks through people—ordinary people, imperfect people—most of whom feel unequal to the task.

Even the Prophet Jeremiah felt inadequate when God called him to preach:

> The word of the Lord came to me saying,
> "Before I formed you in the womb I knew you,
>   before you were born I set you apart;
> I appointed you as a prophet to the nations."
> "Ah, Sovereign Lord," I said, "I do not know
>   how to speak; I am only a child."
>
> (Jeremiah 1: 4–5, NIV)

Jeremiah says, in essence, "Before I was born—before I was conceived—God envisioned me. And God envisioned me not only as a generic person, but as a called person."

What a difference that makes!

Like Jeremiah, any person truly called of God is not unduly arrogant or proud. The more common feeling is, "I can't do this. Who am I to speak for God?"

But feeling inadequate is not bad. Actually it's an asset. In fact, I would call it the first prerequisite for becoming an effective preacher, because that insecurity drives us to our knees. It drives us to reliance upon God.

We might say that feeling inadequate is what makes us adequate in preaching.

Persons cocksure they know how to preach prove by their arrogance that they do not.

Gerald Marvel and I have a mutual friend who was like that. One of the most gifted men I ever knew, he could do anything. Athletics, school work, making money, courting girls, singing, talking, preaching sermons—he excelled at them all. Name it—he could do it better than anyone else

He went into ministry and pastored a church successfully. But he told Gerald one day: "Sometimes I come to church and don't know what I'm going to preach about when I enter the back of the sanctuary and come down the aisle with the choir. While walking from the back of the church to the front, I pick a subject and then get up and preach."

"Sometimes," he would say, "I get an idea out on the golf course, and that's the last thought I have on it until Sunday morning."

Once when he was out of town, he received a call from his minister of music: "I'm planning the music for Sunday's service. What is your sermon going to be?"

"I have no idea," my friend said. "Just choose a text. I'll read it and preach on it when I get there Sunday morning."

Oddly enough, if you heard him preach, you would never guess that so little effort went into his preparation of sermons. He is a gifted improvisational speaker.

But the truth is, he is not preaching today.

Overconfidence in his own speaking abilities cost him a great career and great usefulness, because he lost that sense of awe that every preacher must have if he or she is truly to be used of God.

It is a sad fact that many people who think they are called are merely gifted. They are not called of God. A preacher called of God will have a holy sense of awe. That is what Jeremiah had.

A Divine Partnership

When Jesus wanted to get the message out, he used people.

He chose ordinary people to be his disciples. For three years he invested his life in them, taught them, mentored them, modeled exemplary preaching and ministry before them. Then he sent them out to carry on the work he had begun.

Later, as he ascended to heaven, he commissioned them—and us—to preach the gospel to all people everywhere.

But the key to our success in that mission lies in the promise Christ made to them—and to us: "lo, I am with you always, even to the end of the age" (Matthew 28:20).

We must never forget:
- preaching is a sacred partnership with Almighty God;
- preaching is imbued with the supernatural;
- preaching is, indeed, a God-happening;
- preaching is a key element in God's plan to save the world.

A Handful of Stars

"God, if You wish for our love,
fling us a handful of stars!"

Preaching is, indeed, more than just getting up in front of a crowd of people and talking for thirty minutes.

Whenever we step into the pulpit we stand as God's emissary to the people. Through the message we deliver, we reach into the heavens and grasp "a handful of stars"—the promises of God that offer

> forgiveness where there is sin,
> healing where there is sickness,
> hope where there is despair,
> unconditional love,
> and eternal life.

These we offer to the people as a sacrament—bread to hungering hearts, water to thirsting souls, sight to the spiritually blind, a balm for hurting spirits.

Ours is a life or death mission in behalf of a God who loves and who has chosen to express that love through us.

That same God has promised to be in intimate partnership with us as we deliver his message to the people. God will fill our hearts with love and compassion, imbue our minds with godly thoughts, fill our mouths with godly words. God then will empower us with divine energy and conviction so that we might speak boldly and convincingly what God has given us to say.

Power Surge

Once in a while in the process of preaching, in the delivery, we are made aware of the power—that it is there, happening in the moment. Most often the power is detected on the receiving end—what happens to those who receive the message. But now and again, the power will be revealed to us during the act of preaching. We can sense that "in this moment" it is present.

No doubt many of you reading this book have felt it. You know what we are talking about. Gerald Marvel's moving testimony speaks for us all:

> I have had times in preaching—as I know all preachers have—when I struggle with the message, as if I were building something out of wood. Try as I might, there is no spirit; no life. It feels hollow and empty.
>
> It's horrible to be standing before a congregation of people try-

ing to speak and feeling like that. And even as I am speaking, I am praying, "Lord, if you can get me through this, I promise, I'll do better next Sunday. Just get me through."

Nevertheless, I trust the power of the gospel message.

Invariably when I have one of those panic-attack experiences while preaching, somebody will run up to me after service to say, "How did you know I needed to hear what you said this morning? You've been reading my spiritual mail."

God's power works through us sometimes in spite of us.

Truthfully, we may not always be aware of God's power at work while we are preaching. But every now and then that accompanying power reveals itself during the preaching of the Word of God, and when that happens, it is glorious!

Little wonder we find preaching so hard to define. For the genuine act of preaching the Word of God is a divine mystery.

Genuine preaching possesses a power that goes beyond skillfully constructed sermons and artful delivery. Something happens in the preaching act that is nothing short of awesome. When God takes over the message and the moment, the preacher himself or herself must stand breathless with wonder and feel humble indeed to think that the God of the universe would choose to speak through us.

Chapter 4

Seven Characteristics of Great Preaching

To preach the best I know how has been my life's ambition, as I am sure it is for anyone called to preach.

And I am convinced there is no such thing as a natural-born preacher.

We may call someone "a natural-born preacher," particularly if talking about a Lori Salierno or a Jim Lyon. But I believe preaching is a learned skill, not a natural-born gift.

Granted, God calls men and women to preach, and blesses those called with the spiritual gift of prophecy. But beyond the call and the insights of prophecy are skills to be mastered if one is to be effective in delivering God's message.

Jeremiah's call was definitely divine; and part of that call was God's order to "gird up his loins," meaning that he had work to do before God could complete his purpose in him.

We all can learn to be more effective in the pulpit.

Putting it plainly, we never preach as well as we ought; but each time we preach should be better than the time before. Preaching is a spiritual exercise, but it also involves the mind and the body. While measuring the effect of a sermon is virtually impossible, we can measure the relative effectiveness of our presentation; and doing so may not only avoid a considerable amount of criticism from those who hear us, but also bear witness to a more fruitful ministry.

Analyzing Effective Preaching

From our study of preaching over the years, Gerald Marvel and I have compiled a list of "Seven Characteristics of Great Preaching" in the hope that these may help you assess and strengthen your own preaching skills. We selected words that all start with *V* to make them easier to remember.

We list them here with a brief introductory comment, then delve more deeply into each one in subsequent chapters.

1. Effective preaching is VISUAL.

Of all gateways to the brain, the eye is the most powerful. What we see affects us more than what we take in by any other of our senses. Yet the visual aspect of preaching is often sorely neglected.

In the first chapter of his book about Christ, the apostle John declares: "The word became flesh … and we beheld his glory … as of the only begotten of the Father, full of grace and truth" (John 1:14, NKJV).

This passage includes several aspects of effective preaching, the first being a *visible person.*

Face it, pastor: you are a part of your sermon. The congregation see you before they hear you. They see you all the time they hear you. If your visible presence is contradictory or distracting, you get negative votes.

Dress and grooming, posture, body movement, gestures, facial expressions—all of these contribute positively or negatively to the message you stand to proclaim. They need to be taken into account as you plan for and rehearse your sermon.

Using *visual aids* is another aspect of visible preaching. The more visual your presentation, the better. Whenever possible, for example, I like to use a chalkboard, flip chart, or overhead projector—valuable tools in that not only do people hear what you say, but they also see key words or graphs or drawings or pictures that help them remember.

A third aspect of visual preaching—and the most difficult to master—is the process of *visualization*—what we are going to call "metaphoric preaching." Visualization is a powerful tool for making the message memorable.

2. Effective preaching is VERBAL.

Words are the essence of preaching. Words are the preacher's tools. The more comfortable the preacher is with words—the more skillful he or she is in their use—the more powerfully the message comes across. Words are the heart and soul of the message.

God honors the power of the word. In fact, in the passage from John quoted earlier, God is described as "the Word"—*logos* in the Greek. You know what the word *logos* means. As John uses *logos*, it means more than just a word like these I write here. *Logos* has

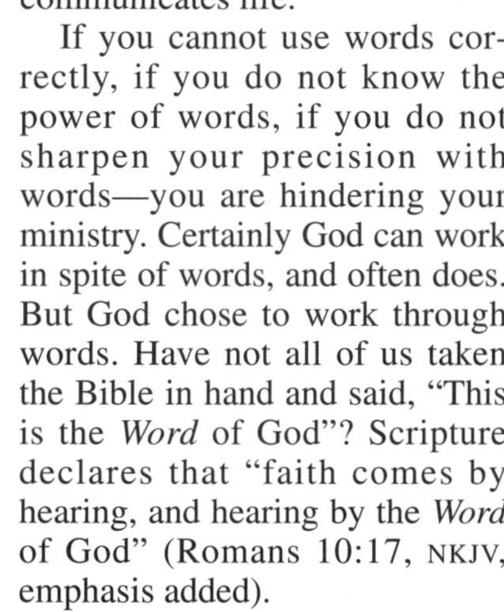

life in it. It lives and breathes. It communicates life.

If you cannot use words correctly, if you do not know the power of words, if you do not sharpen your precision with words—you are hindering your ministry. Certainly God can work in spite of words, and often does. But God chose to work through words. Have not all of us taken the Bible in hand and said, "This is the *Word* of God"? Scripture declares that "faith comes by hearing, and hearing by the *Word* of God" (Romans 10:17, NKJV, emphasis added).

For clear communication, words should be appropriate for the people to whom we speak. The same words will not fly equally well in a college town and in a farming community. One pitfall of seminary graduates, for example, is talking over the heads of their parishioners. All preachers must be careful about using theological jargon without explaining what the words mean. Donald Barnhouse said it well when he spoke of "getting the hay down out of the loft and onto the barn floor where the cows can get at it."

Rudolf Flesch produced a helpful tool for measuring the effectiveness of the words you use for a particular audience. Studying his chart and conscientiously applying it to a sampling of your sermons may reveal some surprising—possibly painful—information about how well you match your words to your audience.

The point is this: while good preaching is more than words, words are important. Words carry the message. Thus, a pastor's verbal skills will largely determine whether or not his or her preaching is effective.

3. Effective preaching is VISCERAL.

This characteristic is one of my favorites. Yes, *visceral* is a pedantic and clumsy word. But it begins with *V*, and it is polite and scholarly. Bringing it more down-to-earth, it basically means to "preach out of your guts."

In other words, preach with feeling! And preach in a way that arouses feelings in your listeners.

The root word for *visceral* relates to the intestines, which the ancients believed to be the seat of the emotions.

It may come as a surprise to many, but preaching is not primarily about facts. Preaching primarily has to do with feelings about the facts. If you do not know how to deal with feelings, you are missing the point of most powerful impact. Plain and simple: it is not the fact that moves people. It is their perception of the fact—how they feel about it.

4. Effective preaching is VERIFIABLE.

Of course, the root word of *verifiable* is the word for "truth." *Verifiable* means that when facts are checked, they prove to be true.

Preachers in general have been accused of having "evangelistic imaginations." People, therefore, are prone to discount what they say. Not all preachers, of course, deserve this reputation. But it is terrible to find a pastor who cannot be trusted to tell the truth. If a person cannot be truthful about earthly things, how can he or she be trusted to tell the truth about spiritual things?

Preaching needs to be well documented. If you don't know for sure that a particular fact or story is true, by all means, tell the people that you don't know if it's true. Before you present something as truth, you ought to have proved to yourself that it is.

One thing you can count on: someone will check it out! If you have checked first, you need not fear that scrutiny. In nearly every congregation, for example, are one or two watchdogs for quotations. If you quote Scripture or a few lines of poetry during the sermon, they will be at your elbow immediately after service to say, "Now, pastor, that's not the way it is. It says this." Well, don't resent that. They can help keep you honest. Preaching needs to be verifiable.

5. Effective preaching is VITAL.

"At last," you say, "one I can understand!" Well, what we mean here by *vital* is the root word for "life." Preaching is related to life.

I don't care how true something is, if it doesn't relate to people, it doesn't do them any good. Actually, if it doesn't relate to people living in your town right now, it just goes right by them. It may be true, but it isn't vital; it isn't related to life—*their life today*. Thus, for them it has little or no meaning.

Vital preaching requires the pastor to be involved with the lives of his people and issues facing them on a daily basis—at home, in their community, on national and world levels. To the men and women in the pew, Scripture is little more than history or pretty words until it is made to "connect" with specific needs in their lives. When they are made to see it as relevant, the Word comes alive and is life-changing!

Vital preaching does not happen by sitting in a study pouring over commentaries and prepackaged sermons or books of topical illustrations. Vital preaching flows out of living with people—walking with them, talking with them, listening to them, praying with them, sharing their laughter and joy, their pain and their tears. Only when a pastor knows what life is like for those God has given him or her to nurture, can that pastor make the Word of God relevant to their experience.

6. Effective preaching is VICARIOUS.

I hope you know the word *vicarious*. Old-time preachers knew the word *vicarious* because they preached about the pope being the vicar of Christ. And they spelled it out. *Vicar* is a Latin word meaning "the representative of."

As we are using it here, *vicarious* means "to experience through a story or other medium what someone else has experienced first-hand."

Vicarious experiences are common when we watch television or read a book, hear a story or see a play, attend an athletic event. We are made to project ourselves into the happening so that we actually experience the same excitement, joy, terror, sorrow, and so forth that befalls the persons directly involved.

The preacher who can take people with him or her on a vicarious journey has learned a compelling secret for gaining and holding the attention of listeners and helping them to experience the Word, not just hear it. Mastering the art of vicarious preaching is like hitting a home run with all the bases loaded!

7. Effective preaching is VICTORIOUS.

God intends life for the Christian to be victorious. Effective preaching, then, should always point the way toward victory in all of life's circumstances. Preaching should reflect a mood of victory. To do that, preachers must possess, must convey, and must inspire a victorious attitude.

The message is that whatever life brings our way, we are to be overcomers in Christ. The heart of the gospel message is victory in Jesus.

Facing Self-Evaluation and Criticism

Those, then, are seven indicators by which to measure effective preaching. They provide a measuring stick for evaluating your own preaching or anyone else's. I suggest, if you are brave enough, that you play back a tape of last Sunday's sermon. Close the door of your study on Monday morning—after you've had some coffee and got your motor running—and say to yourself, "Well, how did it go?"

Lock yourself in, divert or ignore phone calls momentarily, and say, "Nobody's here but God and me. We're going to listen to this thing and see what I do right and what I do wrong—what I can do better."

The good news is this—and it is great news!—most of you are within millimeters of being effective. You may feel that you have to change in some big way to be effective. Not necessarily. It may not be a big thing. Solomon speaks of "little foxes that spoil the vines" (Song of Solomon 2:15, NKJV). You can have a healthy mental vineyard, fertilized well, good genes, and all that. And you may be having a great season—but if you get one little fox in there to chew the vine off at the root, that kills it. You ought to go fox hunting and shoot those foxes!

In other words, when you find something that needs fixing, don't keep on doing it!

You can also solicit helpful suggestions from your spouse or someone in your congregation whose opinions you trust. Share these seven markers with them and ask them to help evaluate your sermons now and then to keep you on track.

Use these seven indicators to measure unsolicited critical comments you get from others. Negative feedback in the narthex after service may lack tact or good taste, and sometimes it may have less to do with your preaching than the person's disgruntled attitude about something else. But it could be that some aspect of your preaching needs attention.

Criticism, I know, is not easy to take. I don't like it any better than anyone else does. But I will tell you this, my critics have been my helpers. Over the years I have come to mind criticism less, because it has forced me to see things about myself that I did not want to see but very much needed to see. Facing up to the truth helped make me a better preacher.

A great philosopher once said, "Your only true friends are your enemies, for who else will tell you the truth?"

In the church all too often we label our critics "troublemakers." In reality, they sometimes tell us things we ought to know about ourselves. And they do it without pay. They do it with honesty and candor—sometimes, I grant you, with more honesty than we would like. But if we listen to our critics, perhaps we can profit from them.

I'll risk sharing one of my gut-wrenching experiences.

When I was in seminary back in the dark ages, we had to preach our senior sermon in chapel. I took homiletics from Dr. Frank Caldwell, whom I described previously as a paragon of preaching. He was a great man and a wonderful preacher, one of the leading preachers in the Presbyterian church.

After I gave my senior sermon in chapel, the next day the students in homiletics class critiqued it—tore it apart. I am sure that ritual still happens occasionally around the world. All my classmates were merciful, because they knew I would critique them later. So their comments contained lots of praise, "Great job!" "Excellent presentation!" "Good points!"

Actually, I was more experienced in preaching than most students in the class. I had been out of school a while before I went back to seminary, and I had been preaching all over the country; so I was not a novice.

After my classmates' reviews, then came Dr. Caldwell's comment. I'll never forget it. Part of it I enjoyed. Part of it was excruciating.

"Mr. Berquist gave us a very interesting sermon," he said. "In fact, homiletically it was perfect. And it was inspirational and well delivered. In fact, I was amazed today at the purity and quality of what he had to say."

I was getting set up. Then he lowered the boom.

"But one thing marred his otherwise excellent presentation. He has an annoying habit of talking down to people … of appearing arrogant … of displaying an air of 'I know this and you don't.' "

Then he added, "That can ruin you."

Well, naturally, my first reaction was to tell myself, "That's not true. The man's got poor judgment."

But then I started listening to myself, playing back my sermons. Sure enough, there it was—an air of arrogance, talking down to people, showing off my intelligence. It was not a conscious thing. It was a habit I had picked up. Fortunately, I saw it. I see it once in a while even yet, though over the years, I have consciously tried to correct it.

I have a few other bad habits I am still working on. If I can get rid of them, it will be so much the better. Better for you, too, if you can become aware of and eliminate yours.

It is painful to look at yourself. But I can tell you this, when Gerald Marvel and I did a preaching seminar for ministers in Washington, more than one pastor said to us some months later, "You know, I've started taking this seriously. Since hearing your presentation, I have changed my whole preaching style. People love it better; they are responding better. The crowds are better, and God is using it more."

And that is good news. Because we want to be effective.

In the Jordan River

Berny and Berk with grandchildren,
Matthew and Lauren Evans

Grandpa Berk with Lauren Evans

Berk, Berny, and Marty (right),
with newlyweds, Lori and Jack Evans

Lori Salierno washes her mentor's feet

Michigan Youth Convention, 1961

Early preaching days

The family in 1977 (from left) Marty, Berny, Lori, and Berk

Chapter 5

Making Sermons Visual

The eye is the widest gate to the brain. For most people, what we see has a greater impact than what we merely hear. Even without visual stimulation, if a presentation has been effective, we exclaim, "I see!"

God understands the importance of seeing:

> The Word became flesh and dwelt among us, and we beheld His glory, the glory as of the only begotten of the Father, full of grace and truth (John 1:14, NKJV).

God has always been God. But it was not until Jesus made God visible that we began to understand the true nature of the Almighty. Even so, God's nature was still not clear to the disciples. Thomas, though he had heard thousands of words from the lips of Jesus, yet prevailed upon him to "show us the Father" (John 14:8, NKJV).

Jesus did not reprimand him for his lack of understanding, his cloudy vision. Instead he explained patiently, "He who has seen *Me* has seen the Father" (John 14:9, NKJV).

Appearance Speaks

Marshall McLuhan's phrase "the medium is the message" is certainly true of preaching—if not for all of the message, at least for much of it.

A preacher may disdain the use of "visual aids," but one's very appearance can be an aid or a distraction. Before the preacher speaks, he or she has spoken! As one sage has said, "What you are speaks so loudly I cannot hear what you say." Preachers make a presentation of the gospel before speaking a single word. We are visible before we are audible.

Gerald Marvel never preaches from behind the pulpit. Neither do I. The reason is simple and goes beyond whether or not you need something to lean on. The pulpit becomes a block between you and the people. The more you are free from that, the more visible you are.

Your body is a part of your message. Away from the pulpit, you stand free to move about, open to the audience so that gestures become more visible to help communicate the message. Your projected image is one of confidence and strength: "I am standing here on my own two feet, not dependent on this pulpit for support." That image alone commands attention.

At Gerald's church in Vancouver, the staging for the proclaiming of the Word is dramatic, well-suited to his style of preaching. The sanctuary is like an amphitheater. On the platform a pulpit stands on one side and a lectern on the other. As Gerald explains to guest speakers, "We have a divided chancel, but we have a central pulpit."

Invariably, that brings a puzzled look to the guest's face and the inevitable question: "How is that possible?"

"Because I'm the pulpit. I'm central."

Gerald then goes on to explain: "I stand at the pulpit and read the scripture. Then I move out to the center of the platform to preach in front of both the pulpit and the lectern. And the Word is central."

It has a powerful effect.

Use of a cordless lavalier microphone enhances the effect, giving him total freedom without the distraction of microphone wires trailing the floor, inviting his feet to get tangled up in them. Sound equipment, while primarily an audio enhancement, is visual, too, and can be visual in a negative way.

Standing away from the pulpit with a microphone that frees you to move has other advantages. In a conference on the use of body language in preaching, Bill Yager pointed out a strategy of movement every pastor can use to advantage, especially in an amphitheater type of sanctuary like the one in Vancouver, with several sections of seating in a semicircle. Yager suggested that when something distracting happens in the audience—a baby starts crying or a child begins struggling with his mother, and everybody turns to look that way—you move in the opposite direction. As you are preaching, simply move to an area of the platform opposite from the distraction. The eyes will come back to you because you are moving.

If movement is a normal part of your sermon delivery, no one will find your move to another part of the platform unusual; and it gives the people involved in the distraction opportunity to calm the situation or exit the sanctuary in a less disruptive manner. The key: *move in the opposite direction of something distracting.*

Your body is also part of your language. Gestures are an important part of sermon delivery. What you do with your hands can help communicate the message by adding expression and emphasis. But to be effective, gestures must be meaningful and controlled. Gestures are an individual thing. What works effectively for one person may not work for another.

You may recall John F. Kennedy's emphatic tapping with a pointed index finger on the podium—or in the air if there was no podium—to stress a point when making a public address or a statement to the press. That worked well for him, was natural for him. But the same gesture might look staged or phoney on someone else.

Some people look relaxed and confident with their hands held in front of them or behind their back or stuffed in their pockets. On another person the same posture might look awkward and distracting, giving a negative rather than a positive effect.

It takes some conscious practice, preferably in front of a mirror, to determine what hand movements are effective for you. The key words here are *natural, relaxed, controlled, meaningful.* Too many gestures or the hands flailing about for no reason at all will not aid communication, but will in fact detract.

The idea is to make our visual appearance support the message rather than contradict or confuse it. Here are some further suggestions:

1. Be worshipful during the worship time.
Fumbling through your notes or gazing vacantly at the back door

separates you from the worshiping congregation. If you are to lead, you must be "with them."

2. Approach the pulpit with confidence.

That does not mean with arrogance or pride, but with confidence that God has called you and given you a message.

3. Study your presentation to eliminate distractions.

A video tape or a spouse may help here. As the poet Robert Burns observed, it is difficult to "see ourselves as others see us."

Thus, we may acquire unconscious habits that distract and send the wrong message. Check yourself for these: constantly shifting from foot to foot, rattling pocket change, meaningless repetitive gestures, leaning on the pulpit, balancing on one foot, aimless walking. Certainly God can use any message—even one that violates all the "rules"—but why penalize yourself or the kind people who have come to hear you?

Add any other visual aids appropriate and available to enhance the message, but your physical presence is your foremost and most valuable tool.

Make Your Method Visual

Jesus wrote with his finger in the dust; and a crowd of angry, would-be murderers silently walked away. With a few fish and loaves of bread he demonstrated his power to bless. With a towel and basin he taught us servanthood. He broke bread and poured wine and thereby imparted the majestic truth of his continuing presence.

The more *visual* the method, the more permanent the impression.

One of the best illustrations of using visuals came to me from India Wassum, a Sunday school teacher in Allison's Gap, Virginia.

India (and that is her real name) did not have the advantage of college or teacher-training. But one day in teaching her class of primary children about Jesus cooking fish for his disciples one morning on the shores of Galilee, she had the presence of mind to bring her electric skillet to class. While she told the simple story of the disciples who, after fishing all night, shared this surprise breakfast with Jesus, India fried fishsticks. When they were ready, she let the class eat them.

Can you imagine any child in that class ever forgetting that Bible story? Not only did she open their eyes to the story, but she involved their other senses as well. Hearing the fish sizzling in the pan, smelling the aroma of cooking fish, touching and tasting the fish—all made the story more real. Those children will never smell fish cooking without thinking of that class and their teacher. A taste will bring back the memory.

Teaching that lasts touches more than one of the senses.

Educational research has revealed valuable information about how people learn:

How People Learn		How People Retain What They Learn
Taste	1%	10 %—of what they read
Touch	1–1.5 %	20 %—of what they hear
Smell	3–3.5 %	30 %—of what they see
Hearing	11 %	50 %—of what they see and hear together
Sight	83 %	70 %—of what they say
		90 %—of what they say and do at the same time

Take note. This is a significant point not always covered in homiletics classes. For preaching that has a long-lasting effect: *the more senses we stimulate in presenting a sermon, the better it will be understood and the longer it will be remembered.*

Visual aids do not have to be elaborate to be effective. I recall one occasion in Vancouver when Gerald invited a friend to preach whom he had not heard before. He was somewhat anxious about it, never having heard the man speak; but he need not have worried. Boyce Moulton turned out to be an exceptionally fine communicator. He carried with him to the pulpit a folder about five inches thick, which he explained to the audience was full of answers to prayers. That was in itself impressive. We all believe God answers prayer, but here was a file folder that proved it.

He picked out one documented case and held it up as he stepped to the side of the pulpit and told a story from the life of George Washington Carver. Then he said, "Now, there's another one in here …" And holding up another sheet, he told about his daughter and how God answered a prayer for her. Then he shared another gem from the folder about the Butcher family, creators of "Precious Moments." And so on.

Granted, he could have told the same stories without literally holding up papers from the folder as he talked. But standing there with the pieces of hard evidence in hand demonstrated more effectively—that answers to prayer are more than hearsay. With each testimony, he wove scripture into the real-life story in a relevant and convincing way. People were touched, as evidenced by a great altar response in both services.

You have to go to some trouble sometimes to use a visual aid with the message; but an object of some kind—a picture, poster, book, Boyce Moulton's file folder—can really make a sermon memorable.

For one particular sermon I used to preach around the country when I was a full-time evangelist, I drew a picture on the board as I talked. Forty years later I have had people say to me, "I remember a sermon you preached one time…" And they go on to describe the picture. But what amazes me and thrills me even more, they remember the message, too—because of the picture.

One of Gerald Marvel's favorite experiences with a visual aid involved a poster he borrowed from his niece's kindergarten class. He had gone to visit little Mary at her school for Grandfather's Day. As he tells it, when he walked into her classroom, the first thing that caught his eye was a large poster on the wall.

It was a map of the United States in black, taken from a satellite at night, and on it were all the lights in all the cities in the United States of America. The lights outlined the country. You could see Los Angeles; you could see San Francisco; you could see Seattle and Portland, Salt Lake City, Detroit, New York, up into New England, Houston, Miami. I looked for my home state, Oklahoma. Sure enough, there were Tulsa and Oklahoma City.

"That's amazing!" I thought.

Later I got to wondering if Mary's teacher would loan me that poster to take to the pulpit next Sunday.

Finally I went to her and said, "Mrs. Kendall, that is really an intriguing poster."

"Yes. We get those," she said, "from *The Weekly Reader*."

All through my childhood one publication I loved dearly was *The Weekly Reader*. How I looked forward to each issue! That intensified my interest in the poster even more.

I said, "What would you take for me to use that poster? I'll mail it back to you or send it by Mary."

They were getting ready for spring break.

She said, "You take that poster and when you're through with it, have Mary bring it back."

So I took the poster. Then I had second thoughts about taking it to the pulpit. I almost didn't do it—thought it was too ridiculous. I was preaching a series from the Sermon on the Mount, and on this particular Sunday I was preaching on "You are the light of the world."

But finally I said to myself, "Oh, why not? You've been here twenty years; all they can do is fire you."

Sunday came. At the appointed time in my sermon, I took out the poster and unfolded it. I told about visiting my little niece at school, and how I came to get the poster. Then I talked a little about the poster itself, that it was taken from a satellite and how it struck me as being a powerful teaching tool.

Then I took out my pen—and I put the poster in my mouth to hold it. No homiletics professor would allow that! And I don't particularly advise it; but that morning, that's the way I did it. I was wearing a lavalier mike, so my voice could be heard from behind the poster.

And I said, "Right here is Portland, Oregon. And here is the Columbia River—just a little line. And right here"—I pointed to a specific spot on the map—"right here ... two of those little lights right here ... two of those little lights ... belong to the Marvel family. One is the street lamp we had installed from the city. The other one is the yard light."

Then came the punchline: "Take note, my friends: I am 'the light of the world.' "

And suddenly, for everyone in the congregation that morning, the Sermon on the Mount took on a new dimension.

They could see the significance of two tiny lights on a satellite map of the United States. Our lives do shine. Our lights do make a difference. It got through to people that you let your light shine, and that's how the world is illuminated—not only physically to be seen in a satellite poster, but spiritually in the hearts of men.

Needless to say, all the elementary school teachers in our church were lined up waiting for me after service.

"Wonderful! Wonderful!"

"You mentioned *The Weekly Reader!*"

"How you touched our hearts, pastor! I had that poster in my room."

Maybe it was a dumb thing to do, especially holding the poster in my mouth the way I did. But it really helped to visualize the message. It had a powerful effect.

Indeed it did. I was there that Sunday, and I can testify that the effect was electric!

We all know the scripture where Jesus called us "the light of the world," but when you look at a map of America and see those lights clearly visible from space ... you never forget it.

So the more visual you can be, do it. Have courage to do "a dumb thing" occasionally.

Don't say, "Well, that's for kids."

Listen. Most of us are kids.

Naively, we think that "audiovisuals" are an invention of modern times. Effective preachers and teachers have always been wise to this axiom of learning. But in our day we have access to many tools unknown to other generations: videos, slides, overhead projectors, sound tracks, photographs—even satellite photos from space! What excuse do we have for not making our method of preaching visual?

Make the Message Visual

Jesus modeled visual preaching, and "the common people heard Him gladly" (Mark 12:37, NKJV). Although he spoke words of eternal truth, he clothed those ideas with pictures. He made them visual. The sower and the seed ... the lilies of the field ... a camel straining to pass through the needle's eye ... a sparrow's fall ... a house built on sand ... a shepherd with his sheep. Not only in the stories he told, but in the very words he used, Jesus was visual. He found a way to put spiritual ideas into earthly terms.

Gerald and I call this *metaphoric preaching.*

Metaphoric preaching, as I think of it, is based upon understanding that the mind thinks in pictures. To use a metaphor here: the mind is a camera; it shows a picture.

The human mind cannot think abstractions. We think in concrete images. If I say the word *mother*, for example, that means something to everybody. It will not mean the same thing to everyone; but it will bring a mental image—a picture—to each person's mind. It isn't just a word, *m-o-t-h-e-r.*

The same can be said for any word: *love, freedom, hope, faith, death, life.* Though the ideas contained within those words are abstract, our mind comes to grip with their meaning through pictures and feelings that we associate with them.

Understanding more about how the mind works has convinced me that preaching that gets through to people must be metaphoric in nature.

Because preaching deals with ideas and ideas tend to be abstract, preachers all too often talk in abstractions and generalities. They talk *about* things without detailed explanations or graphic descriptions. They remind me of the often quoted description of a philosopher: "a blind man in a coal mine at midnight looking for a black cat that isn't there."

If a man leads a tour into obscurity, he will not likely be overrun with followers. He may be deep, but he will also be lonely.

Anchoring the divine idea to the human situation is the essence of preaching. However true the abstractions are, they are subtractions.

The other day I listened to a taped message of a preacher whom

I know to be a good man—an intense, godly, scholarly man. The tape played twenty-five minutes before I got the first picture.

Before we are too critical of him, however, let us remember that we all have been guilty of that. Our sermons are full of abstract jargon:

"What we need today is more sanctification."

No picture.

"We need a genuine deep work of the Holy Ghost."

Again, no picture—unless you count non-Christians in the audience imagining Casper with a halo!

The statements are true. But for most people, those words slide in one ear and out the other. People understand the point better when we present it in real-life, metaphoric terms.

A metaphor, you recall, is a pictorial comparison of one thing to another. It pictures or describes something by comparison. From school days, you probably remember studying similes and metaphors.

A simile compares one thing to another by using *like* or *as*. I'm *hungry as a bear*, for example; or *the night sky looked like blue velvet.*

A metaphor gives an even stronger image by substituting one thing for another in comparison. She's *a tiger when she's angry!* Or, for literature lovers, Alfred Noyes' "The Highwayman" includes this gem: *"The road was a ribbon of moonlight."* Literature is full of such images or pictures—and sermons need to be.

Metaphorically, we might say, for example, that *sanctification* is … not flashing your bright lights at people who don't dim theirs. *Sanctification* is … not getting upset when you cut yourself shaving. *Sanctification* is … not kicking the neighbor's dog when he topples your garbage can to eat your garbage. Sanctification is … feeling as though your cup is full of grace instead of grease.

Understand the point here.

We are not saying you should never use statements like *"Christians need sanctification."* But when you use abstract religious terminology like that, those words need definition, explanation, and some concrete examples from real life to put the idea across.

When you talk in abstractions—without making the effort to translate those abstract ideas into concrete, visual terms—you are just verbalizing, and your listeners are lost trying to follow you.

In short, talk in abstractions, you lose people; talk in pictures, you gain people's attention and hold it—they more likely will understand what you are wanting them to see.

I listened to a preacher just recently, a good preacher supposedly, who talked for forty-five minutes and was totally abstract. I had to force myself to listen to him, and it was a tiring process. I had to do my own visualization … add my own color to it … put my own objects in it. What he said was true. But it didn't paint any pictures.

Preaching without making images is like painting with clear water: no matter now energetically we do it, we leave no lasting impression.

Learning To Visualize

Metaphoric preaching, then, involves tapping into our own mental images (pictorial thoughts) and translating them into words that recreate those images in the minds of our listeners.

It's a skill essential to effective communication, but easier said than done.

The basic stumbling block to more visual preaching is this: our verbal skills are so impoverished, that we lose much of the picture in the translation. The challenge, then, becomes one of learning to verbally visualize pictures.

People of this generation were not brought up with radio, and they are the poorer for it because they cannot mentally visualize. The old radio programs created visual pictures in the mind. Almost anyone over fifty can tell you their image of Fibber McGee and Molly's closet, the screaking door on "Innersanctum", what Sergeant Preston of the Yukon looked like, and so on. Today, television provides pictures for us—in living color, no less. So we no longer visualize.

What that means is that we preachers have to work at retraining our minds to visualize verbally. It takes concentration, discipline, and practice. But you can learn to paint a verbal picture that will help your listeners "see" what you are describing to them. And those metaphoric images will help them remember the message.

Charles Ludwig once made a great point to a young minister

about visualizing: "If you are telling a story about a boy walking down the street, don't just say, 'A boy walked down the street.' Say 'a red-headed boy...' "

"People see that," he said. "It puts color in it. Now don't put a red-headed boy in every sermon. But learn to bring something of color to the mind in a picture and people identify with it."

Good preaching is not an accident. The best preaching typifies the old saying, "Art is art that conceals art." The trick is to retrain your mind to think in pictures and hone your verbal skills to describe those pictures vividly for your listeners.

John Denton was a preacher who developed in himself the power of description. He did it in part by practicing description as he drove around town. Telephone poles, stop signs, convenience stores—whatever he saw, he would describe it out loud to himself the way he would describe it in a sermon. Over time he came to notice the smallest details, so that eventually, he was painting vivid word pictures almost unconsciously. He became an expert at metaphoric preaching, and his sermons were memorable.

Anyone can do that. Lock into a system of visualizing on a daily basis that works for you. Look at things in detail and describe them to yourself until it becomes second nature. Let that become your strong point.

Following Christ's Example

Jesus was a metaphoric preacher.

In the past when I was characterized by people as a "storytelling preacher," I took it as an affront.

"I really preach the gospel," I protested. "I don't just tell stories."

I remember one time a woman in my congregation took me aside and said, "Pastor, you know I love you ..."

After you have pastored for a while, you know that those words more often than not are preface to a lot of trouble. So I braced myself.

"I love you," she said, "and you're a good man and all that. But I have trouble with your preaching."

"Well, I have trouble with my preaching, too; but I'm trying to remedy it."

"You preach the gospel all right," she said, "but you tell too many stories."

Then came the boom: "Why don't you just preach the Bible like Jesus did?"

Well, I took the woman's suggestion to heart and started a personal study of how Jesus preached. Try it yourself. Read the gospels. Guess what you'll find. He told stories! Only he called him parables. In fact, the Bible says that "without a parable he didn't speak to them" (Matthew 13:34, NKJV). If he couldn't paint a picture, he didn't tell it.

Ever since then, I stopped telling stories. I tell parables! And I have been indebted to my critic for her sage advice.

Recently I read an article that said Jesus used fifty-four metaphors in the Sermon on the Mount. Even reading slowly, it takes only about fifteen minutes to read the Sermon on the Mount. That averages out to 3.6 pictures every minute!

Are you open to a challenge? Listen to one of your sermons on tape and pick out the metaphors. How many pictures do you have per minute?

"But I want to be spiritual," you say.

Well, who was more spiritual than Jesus? And if he had 3.6 pictures every minute, you ought to have one every now and then.

When we talk about being visual, you see, we are not just saying bring a map to church and hold it in your teeth—although that helps.

Take a cue from the Master himself. Jesus set a child among them, took bread and broke it, showed them a coin, held up a flower, pointed to a bird and a city on a distant hill, and all these things. Time and again he prefaced his point by saying "The kingdom of heaven is like ..." and then painted a down-to-earth, unforgettable picture: a farmer sowing, a woman baking, a man digging up buried treasure, a merchant finding the perfect pearl, an unforgiving servant, ten girls at a wedding. His illustrations came from real life: a widow's offering; a fruitless fig tree; separating sheep and goats, wheat and tares; pruning grape vines. And his parables were simple, but vivid, spellbinding stories that made an indelible print on the mind and on the heart: a lost coin, a lost sheep, a lost son.

If Jesus was visual in his preaching, shouldn't we be?

As you become more skilled at visual preaching, you won't have to be encouraged to do it. You will be motivated by the positive reaction you will see in the faces of your people and in comments they make that let you know your messages are getting across.

For the courageous preacher, I suggest this exercise. Listen to a recording of any sermon or talk you have given. List all the *abstract, empty* words you used. Then try to replace them with words that paint pictures. Begin to think creatively in pictures.

Now, picture yourself in a wider, more effective ministry.

Chapter 6

Making Sermons Verbal

For thirty years Jesus lived a sinless life in Nazareth, and nobody thought he was anything more than a carpenter's son. Only when he stood to preach in the synagogue—*verbalizing* who he was—did he create a stir.

As powerful as visualization is, preaching involves more than seeing a good example or hearing a good story. Jesus' life in every way was exemplary. But when he read from the scroll of Isaiah that fateful Sabbath and then said, "This day is this saying come to pass in your hearing"—then, the people tried to run him off the brow of the hill.

It was *verbalization*, the speaking of the truth, that aroused them.

People are not won to Christ merely by seeing a good example in the life of their pastor or other saints in the church. God's Word must be proclaimed with power. The great tenets of our faith must be communicated verbally.

Gerald Marvel has an unsaved neighbor who calls himself a "Christian agnostic." Talk about a contradiction in terms! Using this man as an example, Gerald speaks of the importance of verbalizing the gospel:

> I can live a perfect life beside him. He might notice there is something different about me, but that doesn't tell him about the incarnation of Christ. My neighborliness or kindness or generosity or any other admirable traits he may see in my life—none of that tells him about the gospel ... or the atonement ... or the resurrection ... or about the Holy Spirit. My being a good neighbor doesn't tell him a thing about salvation.

Verbalization of the gospel is the number one goal of preaching—the only goal that gives preaching any validity. Our challenge as preachers is to continually search for a thousand ways to communicate verbally that single message in words that are simple, clear, emphatic, moving.

How Many Are You Reaching?

Let me put in a plug for books by Rudolf Flesch. Most are out of print, but a few are still around. An early one was *The Art of Plain Talk.* I bought as many of those as I could find. For years I have given them to pastors, and without exception every one who has studied the book has become a better preacher. What Flesch has to say about words should be a part of every minister's preparation for preaching.

We have already said that preaching is more than words. But preaching uses words. As a metaphoric analogy, think of it this way: a carpenter is more than a hammer, but a carpenter without a hammer isn't much of a carpenter. Words are not preaching, but you cannot preach without them. Thus, the more you know about them and the better command you have of them, the better you can preach.

Rudolf Flesch is a proponent of plain talk. He calls it an art.

If you think people talk plain, you have not heard much preaching, because preachers are masters at obscuring things.

I preached one day in a church in Indiana; and the next morning while I was sitting in a restaurant, a woman I did not know called to me from an adjacent table. She said, "I was in church yesterday morning. My husband was with me. I finally got him to church. He comes once every month or so. I drag him in there. But, you know what, he almost got saved yesterday. You're the first preacher he ever understood."

After that I started listening to preachers as though I were an outsider. Friends, we talk spiritual Chinese and wonder why nobody listens!

Plain talk is not a matter of one given way of doing it. Flesch has been recognized as being perhaps the most astute analyst of the spoken word that we have had in our country. He not only criticizes fuzzy and nonproductive speaking and writing, he gets specific in analyzing what is wrong with it. Here, in a nutshell, is a summary of his directive for "plain talk." If you want to be heard, here's how you do it:

> *Use shorter sentences;*
> *use simpler words;*
> *be more personal;*
> *and you will appeal to more people.*

It's that simple.

First, you'll have to go to the library or to a high quality book store. Ask for one of Flesch's books. Borrow or buy one if you can find it. Any of them is a good investment. In addition to *The Art of Plain Talk*, other excellent ones are
- *The Art of Readable Writing.*
- *How to Test Readability.*
- *How to Write, Speak, and Think More Effectively.*

In each of these you will find help and find it abundantly.

All these books contain a one- or two-page test for readability. For instance, it's on page 309 in *How to Write, Speak, and Think More Effectively*. It's a chart that measures the words per sentence, and gives reading ease scores and other factors.

Using Flesch's chart, you can actually analyze your own speaking or writing. While you are congratulating yourself on your cultured and intellectual approach, pour yourself a cup of coffee and take a closer look at the chart to see what happened to your audience! When you discover your style, you also find out who you are talking to—and who you lost along the way. Rate yourself and see how well you come across as a communicator.

You will find categories of difficulty in the column under *Style: Very easy, Easy, Fairly easy, Standard, Fairly difficult, Difficult, Very difficult.*

You will want to note that words in the *Difficult* and *Very difficult* categories are labeled as *academic* and *scientific*.

Do you realize, friends, that most of us preachers fall into those categories? With our love for theological terms, we are, at the least, *academic*. That means for the average person in the pew we may as well be speaking a foreign language.

For example, you hear people who are into computers talking about computers. If you don't have a computer and don't know anything about computers, they could as well be talking Chinese. They jabber away about rams, roms, modems, bytes, bits, hard drives, software, floppies—all kinds of things. You stand there scratching your head, wondering where you left your floppies the last time you wore them!

It's all perfectly simple to them. But you are totally left out.

That is precisely how it feels for people in your church when you use the language of Zion with people who live in Babylon. That is the picture.

So Flesch has worked out a scientific formula to show that if you are in those upper categories—the *academic* or *scientific* levels— you may be reaching only twenty-four percent of your people at most. If you have a congregation of one hundred, that means seventy-six of them understand very little of what you are saying as you stand there behind the pulpit pontificating on Sunday morning. That should be a wake-up call!

If seventy-six percent of your people got up and walked out on you some Sunday, I dare say you would be upset. But people are not going to walk out on you visibly. They just walk out mentally. They tune you out, that's all.

But if you knew about that *academic* percentage, what would you do?

Would you not say, "How can I get more of them to listen to me?"

And using your head, might you not logically reason, "Let's lower the level a little bit"?

Another of Flesch's charts details the importance of "getting personal." He presents a range of personal references (human interest words: names, nouns, and pronouns relating to people) found in different types of magazines. Their interest rating is determined by their "human interest" score and their appeal to the majority of adult readers.

Interest levels range from *dull* (a term many people associate with scientific journals) to *interesting* (typical of digests of various kinds), to *dramatic* (a quality of fiction, which, by the way, shows the highest "human interest" score, averaging fifty-eight or more personal references in every hundred pages.

Preaching is personal or it is simply mechanical. Short sentences and two syllable words alone won't capture and hold interest.

In summary, Flesch's formula suggests that if you use simple, ordinary language—meaning short sentences, uncomplicated words, and more personal references—you can reach ninety percent of your people.

Probably nothing you do will reach one hundred percent; but ninety out of one hundred is not bad, especially if previously you were reaching only twenty-four.

Now, doesn't it make sense to get more simple?

I grew up as, you might say, an intellectual type. I mean, I used to read the dictionary and I used a lot of big words. And it was impressive. Several years ago when my son and daughter were in junior high school, they were going though my study one day. In some old files they found a recording of a speech I had made in college for one of my classes. That was before tape recorders, so it was on a 78 RPM disk. The kids had put it on the record player and were listening to it when I walked into the room.

Teasing them, I said, "Who is that? Guess who it is."

They couldn't guess.

"Well, guess," I persisted. "Listen. Guess."

Still they couldn't guess.

Finally, I said, "Well, that is your father."

And my daughter, Lori, the younger of the two, spoke up and said, "Wow, Dad! Back then you were smart!"

Well, I listened to that speech; and I knew what she meant. I was using a lot of ten-dollar words and long sentences with involved construction. Fortunately, I'm smarter now than I was then.

By the way, that speech was so complicated, I could hardly understand it myself!

Flesch's chart is fairly straightforward to use. Select a passage of one hundred words from a recent sermon. Count the number of affixes (prefixes and suffixes) in the words you used in that passage. Count the number of words in each sentence. Count the number of personal references. (*I, we, our, you, they, he, she,* and so forth).

In *The Art of Plain Talk* Flesch gives a more complex mathematical procedure for determining the difficulty level of your speech; but he thoughtfully provides a quick method of calculating, as he puts it, "for those who hate figures." We'll use that recipe here:

Take the average number of affixes per 100 words, subtract the average number of personal references in 100 words, and divide by two. Then add the average number of words per sentence. Check the results against this scale:

Very Easy	up to 13
Easy	13–20
Fairly Easy	20–29
Standard	29– 36
Fairly Difficult	36–43
Difficult	43–52
Very Difficult	52 or more
	(Flesch 65)

Try it. See where you come out.

At first glance you might suppose that using simpler words would limit vocabulary. In reality, the reverse is true. Choosing the right words for everybody calls for a greater understanding of words and their use. A part of being simple is being more precise. Your vocabulary will actually expand.

Being simple takes more skill than being complex. Somewhere I read that in the General Motors' laboratories a motto on the wall says, "When the answer is finally found, it will be a simple one." I think that's true. It takes more skill to simplify and clarify ideas than it does to obscure them.

Flesch points out another important principle. To be sure that you are being understood by a particular audience, you should not only use a level of vocabulary they can understand without effort, but you should, in fact, go one step *below* that level.

We need to be clear on a couple of points here: simplifying does not mean becoming trivial; nor does it mean talking down to people.

Flesch is referring to levels of language experience, not intelligence. As you prepare sermons, be aware that most people do not have advanced educational degrees, but never belittle their intelligence. When you master the art of simplicity, highly educated people will understand you and so will ordinary people and even children.

Do not let "fourth-grade level" or "fifth-grade level" of understanding throw you. When you think about it, a fourth-grader can understand quite a lot. They do.

I once did a lecture on "Understanding the Whole Bible" in Hickory, North Carolina. And after the session that Saturday morning, Marjorie Smith from the Drexel church came up to show me notes her son Brent had made on the lecture. Brent was in fourth or fifth grade at the time. He had it right. I only hoped the adults in the class did as well!

You might ask, "Will educated people be turned off by a simple message?"

Not if Billy Graham's crusade crowds are any indication. Truly educated people are not really impressed, most of them, with strings of adjectives and multisyllabic words or sanctimonious jargon. They may understand a word now and then that others miss. But mostly they are interested in ideas and the impact of the message.

Another relevant example comes from the life of Charles Spurgeon. His path as a young preacher was not easy because he had many enemies in London, and they were basically the clergy. That's right—the clergy! Why? Because they thought he was too simple. Catch the irony here. Nobody was listening to them; they were preaching to empty churches. There they were with all their degrees, and Spurgeon came in without a degree of any kind—a boy preacher—and the crowds were overflowing to hear him. The other preachers were mad at him because people heard him.

If that sounds familiar, you may recall that is precisely why the Pharisees were mad at Jesus. They wanted to preserve the rituals and keep the faith all to themselves.

If you take seriously the art of preaching plainly and simply, somebody sometime will likely say of you, "He's too simple for me." If that happens, just remember that with Spurgeon and Jesus, you are in good company.

Polishing Verbal Skills

Another preacher whose books are helpful in developing powerful communicative preaching is J. Wallace Hamilton. He was a Methodist minister who attended Moody Bible Institute in its infancy. He owed his ministry, he said, to a high school teacher who taught him, in his words, "how to walk around a sentence" and view it from different angles. He said that sentence construction became an art to him.

She would say, "Wallace, try looking at it this way. Walk around it. Look at it this way. Walk a little more around it. Try it from this angle."

Of words he said that everybody has them, but it is how we arrange them—the various combinations we make of them—that works the magic.

Granted, that is technical. But anyone can do it. Effective verbal communication amounts to two simple things:

    1. choosing precise, expressive words (semantics);

    2. arranging them into sentences with a natural flow (syntax).

Hamilton was a master at bringing words and pictures together in a natural flow that made his sermons beautiful and powerful. The skills he achieved can be yours, too, if you are willing to pay the price to get them.

If a workman is known by his tools, a lifelong love for words and a growing skill with them should characterize any preacher. Imagine a dentist working with a pair of rusty pliers as his only tool, a surgeon with a meat cleaver for his scalpel, or a watchmaker with a wrecking bar in his hands. Paul's advice to Timothy (and to us all) emphasizes the power of words and the importance of studying words and their use: "Study to *show* thyself approved unto God, a workman that *needs* not to be ashamed, rightly dividing the word of truth" (2 Timothy 2:15, emphasis added).

Recovery of the importance of preaching should reflect a new reverence for the power of words. The Bible says, "A word fitly spoken is like apples of gold in pictures of silver" (Proverbs 25:11). The power of words is awesome when we realize that in one thousand words or fewer we have "The Declaration of Independence," "The Magna Carta," "The Gettysburg Address," and "The Twenty-third Psalm."

Words can instruct, inspire, chasten, heal, encourage, challenge, move to action, and more. On any given Sunday when you step to the pulpit, unthinkable power is available to you through the words you choose and the way you present them. Your power to convince, convict, and stir to action will be limited by the words at your command and your skill—or lack of skill—in using them.

"But," you say, "the Holy Spirit will give me the words to say."

Yes. I believe that, too. The catch is this: God can use only words you already know. You limit God by the limitations of your vocabulary—as we said earlier, being plain-spoken and simple requires an even larger vocabulary than one built on theological terms and abstract religious clichés.

A serious student of words will make friends with a good dictionary and a thesaurus. But the best way to build a strong working vocabulary is avid reading. Words are all around us in newspapers, magazines, books of all kinds. Develop a curiosity and a healthy appetite for new words. Learn a new word a day. Keep your vocabulary fresh and alive.

Discover the fun of word play by exercising your mind with some verbal gymnastics. What is the softest word you can think of? … the hardest word? … the loudest word? … the most beautiful word? … the kindest word? … the hottest word? … the coldest word? … the wettest word? … the most delicious word? … the most bitter word? … the happiest word?

List all the words you know (or can find) for the colors blue … red … green.

How many different words can you think of to say, "The boy *went* down the street"? *Walked, ran, ambled, sauntered, skipped, hopped, limped, sped, flew, dashed, skateboarded.* You get the idea.

The key to being visual is becoming more verbally adept. Speech is a habit—it is easy to get in the habit of using the same words over and over. Conscious word play keeps our verbal muscles stretched and flexible. The result is more vivid, more colorful, more precise, more interesting speech.

Just as fingerprints are individual and may reveal who we are, speech is also a key to identity. A servant girl, knowing only what servant girls know, said to a shivering disciple, "Your speech betrays you" (Matthew 26:73, NKJV).

Speech always does. What does your speech say about you?

I know some preachers—tremendous people, great potential—whose ministries are suffering because of grammatical errors in their speech. They use expressions that are just bad English—every time I hear them I think, "You don't have to say that. Say it another way. Speech is a habit. And bad habits can be broken. With dozens of inexpensive self-help grammar books on the market, why do you keep on doing it?"

I'd love to tell them that! But grammar is a touchy matter with people. All I would do, most likely, is make them mad; and that would accomplish nothing. But how I wish they could see how distracting and belittling of their intelligence these grammatical blunders are. Maybe they will read this book and recognize themselves. We can always hope.

They were kind to my wife and *I.* (should be *me)*

Just between *we* preachers ... (should be *us*)

My wife and *myself* drove down to Dallas. (should be my wife and *I*)

I *done* the work in half the time. (should be *did*)

It *don't* matter what time we start. (should be *doesn't*)

This Bible verse *infers* that ... (should be *implies*)

Everyone was enthused about the program. (should be enthusiastic)

We had *less* people out sick last week (should be *fewer*)

Her idea was *very* unique (omit *very; unique* means "one of a kind"; no degrees)

While it is true that not everyone will notice errors in grammar or diction, be assured that somebody will. For many people, mistakes in grammar are distractions and take away from the overall effect of the message.

If you see yourself in any of the above infractions of the Queen's English, take heart! Poor speech habits can be broken, and grammar can be self-taught. Grammatical errors are like weeds in a garden. Eliminate them!

One last word of caution about verbal description: once you develop a love for words, the natural tendency is to use too many of them. Being verbal does not mean being verbose. Many times people ruin stories, especially humorous illustrations, by describing too much. The fewer words you can use to get the job done, the better it is. As you know, people are way ahead of you most of the time when you are telling a story or describing something. So don't get so flowing with words that you overdescribe. That will kill you—and your audience, too.

On the wall of an attorney's office in Vancouver hangs a quote from Abraham Lincoln: "An attorney's advice and words are his stock and trade." Tending to a legal matter for his church, Gerald Marvel was in that attorney's office for about twenty minutes, and a bill came to the church for more than $500. Later another bill came for a conversation on the phone: $130. The church paid nearly $650 dollars for someone's "advice and words" and about three pieces of printed matter. That is tangible evidence that words are a valuable commodity.

Think of it, pastor. Words are also our "stock and trade." Seldom are we paid $500 for a twenty-minute sermon, but what we have to share is more valuable than anything money can buy.

We are not called to impress people with our sagacity or our prowess with words. But we want to sharpen our verbal skills to express God's message as simply and clearly as we can—so that people of all backgrounds and all ages might understand and respond to God's verbal expression of unconditional and abiding love.

Chapter 7

Making Sermons Visceral

To preach without feeling is to fail at communication.

I can talk about this point. I'm something of an expert on it, because I grew up with a lot of mistaken ideas taught me by my elders.

I was born in 1922 in Kansas. When I was twelve, my mother died. I was the oldest of the boys in our family—a Swedish family. And I was taught by example that boys do not cry. Men do not weep. Men solve life's problems and get on with it.

When my mother died, I didn't cry. A little cotton-headed kid without a mother stood at the graveside to watch the wilting flowers and see the piles of dirt, and I didn't cry. I didn't cry for ten years.

Without Mother, life was hard; but we made our way. I learned to make it. I left home to go to college. There was no point in writing home for money. They didn't have any. I worked my way through school. I was sick and had lots of problems. Finally I graduated and went traveling around the world after the war. I had it rough, but I didn't cry. I was searching for something.

One day in Louisville, Kentucky, I began to preach a revival. And God suddenly said to me, "You know, your heart is hardened. And you cannot preach if your heart is hardened."

Well, I began to pray for God to melt my heart. I went across town to preach that Sunday morning. I stood before the people, and I could not preach for crying. I could not read a text for crying. And from that time on, I began to say, "Oh, God, I thank you for my brain; but help me keep a compassionate heart."

Feelings Open Doors to Learning
and Problem Solving

Visceral is a good word. It may be a little pedantic, but it holds an important lesson about preaching.

The ancients believed that the seat of the emotions was in the viscera—in the stomach and intestines. Later in our thinking we transferred that function to the brain. But now we are learning that the sages of old were probably right. If you worry, for example, it is not your brain that gets sick. You get ulcers in your stomach. If you are anxious, you can't eat; it isn't that you can't think.

We are discovering, too, that learning is visceral before it is mental. Make a note of that. It is an important point for preachers as well as teachers.

Learning is visceral *before* it is mental.

Simply put, what does not get through the emotions, does not get to the brain. If there is an emotional barrier, people are not going to learn.

How is it, for example, that a boy who can't make a passing grade in the classroom because he doesn't understand fractions or the metric system can talk endlessly about the cubic displacement of a motorcycle or expertly rattle off the batting averages of two dozen ball players?

Feeling is the answer. He has bad feelings toward the classroom and good feelings for the open road and the ball field.

While I was pastoring in Daytona, we started a Christian school. When I served for a time as principal of the school, I found my day suddenly filled with discipline problems. From eight in the morning until four in the afternoon, my office was filled with students sent there for discipline. Troublemakers.

This is no life, I thought. There must be some way to overcome this problem. The children, I surmised, were unhappy in the classroom because they were poor students—probably couldn't read. So, I insisted that every student be tested in reading.

My guess paid off. Tests showed that our students averaged two to three grade levels below the national average in reading. Many of them had come to us as problem students from other schools. Obviously, if they could not read, they would not learn. If they were not learning, they were going to cause trouble.

So we started a reading program.

With a little luck and divine guidance I hired a beautiful young woman with a vivacious personality to be our reading "expert." Actually she knew no more about teaching reading than most teachers already on staff. She had taken a couple of reading courses. But I met with her before she began and laid out a secret plan.

She would start with the most delinquent students. My message to her was simple: "Convince these kids that reading is fun and that they *can* learn to read."

You know what? It worked!

In the first place, students were eager to spend time with the personable young woman. They wanted to please her—some to impress her! But the real secret was that she was smart enough to know that the reason these kids couldn't read was not a brain barrier, but a gut barrier.

They had been told by urging, sometimes nagging, parents and impatient teachers: "You *have* to read … you *have* to learn … reading is *hard* work … you are *not putting out enough effort*," and so on—always with somebody holding a ruler over them.

Picture the contrast. Now we have the smiling encouragement of a pretty young woman saying, "Reading is *fun*. It's *easy* to learn. Let me *show you how*."

The students lapped it up. The emotional barrier was down. Within two weeks those kids started to read. They were begging for books. They were taking books home. They were even pulling stuff out of the wastebasket to read! Grades soared. Discipline improved. The faculty was amazed. Parents were ecstatic.

They said, "That girl is a genius!"

I just smiled.

But looking back at it, I see that it reinforces what I am saying here: the barrier was an emotional thing. Solve it there—at the emotional level—and you solve it all down the line. When you address your idea to the emotions, you get through to people.

Perhaps you recall from high school a famous scene from Shakespeare's immortal *Julius Caesar*. The mighty Caesar, popular ruler of Rome, has just been assassinated by members of the Roman senate who feared that the people would make him emperor.

To noble Brutus falls the lot of explaining Caesar's death to the agitated mass of Roman citizens thronging the capital. Brutus had been Caesar's best friend and is highly respected by the people as an honorable leader.

Obviously a left brain, Brutus steps forward and in clear, unimpassioned tones explains logically to the people—in Roman numerals, of course: I, II, III—why Caesar had to die. He does a good job. At the conclusion of his speech, the crowd wants to crown Brutus king.

He should have accepted their offer on the spot. But Brutus, you recall, was much too honorable for that. Brutus, instead, makes two mistakes. First he honors Mark Antony's request to say a few words at Caesar's funeral. His second mistake is encouraging the crowd to stay and listen to Antony.

Antony's speech is a masterpiece of visceral elocution. He knew what Brutus did not—that the battle for the minds of the Roman people would not be won by logic. He knew that the door to sway their thinking lay not in their minds, but in their emotions.

Thus, Antony takes a right-brained approach, helping the crowd visualize Caesar in various scenes of well-doing for the good of Rome. He paints emotional pictures of Caesar as a hero, winning battles and bringing home treasures to benefit every Roman citizen. He creates an image of Caesar as sharing every citizen's pain and sorrow: "When that the poor have cried, Caesar hath wept." And at that point Antony himself weeps before them: "Bear with me; My heart is in the coffin there with Caesar, / And I must pause till it come back to me."

It is a masterful, well-planned, expertly executed speech. And it does what Antony knew it would do. It stirs the people to grief and rage. By the end of Antony's oration, the crowd has become a lynching mob moving off to seek and destroy Caesar's attackers— including noble Brutus.

In the battle of logic over emotion, emotion always wins.

If you as a church leader think you are going to solve a problem on a factual basis, you are wasting your time. It is an axiom of dealing with human relationships: facts don't matter; feelings do!

Somebody comes in saying, "I don't like the way the church is spending money" or "I don't like the way they've organized the choir" or "I don't like the length of your sermons" or "I don't like that story you told."

If all you do is try to adjust the sermon or the song or the paint or the carpet to please them—you, my friend, are in for a long, hard, and rough ride. Because those things are not the problem.

The problem is that those people have some feelings about you that they don't want to admit. These other things are the pretext. Uncover and correct the feelings, and it is amazing how the problems diminish.

The Preacher as a Moving Agent

Clide Fant observed that "it is not in the order of nature that rivers shall flow up hill, and it does not often happen that zeal rises from the pew to the pulpit."

On the other hand, genuine fire in the pulpit will warm the hearts of listeners.

Have you noticed that no one warms his hands at the make-believe flames of the artificial fire in the fireplace? But on a cold night, no one needs to urge people to gather around the flame of a real fire. Jeremiah felt compelled to preach:

> … His word was in my heart like a burning fire
> Shut up in my bones;
> I was weary of holding it back,
> And I could not.
>
> (Jeremiah 20:9, NKJV)

Jeremiah didn't want to preach. His preaching was unpopular. He was being mocked and ridiculed. He wanted to hang it up—to shed the preaching mantle God had placed on his shoulders. But he could not. He *had* to preach. Like fire in his bones, he could feel it!

If you want to move people, you yourself must be moved. If your message doesn't move you, it is not going to move them. A preacher who is moved deeply will be able to move others deeply. A sermon that is merely a dull recital of half-digested truths will have no power to inspire spiritual hunger in the listener.

In discussing the verbal aspect of preaching we said that preachers are prone to use words nobody understands. Let me tell you this: even a baby understands emotion. Even the tiniest baby understands love.

I have to say this, though it pains me to do so. Having served at almost every level of the church—in the state, the national, the international, the personal, big church, little church, and all kinds of places—I have met some men and women who should not be in ministry. They do not belong in a pastorate for the simple and basic reason that they do not love people. The ministry to them is a just a job—like working in a factory from seven to four. The sooner they get through with their "obligations" for the day the better they like it. They don't like to mix or mingle. They hate to visit. They want only the most superficial of relationships with the people they serve.

To make matters worse, these misfits characteristically don't like to share authority. They like being "the pastor"—they like the position and the sense of power they imagine it gives them. They like to dominate and manipulate. But they don't like people. Subsequently, they do a lot of damage to the congregations who hire them, and to the ministry as a whole.

Even a pastor with little or no formal training for ministry can be successful if he or she loves people. That is not to say training is unimportant. Naturally, we all want the best training possible to develop our gifts for ministry and preaching. But I have found that people don't really care as much about degrees as they do about whether or not the pastor is "real" with them and really loves them.

Thornton Wilder wrote a three-minute play called "The Pool of Bethesda." Bethesda, of course, was the place in Jerusalem where the infirm people gathered; and the first one into the pool after an angel troubled the waters would be healed. In Wilder's play, the angel has stirred the waters, and people are rushing to the pool. Among them is a physician with a horrendous wound on his back. He is about to step into the water, when the angel speaks:

> Draw back, physician. Healing is not for thee. Without your wounds, where would your powers be? It is your sorrow that puts kindness in your face and causes your low voice to tremble in the hearts of men. And not even the angels of themselves can heal the wretched like one mortal broken on the wheel of life. In Love's service, only the wounded can serve.

Powerful message in those lines, for preachers as well as physicians. Something within us—call it passion, emotion, deep feeling—must come through in our preaching. And it is living through good times and bad times, times of pain and times of joy, and all that comes in between that puts emotion there. Effective preaching risks sharing our lives with our people, sharing passionately with them whatever life is teaching us, what we genuinely care about, what matters most.

That is not to say that every Sunday we lay out all our sorrows and woes before the congregation. But something deep within our souls must communicate to people that we care passionately about what we are saying.

Haven't you heard sermons preached with absolutely no feeling in them? I have.

Some of them have been delivered eloquently, intellectually, perfectly. But I would have given anything during one of those emotionless dissertations if just for a moment the preacher might have stepped to the side of his bulwark of a pulpit and said, "Let me tell you what happened to me."

Never happens.

For these speakers the sermon is a kind of ivory-towered oration, the delivery of a beautiful thing that is lofty and glowing, but somehow never reaches down to the level of the human heart. And so it soars high above the listeners' heads, a thing to be admired; but because it has no feeling, they don't take it in. They don't identify with it.

People tend to put their pastor on a pedestal. The preacher, it is imagined, lives a pristinely pure life with never a tainted thought or flushed collar. Like the hero in cowboy films of yesteryear, he never gets a speck of dirt on his white shirt in the roughest fistfight, and he sleeps in his white hat.

That's a tough image to live up to.

You need not make this a habit. Please don't. But occasionally, take off your white hat. Let your congregation know how God has been dealing with you concerning your arrogance. Every now and then let them know how God has dealt with your stubbornness. Tell them how God is dealing with you in some of your prejudices. Let the congregation know occasionally about a mistake you made and how hard it was to own up to it—how hard it was, for example, to say to your children, "I was wrong," and to ask for their forgiveness.

Every pastor I know has had to deal with conflict of one kind or another that has resulted in personal hurt. Let's face it. Personal hurt is an occupational hazard for ministers and their families. We are in the people business, and people are not perfect. Even saints wear muddy shoes. Much of the time we can rise above the hurt or the frustration. Dare I say anger? But sometimes, it gets to us, and we lose it. Pastors are human, too.

When that happens to us—when we lose it—we get a first-hand lesson in how God deals with a bad attitude. Our people can learn from our pain, if we have the courage and the confidence to share it.

Even Gerald Marvel is human. Maurice Berquist, too, hard as it is to admit.

Gerald tells a touching story about wrestling with his own humanness. Some years ago, a conflict arose between him and an individual in his congregation that, in his words, "absolutely absorbed me." The conflict moved from debate—trying to find a resolution—into the realm of bitterness. As Gerald explains it:

> I became bitter—so much so that my wife grew concerned about it. Even my children were concerned about it. And they were after me at the table: "Dad, don't dwell on this." We were eating, and they were trying to reason with me. Finally, I couldn't take it any more. I let them know in short order that what I was experiencing they had never experienced. They were not walking in my shoes, and so on. It was so upsetting to me that I got up from the table and walked out of the house.
>
> To the west side of our house was a little five-foot passage, a gravel path; and I went out there just to stand by myself. I stood there. It was one of the most frustrating moments in my whole life. I felt that nobody on this earth understood me. I was totally alone. And totally miserable.
>
> I heard this soft scratching of the gravel, but I never turned around. And my daughter came up behind me and said these words:
> "What about Jesus?"
> Then she turned around and walked back in the house.
> And I had to go in and ask for forgiveness.

A long time passed before Gerald could share that from the pulpit. But when he did, it really touched the hearts of the congregation. He was broken up in telling the story. And the congregation was broken up in hearing it. But that is when God can do some wonderful things—in those moments of brokenness.

We are all mortals, broken on the wheel of life. Sometimes that is how we heal.

So preaching is more than an intellectual exercise in choosing a theme, researching the Scriptures, and tossing in a few jokes to hold attention.

That is not to demean what happens in the head. You can't preach without thinking. But the power to move people comes from what happens at gut level—how you *feel* about the message and how well you can get that feeling across.

One day a woman in our church came to me and said, "I want to sing in the choir."

"Good."

"But I don't think I can," she said.

I tried to reassure her. Our minister of music was excellent. We had an outstanding choir. She had a nice voice. She would fit in. Couldn't miss.

Still unconvinced, she revealed more of her concern: "But right now I'm having such problems at home. My husband is an alcoholic. He has threatened to leave me. My heart is broken. If I got up there Sunday morning in the choir, about all I could do is stand there and cry."

My heart went out to her, and I said, "For heaven's sake, get up there and cry. It might be the best song they hear! The important thing isn't whether or not you can hit high C, but how well people know that you are real. Your tears can move people."

That is not to suggest that preachers or soloists need to be sloppy sentimentalists. For a biblical model of a visceral communicator, take a closer look at the Psalms. David was the most transparent person in the Old Testament—so willing to pour out his soul in prayers and praises to God. From deepest despair to ecstasy, he openly and honestly shared what was happening in his life. He was real. And that is why, in many ways, I believe God singled him out as "a man after My own heart" (Acts 13:22, NKJV).

Our God is a feeling God. Jesus wept with his sorrowing friends, even though he knew that Lazarus would very shortly live again. Time and again Jesus looked with compassion upon the crowds that followed him, feeling their hunger and their pain as they reached out to him for hope and healing.

I like the way one writer put it: "God weeps with us so that one day we may laugh with Him."

Preaching without passion, without intense feeling, is not preaching. It may be a lecture disguised as a sermon, but it is not preaching.

The difference between preaching and lecturing should by now be obvious. Lecturing informs: it appeals largely to the intellect. Preaching stirs to action; it appeals to both mind and heart.

Genuine Feeling Evokes Genuine Feeling

One day, when I was pastoring in Daytona Beach, the church secretary, Nita Garmon, brought me a poem one of our church women had written for Mother's Day.

"Read it," she said. "I think it's good."

"Lay it on my desk."

"Read it now," Nita insisted. "Joanne Long wrote it, and she is out here in the hall now."

So I read it. Then I read it again. Finally, a third time. Then I went out in the hall and spoke to Joanne.

"Joanne, this is a good poem."

"Oh, it's nothing really. I'm no writer."

"Joanne," I insisted, "I think I know good poetry when I see it. And I think this poem is good."

"It's really nothing," she said again.

By this time, I was in earnest about convincing her.

"Joanne, I read this poem three times—and to show you what I thought about it, I cried when I read it."

Joanne looked down at the floor. "Well, I'll tell you something. *I cried when I wrote it.*"

That is what does it. Feeling makes the difference.

Without fire in the pulpit, there won't be much fire in the pew. If you go to sleep writing your sermon, don't be surprised to see nodding heads during your presentation. If you are not excited about the message, your congregation certainly won't be.

The essence of preaching is to light a fire, bring wood to it, and then carry that fire to somebody else.

Ralph Sockman, a powerful preacher of a few years ago, observed that some sermons are like "winter sunshine: brilliant, but cold."

"That's clever," you say. But hear this: nobody gets saved by clever sermons or deep sermons. Sermons that come from the heart—visceral sermons—are the ones that do it.

Don't be afraid to be real!

Chapter 8

Making Sermons Vital

Effective preaching is vital. The root word for *vital* means "life." Vital preaching, then, is life-centered. It comes from life and speaks to life.

The best definition of preaching I know comes from Clyde Fant:

> Preaching is that form of verbal activity that moves between the historical revelation [the Bible] and the contemporary situation [life].

Each word in that definition is important. Good preaching involves the revelation of God's Word through the Bible. But it is more than a commentary on Scripture—as appropriate as that might be in its place. Nor is it merely a problem-solving conversation about life in this century.

Preaching is a verbal activity—it moves. It does not stay on one level ("historical revelation") or the other ("contemporary situation"), but moves between them. And it is that movement that makes preaching, preaching.

In a later chapter of this book, we will talk in depth about expository preaching. Expository preaching, if done right, is the greatest thing in the world. But I want to point out here that probably seventy-five percent of what passes for expository preaching is not preaching at all. It is Bible exegesis. It is commentary. But it is not preaching.

Many preachers have the misconception that they are doing expository preaching when they lead people through a passage of Scripture, reading a verse or two at a time, saying "Now, here Paul is ... and here he says ... and here we see ... and he says here ..." and so on. There is no preaching in that. Such commentary only points out the obvious. The congregation can see that for themselves if they have Bibles and can read.

Some preachers may fill in some background to put the Scripture in perspective, saying, "Now the historic situation was this: Paul was in Rome, but he was in jail"—or wherever. And they document this or that event, and pull in a few Greek or Hebrew words to amplify the meaning. That still is not preaching. That kind of thing is great in the classroom. It is excellent in Bible study. But it is not preaching—not expository or any other kind.

On the other end of the scale is another exercise that masquerades as preaching. Popularly known as "life-centered preaching," it never gets into the Bible at all. The preacher just talks about life. It is interesting, but it doesn't go anywhere. You can read that kind of stuff in *Time* magazine or *Parade* or, if you have the stomach for it, in all those tabloids you can buy in supermarkets. Without the Bible connection, these "sermons" offer little really to help people.

So what exactly is expository preaching? Scripture *and* life— *making the connection.* Tying those two things together makes the difference.

Peter's sermon on the day of Pentecost is a good example of this balance in preaching.

For those who insist that sermons must always begin with the Scripture, take note here that Peter started with the *"contemporary situation."* People were acting strangely. Casual observers thought they were intoxicated. Peter addressed the crowd by first acknowledging the strange happenings and then related them to *"the historical revelation"*: "This is that," he said, "which was spoken by the prophet Joel ..." (Acts 2:16).

This and *that.* The sermon moves between these two points. "That which was written," and "this which we now see." Our job in the pulpit is to show how these two things relate.

Both give meaning to the other.

Jesus constantly made that connection in his preaching.

In his parable of the Good Samaritan, for example, the story begins with a man being attacked as he travels. The robbery, the beating, the bleeding— all are part of the "contemporary situation."

One-sided preaching comes along in the persons of the priest and the Levite. Both, intent on "pursuing the Scripture," pass by on the other side, ignoring the contemporary situation encountered on the road. They, studying the Scripture, miss the spirit of it.

By contrast, a despised Samaritan comes along and, seeing the human need, stops to meet it—not quoting the Scripture, but illustrating it. In his simple act of caring, he brings historical revelation (what the Scripture teaches) to bear on the real-life situation.

Preparation for Vital Preaching

How do we prepare ourselves to do vital expository preaching? The same way we prepare to do visceral preaching. We must leave the ivory-towered study once in a while and get out among the people.

Gerald Marvel does a lot of exemplary things in his ministry, and one of them is trying to train his ministerial staff—especially younger ministers working with him—to develop a sensitivity toward people and their feelings. As a part of that training, he requires each of his eight staff members to make one visit a week, preferably in the home of someone they do not know. It's not a difficult assignment, given the size of the Vancouver congregation and the fact that at least a dozen visitors are present every Sunday. On Monday morning the staff report on calls made the previous week.

Occasionally, a staff member may protest: "What does visiting in homes have to do with my area of ministry?"

Gerald's stock answer is, "It has everything to do with it."

"But my ministry is a totally unrelated area. It has nothing to do with—"

"It has everything to do with it," Gerald persists. "I don't feel right if in a week's time I haven't been in at least three or four homes I've never been in before."

"But why? All of us together can't possible call on every home in the church!"

"That's not the point," Gerald insists. "We do it to get in touch with people. To sit in their house ... drink their coffee ... listen to them."

What Gerald says is so true. Being with your people, pastor, is where you learn to feel the heartbeat of life. Those personal contacts give you that gut-level empathy that will keep you real as you prepare sermons and also when you are preaching them.

Gerald cites a classic example of how visiting in a home holds untold importance:

> A couple of weeks ago at the close of the morning worship service, I said, "I want the altar workers and the other pastors to pray with those who have come to the altar. I need to be in the narthex this morning. Some of you I have never met. I want you to take a little time this morning to meet me."
>
> As I shook hands in the narthex, a man and his wife whom I had not met introduced themselves as Ron and Shirley Thomas. I had seen them, but had not had an opportunity to speak with them.
>
> Ron said, "Pastor, we've been coming here a few weeks. And we wanted to meet you."
>
> They seemed so real and genuinely interested that I said, "Ron, I'd like to get better acquainted with you. Next time you are in the service, fill out one of the visitation request cards. Put your name, address, and phone number; and in that little space provided just say, "Pastor, come see us."
>
> The next week, theirs was the first card my secretary brought in to me.
>
> So I called them. "My schedule is pretty full this week, but I could come out Saturday afternoon."
>
> They said, "We're waiting."
>
> Saturday came. And it was hectic. It would have been really easy to justify not making any visits that day. We had company coming. I had hospital calls to make. A marriage counseling session was scheduled for the morning.
>
> But I carved out some time anyway, made my way to the Thomases' home, and sat down in their living room. And although we had only spoken once—the previous Sunday in the narthex— they just opened the door of their hearts.
>
> Shirley said, "What a year, pastor! What a year we've been through."
>
> "What has gone on?"
>
> "My brother committed suicide. Ron has had two heart attacks that resulted in a by-pass surgery. He has been recuperating."
>
> "And it was just now," he said, "that we came to your church trying to find something."

I was moved to think how God had impressed me to stand in the narthex that Sunday morning, even though many people were praying at the altar after the service, and normally I would have stayed there.

I said, "Ron, Shirley, before I pray with you, let me say that tomorrow I won't be preaching—we have a guest speaker—but I'll be praying."

And he said, "We'll be there. We need the church."

Don't you know that visit made a difference in how Gerald thought about his sermons over the next several weeks? That kind of preparation is precisely what he is driving at when he says to his staff—and to the rest of us:

Get out there—knock on doors, press the flesh, let the baby spit up on your shoulder. Get out there and meet the people. Find out where they are and who they are. Live with them. Get into their hearts, and let them get into yours.

That is the most valuable lesson any pastor can learn. For unless you know what life is, you will never be able to bring the spotlight of Scripture to bear on it.

Spurgeon insisted that the preachers he trained—seven hundred of them—get out in the worst places of life, to smell and see and touch and feel what life is about. You don't get that in an ivory tower or from reading somebody's book. It is when you are out there experiencing the agonies and the ecstasies of life alongside your people, that you yourself begin to make relevant connections between "the historical revelation" and "the contemporary situation."

The crossing point between real-life and Scripture has never been illustrated more effectively than in one of this century's most popular books, one that continues to speak to millions in every land. My home town, Topeka, is not famous for my having lived there; but it is famous for Charles M. Sheldon's being there. Charles Sheldon, you recall, wrote the book *In His Steps.*

Sheldon was pastor of a sleepy Congregational church during the Depression. I didn't even know who he was until I left town. But at one point in his ministry his Sunday night church meeting was on the decline. So, out of his frustration, he decided to try something different. Instead of preaching, he would tell stories, and the stories would all explore the question "What would Jesus do if he were here?"

In His Steps, a compilation of those "sermon stories," has been translated into more languages than any book but the Bible and has sold millions of copies all over the world. It was a revolutionary book. But I didn't learn until recently the secret of the book's power.

Sheldon, you see, did not just sit down in his study and conjure up in his imagination what Jesus would do. During those Depression years—before most of you reading this story were born—jobs were impossible to get; poverty was everywhere. During the week Sheldon disguised himself as a workman, went out to apply for work, and took all kinds of lowly jobs. Life was grim in those days, and he exposed himself to it. He felt it all. He stood in unemployment lines and soup lines. He talked to those who were down and out, struggling through those hard times. Then, during the week, he adapted his experiences into stories and projected the person of Christ into each situation.

Little wonder that millions of people found help from that book. It was the story of their life. It was vital.

Friend, when you are out there in the lines during the week, you don't step into the pulpit on Sunday and preach about the Jebusites. You are forced to think about life.

When you, as Gerald Marvel did, sit down with a family whose first words are, "My brother committed suicide last year, and my husband had two heart attacks and by-pass surgery ..."—you are touching real life. What do you tell these people? If you have sat with them, walked with them, talked with them during the week, when you stand facing them on Sunday morning, you will be less inclined to say, "Now, in the Greek, the word *ekklesia* means 'an assembly of ...' "

Preaching becomes vital the closer you stay to life.

Vital Sermons Live and Breathe

For the beginner, illustrating sermons looks like a picnic. Just buy one of those many books of illustrations already catalogued and indexed. How soon the novice discovers that those books make excellent places to press the flowers from grandma's funeral, but they are little help in preaching. Most of them speak of life in another year, sometimes in another century. Little is there that carries the life and breath of today.

A better alternative to canned illustrations are "living illustrations" and "sermonic sparks,"—those germinal ideas that grow into inspired sermons.

Using Fant's definition, relating *"the historical revelation"* to *"the contemporary situation,"* we can work out a sermon planning chart that might look something like this:

Bible narrative or principle	How it applies	Life situation
		rejection loneliness guilt grief indecision sickness divorce, etc.

Certainly no one would cover in one sermon all the "life situations" listed on the chart. Those are broad and inclusive categories of typical situations, intended merely to illustrate a technique for planning a vital sermon. Any one of those categories will contain any number of specific situations that might be addressed in a sermon. The idea is to list whatever situations you are led to address, and then search the scriptures to find what answers God has for them.

I am aware that expository purists will be horrified by this approach. They will insist that we begin with Scripture and then fit life situations into it. While that approach seems logical and highly spiritual, it can lead to answering questions nobody is asking.

If the Bible tells us not only what to preach, but also how to preach, a close inspection of Scripture will reveal as many examples of preaching that begins with life situations as begins with historical revelation.

In truth, no real conflict exists between these two approaches. If we read the Bible while we are in contact with life, we are nourished by the Word. If we look at life while we are immersed in Bible truth, we find the Word relevant.

Good preaching is like rowing a boat: we need to use both oars. Pulling too hard on one oar takes us in circles. Even if the circles are "perfect," they are unproductive.

How does one maintain a balance between biblical authority and living authenticity? The answer is simple enough. Live!

You are one of the best authorities on what happens to living people because you are living.

Sometimes those who listen to preachers have a hard time understanding that even though preachers are anointed to preach, they are still human. Most of them do not have a clerical collar on their pajamas or bowling shirt. Preachers face the same trials other people face.

Unfortunately, preachers sometimes develop a holy schizophrenia—a sanctified but split personality. They have a "sweat shirt" personality and a "stained glass" personality. When wearing their "sweat shirt" personality, they are down-to-earth and "call a spade a spade." But upon entering the pulpit, for some reason, they refer to that same shovel as "an implement of archeological research."

Stained-glass prayers, in deep resonant tones, begin: "Omnipotent sustainer of life, omniscient solver of mysteries, and omnipresent benefactor of all mankind...."

Sweat shirt prayers cry out: "O God, help me. Hear me. Get me out of this mess!"

Authentic scriptural living will produce authentic scriptural preaching. It will be vital.

We speak of preaching being "incarnational," meaning that it must be clothed in the humanity of the preacher. Vital preaching comes out of the preacher's life.

In the graphic language of scripture: "Out of his belly shall flow rivers of living water."

The effective preacher speaks of what he or she has experienced.

A young preacher came to me with a problem. "I have 'tried out' for a number of pulpits, but the people just do not like to hear me preach."

As I was about to suggest some ways he might make his preaching more interesting and helpful, he said, "I know my sermons are good. I get Gerald Marvel's tapes every week, and I preach the same sermons almost word for word. People love him, but they don't like me. What is wrong?"

The young man's problem is the difference between igniting a firecracker and painting a picture of one. He has not lived the message.

Only sermons that come from life can speak to life. If they come from the heart, they will reach the heart. If messages are mechanically reproduced, the congregation may as well have sent for the tapes themselves and stayed home to listen to them in the comfort of robe and house slippers.

How To Stay Vital

A pastor out of touch with people is out of touch with life. Spend time with your people, if only one visit a week to a home or someone's place of business. You preach better when you know firsthand that there are people sitting before you on Sunday morning who need to feel the presence of God.

And there are other benefits. Even in this modern age, something about a pastor going into someone's home—sitting down and praying with them, maybe reading a few verses of Scripture, and hearing them out—gives him or her more authority and dignity in handling the Word of God on Sunday.

I hope you are getting the idea: preaching is more than thirty minutes of talking on Sunday. It is a lifestyle. And each of these words we are talking about—*visual, verbal, visceral, vital*—is a key to shaping that lifestyle so that inevitably you become a better preacher.

Chapter 9

Making Sermons Vicarious

"If you are leading and nobody is following, you are just taking a walk."

That bit of wisdom was given me by a pastor who felt his work was finished in his present parish. "They are not with me," he said, "and I don't know how to bring them up to speed."

Vicarious preaching might have saved him.

By vicarious we simply mean that the listener is brought along with the speaker—to see what he sees, to feel what he feels, to learn what he learns.

Vicarious preaching is going on a journey and taking people with you. If you speak a language your traveling companions—your listeners—do not know, they don't hear you.

If they cannot feel with you, they won't identify with what you are saying. If your preaching does not relate to life as they know it, they won't understand.

Vicarious preaching brings together all the characteristics of good preaching we have talked about thus far into an unforgettable moment in which the preacher invites the audience to enter his mind and heart and transports them—much as John was transported in his vision of the Revelation—to see and feel things they know not of.

The art of vicarious preaching comes through the power of imagination and vivid description. If the preacher has developed the skills of being visual, verbal, visceral, and vital—the vicarious experience will happen almost automatically.

But the preacher can enhance the effect by being aware of when and where in the message he wants it to happen. For example, involving the audience vicariously to begin a sermon captures attention and pulls people immediately into the mood and framework for the message. Vicarious involvement in the middle of the sermon stirs people awake as an important concept springs to life. It also makes for a powerful, highly motivational ending.

Of course, the gospel message itself is a vicarious experience—that Christ suffered and died for us. Christ being the vicarious atonement for our sins is the heart of the gospel. It should be the heart of our preaching to take people into that experience in a way that makes it real to them—and unforgettable.

Getting People Vicariously On Board

How do we get people on board as we speak? Here are some practical suggestions:

1. Eliminate physical barriers:
Whenever possible, I like to step out from behind the pulpit or podium to eliminate that physical barrier between me and the people to whom I am talking. If it is possible to move down from the dais or platform, I do that, too.

2. Eliminate verbal barriers:
Preachers need to be sensitive to the people in a given audience. It may help to imagine yourself as a tour guide and think about who exactly are the people you expect to board your tour bus on Sunday morning. How are you going to talk to them to make the journey interesting and understandable? What words will you choose to reach them?

Keep in mind Flesch's chart showing how technical words and complicated sentences keep people from listening. Every skilled speaker knows that a key word in effective communication is *simplify.*

Keep in mind that every field of knowledge—including the spiritual realm of Christianity—comes with its own specialized vocabulary or jargon. These unique terms and phrases may be well understood and cherished by believers, but totally mystifying to the unchurched. Being "washed in the blood of Jesus," for example, could be a horrifying or repulsive idea to a visitor who knows nothing about Christianity.

It is difficult to converse with people when you are speaking a language unknown to them. If "religious jargon" is important to the point of the sermon, be sure to translate its meaning in terms understandable to the uninitiated.

3. Eliminate pedagogical posture:

Don't come off as a teacher with a condescending attitude who knows something the people in the audience don't know. Never talk down to the audience or belittle their intelligence. Encourage the attitude of "we are learning this together." Alexander Pope's advice still holds true:

> Men must be taught as if you taught them not,
> And things unknown proposed as things forgot.

4. Identify the interests of the listeners:

If Jesus did it, we should try it. To the woman of Samaria, he talked about "the water of life" because she was interested in water. The topic was timely since she had come to draw water from the town well. Item by item, Jesus showed a familiarity with her world. Soon this woman who had begun the conversation with suspicion and hostility was inviting her friends to come and "see a man who told me all that I ever did" (John 4:29, RSV).

Paul used this approach when he talked to the philosophers on Mars Hill in Athens: "As I was passing through … I found an altar with this inscription: *To the Unknown God.*" Using that connection, which immediately caught their interest, he was able to proclaim to them "the One whom you worship without knowing" (Acts 17:23, NKJV).

If you are looking at a group picture, what is the first thing you look for? Yourself. A hundred people may be in that photograph, but you want to know where you are in the picture. Likewise, no matter how graphically some preacher paints a picture in a sermon, unless you fit into it, you are not highly interested.

A skillful speaker knows where the listeners are, connects with them at that place, and then builds a bridge from there to where he wants them to go. If we convince the listeners that we have walked where they walk, they are more likely to walk with us into new areas of thought and experience.

Preparation for Vicarious Preaching

How does a preacher develop skills for vicarious preaching? In much the same way that we prepare for visceral and vital preaching—become involved with people and life as they see it and feel it. In doing that, we ourselves go through a vicarious experience as we try to put ourselves in their place.

I refer again to Spurgeon and what made his sermons so moving. He went out into the streets of London where there was poverty, drunkenness, prostitution, children homeless, all that. He went among them and ministered to them. And he preached to them.

He devotes an entire chapter in one book to street preaching. Now, that experience is a seminary all unto itself! Not many of us do it any more, but street preaching will teach you how to relate. You don't go out there in your black suit and white shirt with coordinated tie and handkerchief. You won't need a three-point sermon. But you will learn to relate to people and feel their lostness and their pain—to identify with them where they are.

I have made several trips to India, and I preach when I go there. On one of my visits, P. V. Jacobs said to me, "We like to have you come over here and preach, Brother Berquist, because you are not like other preachers from the states. They come with stock sermons, and they preach American services to Indian people. You talk about elephants carrying boards down the streets and rubber trees and washing clothes by the river. Your messages relate to life here."

Well, I had not consciously thought about it. But instinctively I was putting myself into their lifestyle and was preaching from that perspective. We have to do that if we expect people to grasp what we are talking about. In the hinterlands of India it would be silly to talk about jet planes; they have never seen one. Talking about people's golf scores would mean nothing. Teenagers there never heard of Calvin Klein jeans or any other brand-name clothes. If we are to lead people to experience the gospel, we must wrap it in what is familiar to them.

A key, then, to vicarious preaching is this: wherever you are, walk where they walk. Put yourself in their skin. Try to see the world through their eyes. You may not get a full understanding or always agree with their view, but gaining even a little insight into their perspective helps you know where they are coming from and how you might make a connection and lead them toward Christ.

The Power of Vicarious Preaching

In vicarious preaching, a transposition happens. Through the magnetism of the speaker's presentation, the listeners are transported through time and space so that they and the speaker become one in mind and in spirit as the message unfolds. What the speaker sees, they see. They hear what the speaker hears, feels, or finds amazing. Whatever is told becomes so real to them, they experience it, too.

The effect is compelling, powerful.

It can be life-changing.

It is the kind of experience that drew a poor Tennessee mountain boy out of himself and into a new world of music.

Nearly everyone knows of Chet Atkins, one of the greatest guitarists alive today. He is bestknown as a "down home country" musician, and he has made millions at it. But he could just as easily be a renown classical guitarist, for he is truly a virtuoso in guitar. How Chet acquired his passion for guitar and came to pursue his illustrious career in music is less well-known.

His father was a music teacher in East Tennessee. The family was very poor and did not often travel to the city. But one cold winter day, when Chet was just a boy, he accompanied his mother to Knoxville. As they walked down the street, they came to a blind man on a corner playing a guitar. Chet was totally captivated. His mother left him there while she went shopping.

As Chet stood there on the street listening to this man play the guitar, he said that something from that blind man and that guitar came into his heart and into his life. "From that moment," he said, "all I ever wanted in my whole life was to be able to play the guitar good enough that I could stand on the street and let what happened to me happen to somebody else."

Vicariously, that blind man's music got through to a young heart that, in turn, gifted the world with some of the most beautiful and distinctive guitar music the world has ever known.

If only we preachers, as we stand to share the gospel message, could vicarously capture someone's heart as effectively!

Chapter 10

Making Sermons Verifiable

Is it too much to expect the preacher to be honest?

The preacher had better be. However small the crowd that listens, always someone will know whether or not a particular statement is right or wrong—or they will be curious enough to check it out. And if, in the enthusiastic proclamation of eternal truth, the preacher makes statements that are not true, who can then believe anything he or she says?

Good preaching is verifiable. Simply put, friends, that means to tell the truth.

You would think preachers, of all people, would tell the truth. But some have a reputation of not doing it—and that is bad.

In the first place, when preachers lie, it is obvious to most people.

In the second place, it is destructive.

And in the third place, it is immoral.

If people cannot believe in the preacher to tell them the way to heaven, what can they believe about anything?

Surely no one called of God to preach would deliberately falsify facts or illustrations. But preachers can be dishonest in many ways without any intent to lie. Here, for example, are a few of the ways preachers can misrepresent the truth:

1. Repeating stories the speaker has not thought through

For many years Clyde Fant taught homiletics at the Southern Baptist Seminary in Dallas and, consequently, claimed to have heard more sermons than any man alive. Certainly, he heard enough sermons to know what preaching is and what it is not.

Somewhere in literature there is a story that made the rounds some years ago and was used by preachers all over the country. You may have heard it—even used it.

> Once Napoleon came upon an old soldier who had but one arm and still wore his uniform. On the faded uniform was displayed the Legion of Honor.
> "Where did you lose your arm?" asked Napoleon.
> "At Austerlitz, sire," the soldier said.
> "And for that you were decorated?"
> "Yes, sire. It is a small price to pay for the Legion of Honor."
> "It seems to me," Napoleon said, "that you are the kind of man who would gladly have sacrificed both arms for his country."
> "What then might have been my reward?" asked the old man.
> "In that case I would have awarded you a double Legion of Honor."
> With that, the old soldier drew his sword and immediately cut off his other arm.

For years that story circulated as an illustration of fervent patriotism. Then one day someone asked the question you are thinking right now: "How did he do that—with only one arm?"

Impossible story. Yet, I can imagine a number of oratorical preachers out there in their long black robes saying, "Now, there is heroism for you. Devotion to country. Lost one arm and willing to lose the other! What loyalty!"

But you know that story is a lie. Wherever it came from, that story is not true. It is not verifiable.

People see through that kind of lying—and they do not appreciate it.

Before you are too hard on all the preachers who have told that story, however, play back other sermons you have heard. Recall even some of your own and ask yourself, "Have I been careful that everything I have told was truly verifiable?"

If anyone's words ought to stand scrutiny, the preacher's should. If you cannot verify a story, don't use it!

2. Personalizing stories that did not happen to you

Good stories get around. Probably the good story you are about to tell has already been heard by many in your listening audience.

That fact by no means precludes your using the story. It simply means that if you tell it as though it happened to you, you sacrifice credibility.

One time, while I was living in Florida, a famous preacher came to speak at the First Baptist Church in Daytona Beach. I wanted to hear a good preacher, so I went over one night. He got up and told this story:

> The other day I was driving down Highway 1 here in Daytona Beach, and I saw a stand selling orange juice. A sign out front said, "All the orange juice you can drink for ten cents." So I stopped and got me a glass of delicious, cold orange juice. It really hit the spot, so I put my glass back on the counter and said, "I'd like another glass, please."
>
> And the girl said to me, "Sir, that will cost you another dime."
>
> So I said to her, "But the sign says, 'All you can drink for ten cents.'"
>
> "Right," she said. "That's all you can drink for ten cents."

Well, the people in the audience laughed politely. But if you live in Florida, you have heard that story a thousand times. It's an old chestnut.

My mind recoiled as he continued to speak. I could not believe he had personalized that story. Later in his message he told other personal experiences, but I kept thinking about the orange juice.

"How do I know you aren't personalizing the other stories you are telling?" I asked silently. Could we depend on any of them being true? Could we depend on anything else he said being true?

For me, his credibility was severely damaged.

I hear other stories like that all the time in my travels around the country. Some preacher stands in the pulpit and says, "The strangest thing happened to me the other day when I was in the Saint Louis Airport"—and then he proceeds to tell some story from James Dobson.

Whenever I hear that kind of thing, I want to stand up and shout: "Quit lying. The incident is not any better because you tell it about you. If it didn't happen to you, don't pretend that it did."

Why lie when you can just as easily say, "A tourist traveling on Highway 1 saw a stand selling orange juice"? The story is equally funny and makes the point equally well.

Why lie when you can just as easily say, "James Dobson tells an interesting story about an incident that happened in the Saint Louis Airport"? The story will be just as touching.

Dobson may not care whether or not you give him credit for the story in your sermon; but when you do, if the story is not true, the problem is his, not yours. Quite likely, some of your people will have read the same article and they will know where you got it anyway. Giving him credit verifies it in their minds and validates your integrity.

There are legitimate ways to use an unverified story. Simply toss in a disclaimer either before or after you tell it. Admit to the audience that it's a story you heard, but can't prove true. If you read it somewhere, say so. There is no embarrassment in that. If the story illustrates a point, use it. But let the people know that you know that it may not be true.

Above all, don't pretend that it happened to you or to the host pastor or to someone you know in the congregation. Some speakers— particularly evangelists and other visiting preachers—are prone to tell humorous stories, inserting names of people known to the congregation for characters in the story. Doubtless, they think that is a good way to build rapport with the audience. They probably assume that everyone knows it is all in good fun and that the laughter puts people at ease and gets them in a good frame of mind for the sermon to follow.

Bad idea!

That kind of folksiness is tiresome. People see right through it.

More to the point, it wastes good preaching time. Starting off with a legitimate story or getting right into the Scripture text will be more appreciated.

I do not, however, want to leave the impression that using personal illustrations is bad.

Quite the contrary—personalizing sermons is a good idea!

More than just good, it's a great idea!

Personal stories catch and hold interest. They give the sermon life, making it human and vital. But personalizing does not mean taking someone else's worn-out tale and casting yourself or someone else in the lead role.

Within your own life and in the lives of people around you are legitimate stories to illustrate any aspect of Scripture you might choose for a text. We talk more about this kind of personalizing in the chapter on illustration, but I simply want to say here that stories from real life most of the time will touch the hearts of people far more deeply than fiction.

Of course, there are wonderful fictional pieces of literature that merit telling again and again—and poetry, too. But day in and day out, the stories you glean from your own life and the lives of people you rub shoulders with every day make the best "stuff" to illustrate sermons.

Another advantage of a real-life story is that it is easier to remember and therefore easier to tell, because it's your story or the story of someone you know well—and you don't have to worry about verification.

One of my favorite personal stories is this one:

My wife, Berny, comes from a part of the country not very well known. We met at a youth convention in Virginia. I was the speaker there. She came from one of the churches in the area. I met her, and we started talking:

I said, "Where do you live?"

She said, "I live in Roanoke."

I said, "Right in Roanoke?"

She said, "No, not right in Roanoke. A hundred and twenty-five miles from there."

I said, "Well, what's the name of the town?"

"We live in Saltville."

"You live right in Saltville?"

"No," she said. "But that's where we get our mail. We live in Allison's Gap."

So I said, "Well, do you live right in the Gap?"

"No," she said. "Not right in the Gap. We live between Lick Skillet and Pump Log Hollow."

Which is true.

And the only thing it's close to is the ground!

I like to tell that story. But do you know what has been simply amazing as I've told that story across the years? Ever so often in my travels around the country, somebody will say to me, "Brother

Berquist, you remember telling about where your wife came from?"

"Yes."

"Well, you know, what I found out? There really is a Saltville. There really is a Gap—and there really is a Lick Skillet. When I first heard you tell that story, I didn't believe you. Now, I believe you."

See? Even when telling the truth we are suspect!

People do check up on us, and all of our stories should withstand scrutiny.

3. Failing to check the accuracy of information

When I chose to use the word *verifiable*, I checked its meaning in the dictionary to be sure I was using it appropriately. I verified its meaning and, thus, can present the word to you with confidence. So it should be with any words or facts or illustrations you may consider using in your preaching.

Every pastor's study—along with all the pulpit commentaries and other reference books—ought to be equipped with a good encyclopedia. If you are into computers, the miracle of CD-ROM gives fingertip access to a complete encyclopedia right in your computer. In a matter of minutes you can check facts and figures on virtually any subject imaginable. There is little excuse today for any sermon to contain faulty information or half-truths. Again, I appreciate so much the preaching ministry of Gerald Marvel, who will tell you that he always verifies any fact before he tells it, because someone in the congregation will know. He says:

> I am convinced that in my congregation no matter what subject I speak on, someone sitting out there knows in infinite detail far more about that subject than I do—and it humbles me. But I have found that when I approach a subject with honesty about the extent of my knowledge of it, people accept it. It's when you don't know, but pretend to know—or when you stretch the truth to make it sound as if you know when you do not—that you sacrifice your reputation, because people see though that in a minute!

Perhaps you have already discovered, as Gerald and I have, that the people in your congregation make wonderful resources to verify

information. You have literally at your fingertips—via telephone—
experts of all kinds in every field imaginable. Use them. They will
be thrilled to help you. Your people possess all kinds of interesting
information that will add a dash of veracity to Sunday's sermon.

4. Exaggerating for emphasis
If people have to down-size the details of your sermon to make
them believable, they will also down-size the rest of your sermon.
And, in the process, they will probably down-size you.

"Exaggerating to make a point," may have been a mark of good
debate and oratory in years gone by, but today's "with it" generation is more appreciative of plain, simple, straightforward facts.

The new bywords are "Keep it simple; keep it honest."

5. Perverting the text to say what you want it to say
Most assuredly the Bible has been quoted to support almost
every argument and every lifestyle. When we build a sermonic
house on a shaky foundation, we should not be surprised if it does
not withstand the storm of investigation. Nor should we be surprised if few people want us to be their spiritual architect.

> Some boys, so the story goes, wanted to trick their biology
> teacher. Knowing that this particular teacher was able to identify
> almost every kind of insect, they concocted a "new specimen."
> Using the body of a grasshopper, the wings of a butterfly, and
> the antenna of a cockroach, they made up a composite bug which
> they brought to the teacher and asked him to identify it.
> "Gentlemen," he mused, "you have a rare specimen here. It's
> called a humbug."

Playing "homiletical hopscotch" through the Bible to find a sen-
sational text or a proof for some personal idea gives rise to "humbug" preaching. And one doesn't have to be a Scrooge to say in
disgust, "Bah ... humbug!"

Reputations At Risk

A story I have heard—and wish I could verify, but cannot—
illustrates well the importance of verifiable preaching:

A missionary in the tropics wrote his board to ask for a refrigerator that would make ice.

"It's not for my pleasure," he said, "but for the sake of the gospel. If I don't get this refrigerator, I may as well come home and not try to preach to these people."

Naturally the mission board was curious. Why should a refrigerator be so important? Besides, the board's policy was that missionaries should live simply, adapting to the basic lifestyle of the country in which they serve.

The missionary explained. "I have been teaching these village people about the Trinity—the Father, the Son, and the Holy Spirit. I have told them that they are three persons, and yet they are one. To illustrate this mystery, I told them that water could be fluid. This they knew. Or it could be gaseous like steam. This they also knew. And that it can also be ice—hard as stone. This they could not believe. They have never seen ice.

"So, now all my preaching is suspect," the missionary wrote.

As ones called to prophesy, we are given a sacred trust to represent not just our own truth, but God's Truth.

Prophets of old wore that mantle with integrity and honor. And so should we.

Thus, every word we speak should be carefully weighed on the scales of honesty and truth. If people are to believe God, they must find ambassadors of God believable.

Chapter 11

Making Sermons Victorious

Charles Spurgeon was not only an effective preacher, but he inspired others to preach. He trained seven hundred preachers during his long pastorate in London. From what we can read, he not only inspired them, but also kept his hand on their ministry and coached them as they preached.

One day a young pastor came to Spurgeon greatly troubled and said, "Dr. Spurgeon, I'm worried about my preaching because sometimes I preach and nobody gets saved."

"Certainly you don't expect people to be saved every single time you preach, do you?" Spurgeon asked.

"Well, of course not," the student replied.

"Ah, that explains it," said Spurgeon.

Expecting Victorious Results

If you expect to see results from your preaching, you must *expect* to see results from your preaching.

Victory in preaching begins with a victorious faith. We are not talking about empty self-confidence here, but faith—faith in the call, faith in the process, faith in the promise that God rewards obedience.

One day when Gerald and I were discussing the main elements of effective preaching, I recalled a particular sermon I had preached scores of times while I was traveling as an evangelist. Wherever I went, this particular sermon was effective. Big church, little church, young church, old church—it didn't matter. Whenever I preached it, the response was phenomenal. It never missed. That may explain why I preached it often.

Then one day I noticed that over the years I had changed everything about the sermon. I had changed the text. I had changed the illustrations. I had changed the approach and the process. I had changed everything. Truly, from Point A to Point Z, nothing remained of the original. Yet it still worked.

That reminds me of the man who said he was still using his grandfather's axe, but he had replaced the head seven times and the handle fourteen times!

When I pointed out to Gerald that I had replaced everything in that sermon, we both had the same question: "Why did it still work?"

What do you think the magic was?

We summed it up in one word: *Victory!*

Nothing remained of the original sermon—except the confidence.

I had come to expect that sermon to produce results.

Whenever I got up to preach, the time frame varied—sometimes the sermon was short because time was limited; sometimes it went longer because we had more time—but I knew from the moment I started that I was headed for a victory.

Nothing is more transparent than the attitude of the preacher.

I recall a particular evangelist we invited one time to my church in Florida. He was a fairly popular fellow and a good preacher. But after the first sermon, I would have been glad to pay him to go home, because he was defeated. He told my people how bad the church was, how bad the future was, and how powerful the devil was. As the week wore on, crowds kept getting smaller and smaller. Strange to say, I was grateful. I hated for him to contaminate any more people than he had to.

But sitting there night after night listening to him preach, I learned something: if I go anywhere, God, please let me go with VICTORY.

Victory is an attitude you carry with you. Whether your congregation is one or a thousand or ten thousand, you set the tone by your attitude of expectancy. If you don't expect much, that is exactly what you will get.

One time I began a revival in a certain city in the United States. I arrived at the church on Saturday. The pastor gave me a tour of the church building, then seated me in a pew and said, "Now, Maurice, you and I are friends."

"Up to now, yes."

He said, "You're here for this meeting."

In those days meetings went for two weeks.

"As a rule," he said, "you have a response to your preaching. You're an evangelist, and you expect things to happen. But you're in a different place here, so don't feel bad if nobody gets saved in this meeting because that just doesn't happen much around here."

He then described the situation.

"We have a men's Bible class. A kind of a social event, I guess. The men come on Sunday morning, and there's a good group. But most of them aren't saved. They leave before church. And they won't come to hear you preach. But don't let it get to you."

Well, I listened to him.

Then I said, "Well, let me just stay around the church a while and pray … kind of get ready for tomorrow."

I will never forget praying there in that church.

I said, "Lord, if we have revival, it certainly will be in spite of this man, not because of him. Not for my own personal aggrandizement, but because I think I am called to preach and to win men and women to Christ, I pray you will make his prediction become untrue."

God laid a burden on me, he really did.

God said, "I want you to expect a miracle."

I began with that. I can tell you this—God did a miracle!

In that meeting we had fifty men saved. They are the core of that church today. The whole church was turned around. It was an exciting story.

But it taught me a lesson: if we don't preach with a sense of victory, we needn't expect miracles from God.

Clyde Fant observes: "He who declares what may or may not be true, and what he considers upon the whole to be as good as any other form of teaching, will necessarily make a very feeble preacher."

Friends, we have the greatest message in the world when we communicate Christ. But if we feel that what we have to say isn't worth saying, we have already conveyed that message before we speak the first word.

Consider the man who got up to preach and said, "Now, before I preach, I've got something I want to say!"

Listen: we are called of God, we are equipped of God, we are guaranteed by God that what we do will not return void—why then can we not expect something to happen?

If we do not move in faith, we accept defeat.

Great preaching is victorious! And victory is an act of faith.

Developing a Victorious Attitude

How do we develop a victorious attitude? These suggestions should help:

1. Remember that we are called.
A victorious attitude begins with confidence—confidence in God and in ourselves because of what we believe God wants to do, can do, and will do through us.

God, who knows us better than we know ourselves, has called us. Though we may feel that we are the "least of the called," we are at least among the called.

Don't be like the goat being shipped on the railroad, who, as he journeyed, ate his shipping tag. Preachers who belittle or destroy their sense of being called will certainly have doubts about being qualified to preach, and that self-doubt will most certainly be picked up by their listeners.

Always remember: "He who calls you is faithful, who also will do it" (1 Thessalonians 5:24, NKJV).

2. Remember that planting and reaping do not always happen the same day.
Once when I was in northern Indiana in the springtime, an unusually wet season kept farmers waiting for weeks to get out into their fields. Rainy weather kept them from plowing and planting. Then a few days of wind and sunshine dried the fields enough to let the tractors in. Although not a farmer myself, I could empathize with these farmers' saying, "I can hardly wait to get out in the fields to plant."

The farmer plants in hope. From year to year there are no guarantees, but there is always hope. Hope keeps the farmer going.

Like the farmer, the preacher is a planter. But there's a guarantee.

He who continually goes forth weeping / Bearing seed for sowing / Shall doubtless come again with rejoicing / Bringing his sheaves with him.

(Psalm 126:6 NKJV)

If we had never seen the miracle of planting and watched a farmer take a bushel of corn and bury it in the ground, we would say, "That's a stupid thing to do. The farmer could sell the corn or eat it or even feed it to the pigs." But instead, he or she takes it out, scatters it all over the field, and leaves it.

Of course, having seen crops grow, we are not alarmed by the farmer's peculiar behavior. We know he or she is planting the corn. We know that when it is scattered out and left, in a matter of weeks it will come up, giving the farmer back not only one bushel of corn, but fifty or sixty or a hundred bushels to the acre as the result of the investment.

That is such a simple illustration, I am almost embarrassed to use it. But we can learn a valuable lesson from the farmer.

We preachers tend to measure success as an immediate, physical response. We know better. I know better. I keep telling myself better. The ministry of preaching boils down to planting: we take the eternal word of God, and we plant it. One of us sows; another reaps; but God gives the increase—and we never know what is going to work.

We plant in hope. We plow in hope. We preach in hope. We reach in hope.

There are planting sermons and there are reaping sermons. Both are victorious sermons.

3. Remember that there are many kinds of victories.

Paul, in writing to the Corinthian church about the gift of prophecy, indicates three results of preaching: *"edification* and *exhortation* and *comfort"* (1 Corinthians 14:3, NKJV, emphasis added). Later he says that an unlearned man, hearing the prophecy, is *"convinced by all,* he is judged by all" (1 Corinthians 14:24, NKJV, emphasis added). Jesus said that the Holy Spirit would "convict the world of sin, and of righteousness, and of judgment" (John 16:8, NKJV).

Clearly, there are many results of preaching. They do not all happen at the same time or in the same way.

As we have said from the outset, recognizing the importance of the prophetic ministry is the first step in effective preaching. We never know what God can do through a simple sermon. But if we place little value on it, God will not do very much.

One reason Gerald Marvel's ministry is so effective is that every time he preaches, he says to himself: "Somebody out there is hearing me for the very first time."

That perspective is valuable in several ways. For one thing, it keeps the pastor from being provincial—talking to the congregation as "just family" with no strangers present, thereby assuming that everyone knows what the preacher is talking about. That's a bad habit preachers have, particularly in a small congregation or in any size church after the pastor has been there a while and knows everyone.

Familiarity brings the assumption that "we are all just family here; nobody really needs any spiritual help." With that mentality, a pastor falls easily into a pattern of just going through the motions—and that is deadly.

Tremendous opportunities may be missed when pastors "fall asleep at the wheel," so to speak.

It was a Sunday night in Africa. A preacher in a little church went to the service; and, as was customary there—as it is in America for that matter—not many showed up. He really would not have preached at all except for the fact that it was his job and they had a scheduled service.

When he laboriously finished the sermon, he trudged home and said to his wife, "It's just hard being in an obscure place like this where nobody seems to care what happens. I'm not accomplishing much."

What this dispassionate pastor did not realize was that one visitor had come that night to his church—a young law student who had been studying in England and was now in Africa, a young man who was casting about for something to believe. He sought out a church because someone had told him the Christian church had a message. But he walked away deeply discouraged, saying to himself: "That man not only had nothing to say, he didn't want to say it.

Obviously, it was not very important to him; so it couldn't be very important to me."

That preacher did not know—and the young student did not yet know—that the destiny of millions would be affected by that sermon. The student's name was Mohandas Gandhi, later called "Mahatma" (the Great Soul Gandhi), who influenced a nation and a world as much as any one man who has lived in recent times, whose shadow was cast over millions of people, and who said repeatedly of Christians: "I cannot accept your Christianity, although I have to admire your Christ."

He did not see much of Christ's victory in us.

Even as I tell that story, cold chills sweep over me—to think how many times I have preached saying, "Well, it's just another sermon, another Sunday. Not a big crowd; not a big service."

But you never know what God can do.

Who knows what great doors swing on little hinges?

In another small church in another place, God used a simple man to make a giant leap for Christianity in the twentieth century. What happened there on a cold, snowy Sunday morning was the epitome of victorious preaching and its powerful effect.

Probably no other Christian preacher in the last few hundred years has influenced the world more than Charles Spurgeon. Called by many "the prince of preachers," in his early twenties he pastored one of the largest churches in London. It numbered about a thousand members when he started and grew to about ten thousand. His sermons were so vital, they were sent by wire across the Atlantic each week to be published in full in the New York papers on Monday. Even today, the shadow of Spurgeon continues to influence.

Reared in a Christian home, Spurgeon was a scholarly young man who had heard the great preachers, read from the Christian classics, and even debated theological issues as a teenager. But he was not saved. Spurgeon was not saved until he was sixteen. How he came to find salvation is a dramatic story no one tells better than Spurgeon himself:

> I sometimes think I might have been in darkness and despair until now had it not been for the goodness of God in sending a snowstorm on Sunday morning. While I was going to a certain

place of worship, I turned down a side street and came to a Primitive Methodist Church. In that chapel there may have been a dozen or fifteen people. I had heard of the Primitive Methodists, how they sang so loudly that they made people's heads ache; but that did not matter to me. I wanted to know how I might be saved.

The minister did not come that morning; he was snowed up, I suppose. At last a very thin-looking man, a shoemaker or a tailor, or something of that sort, went up to the pulpit to preach. Now it is well that preachers be instructed, but this man was really stupid. He was obliged to stick to his text, for the simple reason that he had little else to say. The text was—"LOOK UNTO ME AND BE YE SAVED, ALL THE ENDS OF THE EARTH."

He did not even pronounce the words rightly, but that did not matter. There was, I thought, a glimmer of hope for me in that text.

The preacher began thus: "This is a very simple text indeed. It says, 'Look.' Now it don't take a deal of pain. It ain't liftin' your foot or your finger; it is just 'Look.' Well, a man needn't go to college to learn to look. You may be the biggest fool, and yet you can look. A man needn't be worth a thousand a year to look. Even a child can look.

"But then the text says, 'Look unto me.' Ay," he said in broad Essex, "many of ye are lookin' to yourselves, but it's no use lookin' there. You'll never find any comfort in yourselves. Some say look to God the Father. No, look to Him by and by. Jesus Christ says, 'Look unto Me.' Some of ye say, 'We must wait for the Spirit's working'. You have no business with that just now. Look to Christ. The Text says, 'Look unto Me.' "

The good man followed up his text this way: " 'Look unto Me; I'm sweatin' great drops of blood. Look unto Me; I am hangin' on the cross. Look unto Me; I'm dead and buried. Look unto Me; I rise again. Look unto Me; I ascend to the Father's right hand. O poor sinner, look unto Me; look unto Me.' "

When he had managed to spin out ten minutes or so, he was at the end of his tether. Then he looked at me under the gallery, and I daresay with so few persons present, he knew me to be a stranger.

Just fixing his eyes on me, as if he knew all my heart, he said, "Young man, you look very miserable." Well, I did, but I had not been accustomed to have remarks made from the pulpit about my personal appearance before. However, it was a good blow, struck right home. He continued, "And you will always be miserable—miserable in life and miserable in death—if you don't obey my text; but if you do obey now, this moment, you will be saved." Then lifting up his hands, he shouted, as only a Primitive Methodist could do, "Young man, look to Jesus Christ. Look! Look! Look! You have nothing to do but to look and live!"

I saw at once the way of salvation. I know not what else he said—I did not take much notice of it—I was so possessed with that one thought. I had been waiting to do fifty things, but when I heard that one word, "Look," what a charming word it seemed to me. O, I looked until I could almost have looked my eyes away.

There and then the cloud was gone, the darkness had rolled away, and that moment I saw the sun; and I could have risen that moment and sung with the most enthusiastic of them of the precious blood of Christ, and the simple faith which looks alone to Him. Oh, that somebody had told me this before, "Trust Christ, and you shall be saved."

I thought I could have sprung from the seat in which I sat and called out with the wildest of those Methodist brethren, "I am forgiven! A monument of grace! A sinner saved by blood!"

My spirit saw its chains broken to pieces. I felt that I was an emancipated soul, an heir of heaven, a forgiven one, accepted in Jesus Christ, plucked out of the miry clay and out of the horrible pit, with my feet set upon a rock and my goings established.

Between half past ten o'clock, when I first entered the chapel, and half past twelve when I was back again at home, what a change had taken place in me! Simply by looking to Jesus I had been delivered from despair, and I was brought into such a joyous state of mind that, when they saw me at home, they said to me, "Something wonderful has happened to you," and I was eager to tell them all about it. Oh! There was joy in the household that day, when all heard that the eldest son had found the Saviour, and knew himself to be forgiven.

You get the picture.

He was a frail-looking working man. He didn't plan to preach. He certainly would not have dignified his name with any titles. He came to church because he believed that was where he ought to be on Sunday. A snowstorm prevented his pastor from coming, and somebody said, "Well, we ought to have a few words."

"I ain't no preacher, but I can at least lift up the Word of God."

He didn't preach an hour. He struggled to get through ten minutes. When he was at the end of his tether, he reached out his hand to a stranger, and did not know—as you and I do not know—that he was reaching out his hand to the world.

Do not disdain the spindly cobbler with shoe polish staining his fingers. Do not take lightly the little chapel, banked high with snow. Listen well to the songs of the dozen worshipers who have braved the cold to listen to a ten-minute sermon.

History is being made.

Though he does not know it, the thin man with the inelegant dialect of Essex is speaking to the world. His Primitive Methodist shout reverberates not only under the chapel gallery—it is echoing around the world.

This is the victory!

Chapter 12

Creating the Creative Climate

With determination and persistence, it is possible to make the gospel dull and uninteresting. Difficult, yes, but possible. Countless preachers manage to do it.

The same exciting news that filled Judean skies with a host of heavenly choristers shouting, "Glory!" and sent shepherds rushing to Bethlehem, now drives thousands to the golf course on Sunday morning and lulls the righteous remainder to sleep on upholstered pews.

Amazing, utterly amazing!

It is hard to imagine that preachers can load their homiletic artillery with the gunpowder of miracle and then defuse it to explode with the impact of baking powder!

But such is the plight of preaching in far too many pulpits—dull sermons falling on deaf ears.

Little wonder the prophets of doom predict that "preaching as we know it is a thing of the past." In spite of the rankling in our souls as we hear this dirge, we have to admit that *preaching as we know it* may indeed be wending its weary way to the cemetery of memory. If we listen to its detractors, their arguments are convincing that preaching is no longer a viable way of communicating the gospel. But we know better.

That we have let tradition and tiredness take the excitement out of proclamation is more of an indictment upon ourselves than upon preaching. If we have built our own caskets and crawled into them to die, we cannot cry, "Murder!" It is suicide.

The phrase *as we know it* is the clue. Perhaps that kind of preaching is dead and deserves a decent burial. But what of preaching *as it should be—as it can be*? Will it not have meaning and acceptance? In reality, all spoken and unspoken obituaries for preaching are merely calls for creative preaching.

Dullness is a human invention. Relieving it involves divine creativity.

Creativity, you see, is not an additive to the gospel. Creativity is the very nature of God and of the gospel about God.

Preaching must be creative.

If the Creator called us to preach and through proclamation promises to lead persons to Christ—Who can make of them "a new creation"—then those called to preach must themselves be creative. One does not call a mortician to deliver babies.

At the risk of being repetitious, preaching simply must not be dull!

"Dull preaching" is a contradiction of terms—like cold fire or old news. "The Word of God is quick, and powerful, and sharper than any twoedged sword" (Hebrews 4:12, KJV). Something quick, powerful, and sharp, cannot at the same time be dead, weak, and dull.

For the "Word of God" to be the "Word of God," it must be more than words about the Word of God. "The letter kills, but the Spirit gives life" (2 Corinthians 3:6, NKJV).

J. B. Phillips experienced that truth firsthand. In working on his first translation of the New Testament he testifies that he felt as though he were an electrician rewiring an old house with the current still turned on. The words about the living God were themselves alive!

A droning recitation of Bible texts is not preaching. However scholarly, a collection of Bible verses all saying the same thing is not preaching, not expository preaching or any other kind. Only when divine truth is clothed in flesh—both in the flesh of the preacher and in the experience of the listener—is it truly preaching. Only then is it creative.

Preaching Must Be Forever New

The gospel is good *news*. It is not the "good *old* gospel." The nature of preaching is to be new. Sometimes this newness brings problems—as it did in Jesus' day.

When Jesus picked up the scroll of Isaiah's prophecy and began to read, no one was surprised; he was, by Hebrew law, old enough to read the Scriptures. But when he sat down to preach, alarms began to sound.

"This day is this Scripture fulfilled in your ears."
That was new!

From that ancient parchment, the Word of God had moved into the flesh of the young carpenter.

The response of the people of Nazareth was not affirmative, but it was definite. They responded angrily, of course; but they did respond. Preaching was a living thing, and it was creative. It created a crisis.

Preaching will not be creative if we assume that creativity is optional—a matter of choice or a talent given only to a few, a gift some have and some do not. On the contrary, our creative God calls all of us to be creative. And those who listen to us watch for any signs of creativity as blind men long for light.

Newness is the law of life. It is impossible to grow an old blade of grass or an old leaf on a tree.

A popular singer captures a powerful truth in these words: "He that is not busy being born / Is busy dying."

If, as its critics predict, preaching is dying, perhaps preachers who recommend the "new birth" to their listeners should apply their sermons to their sermons—giving them new birth. If the Spirit of God could come upon Abraham and Sarah, making them fruitful in their old age, is it too much to hope that the same Spirit will come upon preachers who have been telling the Abraham and Sarah story?

God says: "Behold, I make *all* things new" (Revelation 21:5, NKJV emphasis added). That promise includes preaching!

Tuning in to the Creative Process

Let's look now to some practical aspects of creativity—understanding what it is and how we can tap into it for preaching. A logical place to start is with the Bible's first reference to creativity: "In the beginning, God created" (Genesis 1:1, NKJV).

The opening words of Scripture proclaim that God is creative. If you become creative, you will learn something about God.

Let me be clear. We are not talking "technique" here. We are not referring to prepackaged formulas or instant recipes of "do this and this and this and you'll be creative." We are not thinking of slick audiovisual tricks to make a humdrum sermon look creative.

We are speaking of creativity as a spiritual exercise in letting God work through you.

When you enter with God into the creative process, the Word again *"becomes flesh"*—through you. In you, God's Word comes alive! And the gospel is once again "good news."

That is the essence of preaching: to tell "the old, old story" without letting it get old. It is just that simple. As the angel told John in his vision of the Revelation, "The purpose of all prophecy ... is to tell about Jesus" (Rev 19:10, LIVING BIBLE). We are not to change the content of the gospel, but we must change the way we tell it to keep the story fresh and relevant to the times in which we live.

As one contemporary writer put it, our challenge is to "tell the never-changing Gospel to an ever-changing world."

Steps to Creative Preaching

So how do we start down the path toward more creative preaching? By realizing first that creativity is an attitude. At the heart of creativity is simply allowing ourselves to be creative.

You may have said, "I'm not creative."

And I must protest, "Oh, but you are!"

You may have let yourself fall into the pattern of other people's lives and thereby denied and thwarted your own creativity. But you were not born that way.

Human beings are born creative. Young children are ingenious if left to play creatively. They are full of inventive ideas. But gradually, as they get older, they are pulled more and more into the confines of tradition and cultural mores, where they are taught to color within the lines and to do everything the way it has been done before. Thus, potentially creative minds and spirits become imprisoned by convention and culture. Nevertheless, a spark of creativity remains in every person.

When you listen to a creatively inspired preacher and respond to the sermon, your first thought may be, "Isn't he or she a great preacher!"

But you also think, "Isn't God a Great God!"

That should be the objective in all our preaching: to glorify God and make him real and approachable for our listeners.

In the presence of a great preacher, one in whom the Spirit of God is flowing freely, we can sense a creative interchange taking place even as the sermon unfolds. Something happens during the delivery of the message—an explosion and implosion of God's power in the process. You can feel it when it happens. The speaker can feel it; the audience can feel it. God has taken over and the preacher has become only a speaker system for the voice of God to command.

When you are listening to another preacher and you see that transformation happen, you say, "This is preaching. This is what it is! I wish I could do that."

It doesn't always happen; but when it does, you wish it could happen all the time.

The secret is in the *process*. In the *process of preaching*, we allow God to take over. For that to happen, the preacher must be open to it.

That is why Charles Spurgeon and Clyde Fant and other reasonably good preachers have disparaged preaching from a manuscript. Once every word you plan to say is locked down in writing, and you rigidly adhere to that script on Sunday morning, there is no room for God to add anything new or fresh in the moment of preaching. All too often what has been prayerfully and carefully prepared and rehearsed early in the week has gone stale by Sunday, and the effect for the congregation is like eating yesterday's mashed potatoes.

I know this idea is upsetting to some people, but the point I want to make is simply this: you cannot lock your sermon up in a box and still be creative.

You may say, "Can't God inspire me in the office on Monday?"

Yes, God had better inspire you in the office on Monday—and Friday, too. But any preacher can tell you this: something magical—supernatural—happens when what you have prepared earlier in the week is touched with the power of God on Sunday and becomes a living thing.

Hearing a "canned" sermon is a little like going to a mortuary to view a corpse.

People say, "Doesn't he look natural?"

Well, most corpses don't. They look better than natural! I've seen dead men in coffins decked out in suits who never wore a suit in their lives. I've seen hands folded that never were that way before. They never looked so good! But that's not natural.

You say, "Well, he has hands, a nose, and two eyes. He looks pretty much the way he's supposed to look."

And that's all true. But he's dead! He is *dead.* Touch him and you will jerk your hand back, because he is as cold as a backslider's testimony. He—it—is not living.

Now, much as we don't like to admit it, just to haul into the pulpit what was manufactured in the study on Thursday and try to breathe life into it on Sunday usually doesn't work. It may look like a sermon. It may sound like a sermon—three points with alliteration in the key words and all that. But without that inward, divine spark of creativity, it will be stone dead and will likely fall on deaf ears.

Saying that in no way is meant to imply that you should not prepare ahead of time for the sermon. I don't mean that at all.

What I am saying is this: *it is the process that is creative.* And we need to allow that creative process to work before the sermon is ever conceived, while it is being prepared, and during the moments of its delivery.

Abort the process too soon by solidifying the sermon into a manuscript that you restrict yourself to on Sunday morning, and you limit what God can do in the power of the moment when you stand to deliver God's message before the people. When you enter into the spontaneity of the moment, allowing God to speak freely through you as you "connect" with the people, you can feel it. Your hearers will feel it, too. It is an exhilarating moment that can happen to any of us, because God is creative. God created us to be creative.

How, then, do we become more creative? How do we unleash the creativity within? Here are seven suggestions:

1. Welcome Creative Chaos.

Let's take a clue from the Genesis account of God's creativity:

> In the beginning God created the heavens and the earth. The earth was without form, and void; and darkness was on the face of the deep.
>
> (Genesis 1:1–2, NKJV)

Out of chaos God created the world. From what did God do it? Latin scholars had a word for it: *ex nehilo*; that is, "out of nothing." There was nothing out of which to make something and no place to put what was made. *"Without form, and void"* is the Bible phrase, and that is about as unstructured as it gets. *"Without form"* means no lines on the outside, and *void* means nothing on the inside. Like a circle without a line, there were no outside parameters and no inside contents. Empty on the inside and unformed on the outside—the ultimate of nothingness. Out of this nothingness, God created.

No outside limits and nothing within the limits. Absolute zero.

When the local pastor begins with "absolute zero," he or she borders on nervous collapse. "Here it is Friday, and I have no idea what to preach on Sunday." That is scary.

Of course, there is always the file of used sermons—the pastor's or someone else's. From this repository of yesterday's manna, the pastor can lift a sermon. Putting it in a mental microwave, he or she can reheat it and serve it up as a creative message. That warmed-over sermon may succeed in filling the pastor's expectations, but it also drives him or her deeper into the rut of noncreativity. That pastor becomes increasingly fearful of the chaos out of which creation comes.

I have observed that people who tend not to be creative are mortally afraid of chaos.

They are terrified of starting from nothing. They say, "Where do I begin? Where are we going? Who did it before? How do you want this done? How many pages do you want? How many words? What should I talk about? Give me some parameters, some guidelines. I want to color inside the lines."

Certainly the world will provide those lines for you, but you are not creating when you accept those parameters. Furthermore, if you want something new, you most likely will have to tear down something old to get it—and that dynamic creates another set of concerns.

Walk through a little scenario with me for a moment here and see if it feels familiar.

You have to preach on Sunday, right? So you go into your study, sit down behind your desk, and you say, "Now, what should I preach about?"

If you are a normal, average pastor, you pull a topic out of the air and say, "I wonder what Swindoll has written on this?"

Or you search through your files asking yourself, "Who's done a sermon on this?"

Or you reach for William Barclay's commentary or a collection of sermon illustrations saying, "Where have I heard something on this subject before?"

You start pulling down books and collecting quotes from various sources, all the while telling yourself, "Now, this gives me a starting point."

What really happens, however, when you start with somebody else's stuff, is that you wind up re-thrashing the same old sawdust somebody else sawed. And it comes out even drier than it was the first time.

"Hey, wait a minute. Give me a break," you say. "I've got to start somewhere."

Yes, that is true. But to be creative, you have to start with chaos.

Sometime back I read this statement made to building contractors: "If you build houses this year the way you built houses last year, you will not be building houses next year."

Anyone who has gone through more than one building project can tell you that building codes change. In fact, everything about the building process changes so rapidly that the only constant appears to be change, change, change.

In paraphrase, I see an important corollary here: "If you build sermons this year the way you built sermons last year, you probably shouldn't be building sermons next year."

Effective preachers must constantly be on what I call "the cutting edge of change." True, the gospel never changes. "Jesus Christ is the same yesterday, today, and forever" (Hebrews 13:8, NKJV). But the packaging of the message—the way we proclaim that truth—has to change because we live in changing times.

Staying on the cutting edge in presentation requires creativity.

I suppose the most frustrating aspect of creativity is learning to live with ideas in a state of flux, always being open to fresh material and organizational shifts as the sermon takes shape—even up to the last minute before delivery.

This is not a plea for procrastination and indolence, but it is a plea for this: "If [the vision] tarries, wait for it" (Habakkuk 2:3, NKJV).

No one believes that such waiting is without anxiety, but such anxiety seems to be the mark of great preachers.

Author Frederick Buechner tells an interesting story about Henry Ward Beecher, famous New England pastor who was to give the first Lyman Beecher Lecture at Yale University. Buechner's description of this scholarly man should make us all feel more comfortable when we have to wait for the vision.

While waiting to give his first lecture at Yale, Beecher was in the wash room shaving. With razor poised, he suddenly had an idea that he knew just had to be included in the lecture. Naturally, in his haste, he nicked his face. He responded by reaching simultaneously for a pen and a steptic pencil, one to capture the idea and the other to stop the flow of blood.

Could it be that this gifted orator was unprepared for one of the greatest preaching assignments of his life? Not likely unprepared. But apparently not yet "inspired." No doubt he had prepared as best he could, but was waiting—still prayerfully expectant for that illusive key point, idea, or thought that would drive the message home. He had the wisdom to know that when he had labored long and faithfully, he could count on divine inspiration, even though it had to come at the last moment.

As you learn to create, one of the first lessons is that originality is almost always accompanied by chaos. Most original sermons— even those that in delivery seem the most logical and carefully planned—grow out of chaos. They begin as seed thoughts. Then, as preparation progresses, bits of information and illustration begin to come together, haphazardly at first. Finally, there is a clicking and dovetailing and fitting together that come in the mix of mind and Holy Spirit, and the sermon takes on a life of its own. It begins to preach itself through you, rather than you consciously preaching it.

But for that creative process to happen, you must be constantly feeding your mind with information and processing real-life experiences—for that is the "stuff" creative sermons are made of.

Gerald Marvel likes to say, "Creativity happens in the going." And to illustrate that notion, he tells of an experience he had some years ago while holding a revival in a small town in northeastern Louisiana.

The community of New Hope was out in the soybean fields. With few meetings during the day, the pastor, O. J. Adams, took me out to explore some old cemeteries in the area—old Indian mounds.

It was fascinating. I was really into it. But on every trip, after twelve o'clock the pastor would say, "We'd better go. Gotta get you back to the house."

Finally I said, "Something goes on here in the afternoon you don't want me to know about. You keep me housed up."

"No," he said, "you have to get ready for tonight."

"Look," I said, "you just get me back a couple of hours before service. This is a revival. I'm not preaching sermons I haven't preached before. But I'm open, and I always try to bring in some new things. I'm gaining some good stuff from these Indian mounds. Let's keep going."

Well, he looked at me, and—I'll never forget it—he said, "You do a lot of thinking on your feet, don't you?"

I said, "That's right, O. J. Get it as it goes! If you don't have your antenna up, you won't get the frequency."

I know for a fact that Gerald is never without his pen and a supply of cards in his pocket to record ideas on.

"Learn to glean information as you go," he says, "and keep it. Stash interesting facts and stories in your mind someplace. They'll come in handy sooner or later."

That's good advice.

You may not use a particular fact or experience from your mental storehouse this week or this month or even this year. But at a precise moment, it will fall into place. One day you will find it fitting perfectly into one of those "wild" sermons you are constructing. As you pray over a text and begin to ponder how it might speak to your people, the Spirit will call to your mind the precise illustrations you need to put the message across—*if you have stoked the furnace in advance.*

Creating an original sermon means being able to trust a little confusion in the process.

If everything about the sermon is bolted down, anchored, and closed tight, the Holy Spirit has no room to move. But in preparing the sermon, if you can begin the thought process and cultivate it in an atmosphere of freedom—allowing space for the ideas to be floating there—the Holy Spirit will move in and will bring order out of chaos.

Just remember that order comes after confusion. For the Holy Spirit is at work and can bring order out of the chaos of creativity.

2. Don't Expect to See the End at the Beginning.

If we insist on seeing the end before we see the beginning, we will never start. If we cannot travel without a map of someone else's journey, we will miss many creative experiences. No one who travels into the realm of creativity pretends that uncertainty of chaos is pleasant, but all testify that they have found many treasures "off the beaten path."

If Abraham, the patriarch of our faith, journeyed *"not knowing where he was going,"* it is not surprising that we preachers are called to live on the creative edge.

Many people, especially left-brainers or those with structured personalities, consciously or unconsciously feel uncomfortable in situations where everything is not spelled out in advance. They say, "I can't stand the uncertainty. I can't stand not knowing where I'm going." Personally, I don't like uncertainty either, but I am not uncomfortable with it.

As children of Abraham, we need to take a lesson from our noble ancestor. Abraham never did know where he was going, but he journeyed nonetheless. Though the final destination was uncertain, he journeyed with confidence—because he knew that God had called him. Because Abraham journeyed in faith, everything came out all right. If we look at sermon building as a journey of faith, it, too, should come out all right.

Often in life, in decision making, we get too hung up about not knowing precisely what we are supposed to do or where we are supposed to go at a given point in time.

Listen, I have learned that it is far better not to know where you are going and know that God is guiding you than to say, "I have made up my mind where I am going to go. Come hell or high water, this is what I am going to do!"

Loosen up a little and leave room for God to lead you. In the creative process, remember, the greatest inventions have come out of the turmoil and the uncertainties of life. God can guide those who walk step by step in faith—even though we may not at the moment see the ultimate product or destination.

Many times you have an idea for a sermon but are not at all sure where it's coming out—not sure *if* it's coming out. When it finally does turn out well, you are surprised!

Sometimes we need to ask God to do something not in the bulletin prepared on Thursday. Not that I am against worship folders or programs. They can be valuable tools for meaningful worship. But I am opposed to becoming slavish to what is printed there. The Holy Spirit needs a little elbow room. We need to stay flexible enough to go with the flow of the moment, to allow God to lead even in a different direction from what we had anticipated. When we predetermine how everything is going to go—and feel uncomfortable if every minute of the service is not detailed ahead of time—we may squelch the Spirit and set limits on what God can do.

I remember one Easter Sunday down in Daytona. We had a huge crowd, and I had prepared what I thought was one of my better sermons. I had on a clean shirt, freshly pressed suit—the works. The choir had special music—wonderful music! We had a full program.

Everything was going along fine. I was getting ready to step forward to preach my Easter Sunday morning message when, out of the blue, some young man came running down the aisle and fell at the altar to get saved!

You know what my first thought was: "Hey, buddy, you can't do that! It's not time for the altar call. Somebody tell him! Hasn't he read the bulletin?"

I suspect that most of the congregation felt the same way.

But I quickly monitored my thought. This, after all, is why we are here. We are not here to listen to an Easter sermon or follow a schedule. We are here to meet people's needs.

So I said, "Here's a man who wants to find the Lord. Let me get down here and pray with him."

I stepped down and knelt at the altar and prayed with him till he got right with God. Then I went back to preach my sermon.

Being creative means leaving room in the journey for surprises along the way.

3. Don't Allow Form to Become Sacred.

That Easter incident showed me how easily we make form sacred and then feel uneasy when things don't go according to our plan. Furthermore, if we hang onto old forms and ideas, we lock out the new. When form becomes sacred, we automatically reject any idea that doesn't fit the old pattern.

In Denmark a few summers ago, a pastor said to me, "I don't think we can have church anymore because our piano player is leaving, and we have no replacement."

"Wait a minute," I thought. "Where in the Bible does it say you must have a pianist to have church?"

You don't even have to have songs to have church! If you need piano music, record some; play it from a tape. Singers do that all the time. But my Danish friend had a mental block there. And Danes are hard-headed. I can say that because I'm a Swede. I know how we are. We are all hard-headed. But his remark is typical of what happens when a certain practice becomes tradition. We wring our hands and with grim resignation announce: "We've done it this way for fifty years. What are we going to do if we don't have somebody playing the piano to start church?"

Well, have church without it! Sing *a cappella*. I preach without notes; sing the same way. It could be refreshing. Who knows, you might start a new tradition!

Sometimes we have to give up some old practices—even ones we are fond of—to make room for new ones. Those moves are not always popular, because people resist change. But keeping on forever with the "same old same old" can lead to stagnation and early death. To stir your thinking further in this regard, do some reading about paradigms. Several good books and videos about the subject are on the market. Breaking our paradigms (old patterns of thought) calls for approaching things from totally different angles from established practices. In sermon construction, the less well-traveled road is often the best road to take.

When form becomes sacred, we kill all chance for creativity.

When we insist on familiar forms and predictable patterns, we can miss the creative message. At the time of Jesus' birth, devout Jews anticipated the coming of the Messiah. Yet, when he came, they did not recognize him. Why? Because they already had a pattern of how he should come, and Jesus did not fit into that picture. Their "king in a castle" mentality would not accept the "babe in a barn" reality.

Any preacher who has a "standard" outline and merely waits for God to "fill in the blanks" will have a guaranteed dull predictability—dull and deadly.

"As soon as I hear the first point of my pastor's sermon, I know exactly where he is going," said one layleader.

That was never said about the preaching of Jesus. His listeners testified, "No man ever spoke like this man."

If you want to have something new in your preaching, you must leave room for it. And—fearfully I say it—you must not be frightened by the "pregnant pause" that unnerves ordinary prsons. If you want a miracle, you may have to wait for it. God has promised it, but not necessarily on your schedule.

God specializes in the unorthodox.

Again, Abraham provides a parallel. God had promised Abraham a son. As the patriarch grew older, his hope grew dimmer. Fearing to wait for God's timing, he (with the encouragement of his wife) proceeded to sire a son by his wife's handmaid. Ishmael, Hagar's son, was a child of human desperation. As might be expected, conflict came—and history was forever changed.

In time, God did fulfill that promise: Isaac was born. The miracle did happen.

We should not judge Abraham too harshly for his impatience. How many times have we said, "Do something, even if it's wrong." And how many times have we paid for our impatience?

For the preacher, there is the temptation to "put the sermon to bed" so he or she can get on with other duties clamoring for attention. Unfortunately, sermons that have been "put to bed" by Thursday often carry their soporific power into the pulpit and pews on Sunday.

Emerson's comment, "A foolish consistency is the hobgoblin of little minds, adored by little statesmen and philosophers and divines," fits well the dull predictability of consistent formats that do not allow for creative chaos.

4. Welcome the Catalyst

From seminary days I remember only two chapel sermons. One was by the well-known Methodist preacher Clovis Chapel. The other was by a senior who before coming to seminary to become a preacher had been an industrial chemist. He gave us in his sermon one of the most useful analytical tools I have ever come across.

"Today," he said, "I am going to preach a sermon on the process of chemical change. There are four steps in a chemical change—whether you are talking about a new plastic or a pan of biscuits." He listed them, and I made a note in my testament:

Four Steps in Chemical Change
1. Stable but unsatisfactory solution
You have something stable, solid, predictable—not what you want, but you know what it is and how it will react.
2. Entry of a catalyst
You inject something to stir up that stable equilibrium.
3. An unstable solution
Now you have confusion and instability; everything is all mixed up. In other words, things are a mess! But there will be a change for the better.
4. A new equilibrium
Voila! A new product. The journey was painful, but the destination worth it.

What he said is not only true; it also holds the key to creativity in any situation. To see more specifically how the process works, consider what happens in baking a cake.

At the outset—*Step 1*—all the ingredients are labeled and in their proper places. You have flour in a sack, baking powder in a can, vanilla extract in a bottle, eggs in their shells. You have these and everything else that goes into a cake sitting out there on the counter—all neatly packaged and labeled. The ingredients are all predictable, and they are stable. The baking powder isn't going anywhere; the flour isn't going anywhere; the eggs aren't bouncing around; the milk isn't churning. Everything is stable.

But then, you stir it all up. And you put in a catalyst—the baking powder or the soda or whatever leaven you are using. That's *Step 2*.

Now those ingredients are all mixed up—and messy! Not only that, but your once spotless kitchen now looks—in *Step 3*—like a war zone! Bowls are messed up; spoons and spatulas are coated with batter; cake beaters are full of goo; counter tops are splattered. The place is a wreck!

Finally, you pour the concoction into a cake pan and, with a sigh of relief, place the confection in the oven to bake. Like magic, all those ingredients work together. And fifty minutes later—*Step 4*—you pull from the oven a delicious cake.

Obviously, you cannot make a cake by keeping the ingredients neatly stashed in the containers. Therein lies the trouble I have with most filing systems. I'm not opposed to having a system. I could use more of it. But for a right-brain like me, filing illustrations away limits my creativity.

When I look around my office, I take comfort in a statement I read one time: "You can't raise much beef in a clean stall."

Try telling my wife that!

We have to face it. Creativity is messy.

Every change made in a church is going to cause some confusion, no matter how hard you fight it. Building programs are classic examples.

Berny and I were attending Gerald's church in Vancouver when they were in their most recent building program. Gerald—or most any other pastor who has gone through a building project—will tell you that it would be much easier not to build! Confusion abounds even when the building program is managed well and is being carried out by expert contractors. Some people like it; others do not. The parking lot is torn up. People can't find a place to park, even if they are not running late on Sunday. Ditches criss-cross the parking lot; dirt and gravel everywhere. The builders have torn down fences and trees. The place is a mess!

Everything was stable before the building began. But we wanted a new equilibrium. We wanted a new building. So we had to endure the chaos of construction to get it.

Likewise in sermon construction.

It is important to keep a creative part of your mind on an open channel to receive information and stories—even wild ideas!—and have them continually stirring around in there. The process involves cultivating a chaotic part of your mind—a stew pot of ideas out of which creativity can come.

5. Nurture Your Mind.

Creativity involves discipline—and that one factor often

becomes a stumbling block for people in realizing their creative potential.

Be assured, you *do* have creative powers. Everybody does. But it may be that someone, perhaps someone in your own family, has convinced you—or through some failure or sensitivity you have convinced yourself—that you are not creative. Wrong! You *are* creative.

To classify only certain people as creative, as though creativity were a gift for only a chosen few, is a misconception. While it is true that some people may tend to be more creative than others in areas of art, music, drama, or invention, the fact remains that we all have more creative capabilities than we give ourselves credit for.

Learning to have confidence in the power of your own mind and in the power of the Holy Spirit to work through your mind is to begin to unlock your creative potential.

Considerable research has been done in recent years to understand more of how the mind works and how we can more fully tap into our mental resources. It has been said that the human mind is capable of memorizing the entire *Encyclopaedia Britannica*; that even a person of average intelligence has the mental capacity to become fluent in twenty-five foreign languages, keeping them all separate and distinct.

Twenty-five years ago I heard Dr. David Gaulke, speaking at Gulf Coast (now Mid-America) Bible College, present a claim of science that if we could build a computer to do all the mental calculations and functions the human mind is capable of, housing it would require a building one hundred stories high.

More recently I have heard that figure adjusted to say that if, indeed, a computer could be built to do what the brain can do, it would not only require a building a hundred stories high, but that building would be as big as the state of Texas!

Actually, science has found no accurate way to estimate the capacity of the human mind. Every new report pushes the parameters farther and farther out.

Never fear exhausting your creativity. You and I have more creative potential housed in our craniums than we could possibly use in a lifetime.

So why are we not using it?

Well, once you realize the potential is there, there are only two things standing in your way: lack of discipline in programming your mind for creativity and lack of faith in trusting God to help you unleash your creative potential.

So how do we "program" the mind?

Your brain is a fabulous computer, more wonderful than any machine yet conceived by humans. Through your senses of sight, hearing, touch, taste, smell, and the sixth sense of faith or intuition, information comes into the brain. Some of that information you immediately record on paper and put away for future reference. But in actuality, the majority of that information is stored in the computer of your mind. Everything that happens to you, what you see or feel or hear that you consider important enough to put in long-term storage—either consciously or unconsciously—is recorded on a memory track in your mind. You might say, it puts a new wrinkle on your brain.

The problem, then, becomes one of retrieval—how to tap into all that information when you need it. Here is where the dimension of faith comes into creativity. Jesus said the Holy Spirit, would *"bring to your remembrance all things"* (John 14:26, NKJV, emphasis added). I believe that. Aiding memory is part of the Holy Spirit's work in your life, part of the creative process.

So honor your own creativity. The more you feed your mind, the more creative you become. If you put only two ideas in there, you don't give the Holy Spirit much to work with.

I know that as pastors we want to be Spirit-led. But there is more to being led by the Spirit than merely praying, "Here I am, Lord; lay a message on me!" That is not the way it works. The Bible also says that we are to study in order to be "approved unto God." Are you willing to pay the price of study to be creative?

Near the turn of the century many church groups got off base on formal education, feeling somehow that educational institutions were substituting human reasoning for divine inspiration. But historical research shows that, in many cases, the pioneers of various movements and denominations in America were highly educated.

In the Church of God, for example, many of the movement's early leaders—D. S. Warner, E. E. Byrum, Russell and Bessie Byrum, and others—attended college and, in fact, helped found the Bible training school that still exists today as Anderson University in Anderson, Indiana. They knew the value of education and eagerly pursued knowledge, not only for themselves, but also for other generations.

Education is a pastor's best strength. The more you put into your mind of reading and study and life's experience the more creative you can become. The Holy Spirit can only work with what you put in there. You are not going to step into a pulpit without any knowledge, without any study, without any creative juices flowing and become a Harry Emerson Fosdick or a Dale Oldham or a Billy Graham. Pulpit giants are always reading, studying, learning—always stoking the fire.

Of course, not all knowledge is gained through formal education. Filling your mind with information and ideas is a lifelong process. That is the discipline of always being a student—the discipline of constantly reading, the discipline of thinking creatively. The more information and ideas you put in, the more the Spirit will bring to your remembrance, and the more different arrangements he will help you put together.

One of the most respected ministers of our day has been Dr. R. Eugene Sterner, former speaker of the Christian Brotherhood Hour radio broadcast. The depth of Sterner's understanding of Scripture is awesome.

His wife, Millie, once said to someone expressing admiration for Sterner's preaching and teaching skills: "People admire the depth of his understanding, but what they don't see are the countless hours of personal sacrifice and discipline devoted to prayer and study of the Scriptures."

When does a busy pastor find time to read?

You probably won't find time unless you give it priority. In his weekly schedule, Gerald Marvel has one hour set aside—7:30 AM—8:30 AM every Monday, Tuesday, Wednesday, Friday, and Saturday—that everybody knows is "his time" for prayer, Bible study, thinking. He is quick to say that is not the only time he reads and studies during the week, but that hour is consistently there.

Maybe your time is late at night. Or during bathroom breaks. Turn off television. Learn to use odd moments while standing in line or waiting to be served in restaurants or sitting at stop lights. Carry in your pocket something to read. I read while my wife shops.

Gerald Marvel takes advantage of airplane travel. He says:

> I don't know of anything more boring than riding an airplane. I have to do something to pass the time. So whenever I fly, I always carry this beat-up folder with me. It's been on airplane trips going on thirty years now.
>
> For some reason, I don't read well on airplanes, so I use the time to memorize poetry. I like a little dash of poetry stirred into a sermon. It's a creative way to hold interest. So, through the years, whenever I find a poem or even a few lines of verse I like, I write it down. I keep them in a sack that travels with me everywhere. So while I'm on the airplane, riding along, I rehearse poetry. Even on trips to the Holy Land or somewhere else overseas, the poetry sack goes with me. I get in lots of practice on those runs!

Gerald is "stoking the furnace." That is the point. The more fuel for sermons—poetry, stories, Scripture passages, information—that you put into your memory bank, the more the Holy Spirit will activate it.

Nourish your creativity. You have it. Work at cultivating it and using it. Keep an ongoing record of things you want to remember. Rehearse them. Then they are ready at a moment's notice to become part of a creative sermon.

6. Honor Your Own Creativity.

From Ralph Waldo Emerson comes this disturbing thought, which I often quote in talks I make around the country:

> In every work of genius we recognize our own rejected ideas. We reject them precisely because they are our own. One day we will hear from the lips of another the ideas we cast aside, and they will come back to haunt us with a certain alienated majesty.

I can never forget that quotation, because I hear it echoed so often in life. People often will say to me, "I have an idea, but then it's probably not very good because I thought of it."

Don't say that! Your mind is as good as anybody else's mind! You can think anything anybody else can think. You have great ideas! But if you demean them and cast them aside, you will wait around, and somebody else will run with the ball. They will say the very thing you are thinking or do the precise thing you were thinking of doing. Inevitably from the sidelines you will hear yourself say, "Why, I thought of that … I had that idea … I could have done that."

But you didn't do it, because somebody told you creative people were a special kind of people.

All the time I hear preachers say, "Well, I'm not Gerald Marvel."

Listen, you don't need to be Gerald Marvel. We have one Gerald Marvel, and that is plenty and sometimes a little much! (Just teasing, Gerald.)

You are not supposed to be anybody but yourself.

Another gem from Emerson's essay on self-reliance speaks to this point:

> There comes a time in every man's education when he realizes that envy is ignorance and imitation is suicide.

When you want what somebody else has—when you covet it or envy it or imitate what they do—you are committing suicide without putting a gun to your head. Trying to be like someone else destroys the unique person you are supposed to be.

The call to preach is personal and unique. Preaching is as individual as there are individuals preaching—or should be.

When God calls you, he wants to use your unique personality and abilities in the pulpit. Remember, God created your personality and also designed a special package of spiritual gifts just for you to use in ministry. God does not intend that you be another Billy Graham—not that there could ever be another Dr. Graham! God does not intend that you be like any other preacher period. He expects you to develop your own personality and personal gifts to the best of your ability. But imitating others is not the way to success in the pulpit.

In calling you to preach, God entrusts the divine message to the personality God created for you. When you trust God enough to be yourself in the pulpit—when you are not tied up in knots trying to preach like somebody you are not—you will experience the freedom of God's Spirit and the power of your personality will come through.

Many good preachers—who had the feel, the urgency, and the

fervency of the message and the love of God and the love of people—were doing well until they took a course on how to be a proper public speaker, and they killed it. Their personality was squelched, spontaneity shattered.

Many preachers mistakenly try to imitate other preachers or try to preach strictly by a formula learned in school or from a how-to course or some other conference.

Do not misunderstand the point here. Seminary training, preaching clinics, public speaking classes are not undesirable. Quite the contrary! Good preachers never stop working to improve their preaching ability.

Once when I walked into a room to lead a conference on communication skills, I was stunned to find sitting on the front row none other than Dr. Dale Oldham, speaker of the Christian Brotherhood Hour radio broadcast for more than twenty-five years, preacher par excellence whose voice was known around the world.

Good speakers never stop learning and growing. No matter how good last Sunday's sermon was, next Sunday's effort can be better. Constantly developing the ability to communicate with people the message of God is the preacher's stock and trade. But in the process of self-improvement, we must ever be mindful not to kill the passion and personality that makes our delivery unique.

Get off the "copy cat" merry-go-round. Get on your knees in the closet and say, "Holy Ghost, I am here. I am as bright as anybody else. Show me the unique ministry you want me to have in this place."

Holy Spirit direction does not come in a kit or a box. You cannot substitute someone else's vision or program for your own personal, prayerful, searching for the specific ministry God wants you to do with a specific group of people in the place where God has called you to minister.

Don't tell me, "But I'm in a little country town out here in the middle of nowhere with nothing but a filling station and a few old people, and I can't do anything."

If you believe that, you're sunk!

Trust yourself.

To honor your own creativity means being delivered from the bondage of imitation. You do not have to be like anyone else. You do not have to envy anyone else, and you do not have to criticize anyone else because he or she is not like you.

Amazing, isn't it? We all want to be individuals, to be ourselves; but at the same time we think our mission in life is to help everyone else be more like us!

Truth is, we are all unique. When will we realize that our uniqueness is part of the Creator's design. We are "fearfully and wonderfully made"—each one of us with an intellect capable of unfathomable creativity.

Don't be afraid of what your mind can do. Trust the ideas God gives you. After all, if you believe God gave them to you, why should you be ashamed of them? Why should you mistrust what God has given you? But that is the pattern I see all the time.

I take a different approach to most things. I have written several books—on Psalm 23, Psalm 103, Psalm 91, Ephesians, and other Scriptures. And my preacher friends often say to me, "Berquist, where did you get those ideas?"

"From God."

They look at me strangely, but that's where I get them. From God.

Invariably, comes the next question: "But who else says that?"

I don't care who else says it. I didn't research the book to re-digest somebody else's ideas. I read a lot, yes. But what's wrong with my ideas? Are you going to tell me that somebody else who has written another book is smarter than I am? They may be, but the ideas that came to me are genuine. What I have written or what I speak is real and true, because the Word of God says it.

Still the questions persist: "Well, who else is doing it that way?"

What does it matter who else is doing it that way? I am an authentic person in my own right.

And so are you.

Emerson hit the nail squarely on the head in his essay "Self-reliance," one of the great documents in American literature: "Trust thyself; every heart vibrates to that iron string."

If you don't trust yourself, no one else will trust you either.

And that kind of confidence is neither arrogance nor vanity, but is simply a matter of affirming what the Bible holds as true: "I am called of God; I am conditioned by God; I believe God can lead me; and I trust what He tells me."

Henry David Thoreau, Emerson's contemporary, voiced the same idea: "If a man does not keep pace with his companions, perhaps it is because he hears a different drummer. Let him step to the music which he hears, however measured or far away."

So, march to the drumbeat of God's call upon your heart, and honor your own creativity in the process.

Chapter 13

Sermon Construction

Words like *creative chaos,* being *led by the Spirit*, and *spontaneity* might lead one to assume that taking a creative and open-ended approach to sermon development means never following an outline or never writing anything down.

Nothing could be further from the truth.

Conceiving sermons in the "chaos" of creativity in no way means that they are not organized before the moment of delivery. For just as creativity is a vital part of the process of sermon construction, so is organization.

Back in the Sixties, Gerald Marvel found in a book by Bishop Gerald Kennedy of the Methodist church a simple statement that profoundly affected the method he has used to develop sermons for more than thirty years:

You rise or fall on your basic outline.

As Bishop Kennedy explained it, designing any sermon hangs on a fairly simple process:

1. You have to know how to get into it.
2. You have to know where you are going after you get into it.
3. You have to know how to get out of it.

Starting with a Purpose

Every good sermon has a purpose and a sense of direction.

We have all painfully sat through marathon sermons in which the preacher starts with Genesis and rambles his way through the Old Testament and the New looking for a point that forty-five minutes later still is not evident to anyone.

We have also endured three-strikes-you're-out sermons. The preacher can't decide which of three sermons to preach, so he pitches them all. But the game is a no-hitter. He wears the congregation out before anyone gets on base.

We have heard sermons that stall out at the beginning. The preacher just can't seem to get started.

And we have all been guilty of wanting to pull the plug on preachers who present a good sermon—but then can't find a stopping place. They go on and on beyond the end of their sermon for ten, fifteen, twenty minutes—generally repeating themselves. If saying it once was good, saying it three or four times must surely be better!

Sad cases all. But not necessarily hopeless. Not if those preachers are willing to apply a few simple tricks of the trade.

Preachers can take a lesson from America's short story master, Edgar Allan Poe, in his innovative and effective design for writing fiction. The perfect short story, according to Poe, *is short enough to be read in one sitting and strives for a single effect.*

Poe followed his own recipe. He determined at the outset what "single effect" he wanted his story to have on his readers. Then every element of that story—mood, setting, characters, plot, description—was carefully planned to contribute to that over-all effect.

A good sermon, like a good story, is designed to have an effect on its listeners. It will move in a particular direction to achieve that effect.

The bottom line in determining that direction is this: *what does God want people to think or do differently after they have heard the message?*

That directive—the answer to that question—may not be immediately evident as you begin grappling with a text and gleaning material on a particular topic. In the early stages of sermon construction, you keep turning the topic around in your mind like an uncut gem, a diamond in the rough. You keep rethinking it and redoing it.

Even the most seasoned preachers will tell you that not every sermon comes in a flash of insight, full blown and ready for delivery. Not by a long shot.

One Easter Gerald Marvel had developed a sermon he just knew was a masterpiece. He could feel it in his bones. He had it ready to go and eagerly tried it out on his wife Saturday night. He was so carried away with his idea that he was more than a little stunned when, after a long pause, Rena's only comment was, "Isn't it a little heavy?"

Every preacher knows how Gerald felt at that moment.

You have worked for days on an idea you believe in, have it all ready to present, confident that it's going to really move people; and then your spouse pops your balloon of enthusiasm with a comment like, "Isn't it a little heavy?"

And it's Saturday night. Midnight.

What do you do?

Well, truthfully, Gerald says, although he hated to admit it, he had been feeling the same way. So he went to bed thinking, "How can I lighten this thing up?"

The sermon he thought had been "set" was suddenly in a state of creative chaos again—and at the eleventh hour, so to speak.

But as he drifted off to sleep, the pieces wondrously began to rearrange themselves, almost like magic. His zealous confidence that his "brainchild" was a masterpiece had blinded him to more creative options. So God used Rena to say, "You're about to mess up here. Reconsider."

In his sleep, Gerald sensed God saying, "Just do this ..."

God showed him that the ideas he had thought were central—"death is not final ... love conquers all ... and you can have a new beginning"—were to be there, but not as the major focus.

"Just tell what happened," he felt God saying. "Make that the focus. Take those points you were going to use as the body of the sermon and make them subordinate. Let them simply evolve out of the story to be discovered by the audience in passing."

The result was something memorable and truly moving.

Being open to that kind of reshuffling of ideas even up to the time of delivering the message—and even while preaching—is dealing creatively with the mechanics of sermon construction. And that kind of flexibility comes not so much from what you have written out or what you have memorized, as from what has been germinating in your mind all week.

Gerald has shared that on another Easter Sunday, as he walked into the church, an idea came to him that changed one whole section of his sermon.

He says, "I certainly didn't get up and tell the church, 'Section Three of my sermon underwent a major revision as I walked in the church door this morning.' Persons in the pew don't care about that. They just want to hear the Word effectively proclaimed."

Mapping the Sermon

All good sermons, even sermons preached without notes, have a skeletal framework—an outline, if you will. It may not be long and formal or in great detail with headings and sub-headings, but it is an outline nonetheless. That outline becomes a kind of map that assures you of getting you and your audience to the desired destination.

Gerald uses a simple and effective method of outlining, which he describes as follows:

When I am ready to outline, I draw a line down the middle of a sheet of paper, dividing it in half lengthwise. Then I try to outline the whole of my sermon on the front of that paper.

Starting on the left-hand side, I title it, note the scripture text, and jot down a brief introduction—what I want to say to open the sermon.

Sometimes I may have only one word for the introduction, just enough to spark my memory. Other times I may have two or three sentences there, if I want to be sure to start out a certain way.

Many Sundays my outline will have a lot of empty space because I don't need it. On other Sundays the outline may spill over to the back side of the sheet.

If I'm doing, say, a classic three-point sermon, my first point goes in right after the introduction. Then down at the bottom of that first column is a key spot on my outline. I want to remember what I write at the bottom of this column because it is a transition phrase connecting me to point Number Two.

It does something else very important: it keeps me from saying, "Well, now, my next point is …"

Remember, the skeleton of your message should not be obvious. It may come as a surprise to you that people in your audience couldn't care less about "your next point." They just want to hear the message. You, not your listeners, are the one concerned about points. They don't need to have the outline pointed out to them. Let the message flow without calling attention to its organization. For example, don't point out the obvious:

"By way of introduction let me say ... ";

"Today my sermon has three points ..." ;

"Moving to my next point ...";

"In conclusion ..."

Such phrases diffuse the punch of your ideas, detracting rather than adding to the overall effect.

For my sermon titled "How Big Is God?" the transitional statement at the bottom of my outline was, "God says, 'I'm going to show you how big I am.' "

Then at the top of the right-hand column I listed the three ways God showed Isaiah his greatness:

1. God is a big giant.

2. God is powerful.

3. God is worthy of praise.

Now, there is an outline for a classic three-point sermon.

But who said you have to have a three-point sermon? Homiletics professors!

Three-point sermons work fine in the classroom. Sometimes they also work in the real world on Sunday. But you need to know that some great sermons don't have three points. Some sermons don't have any points per se. In those, you are off and running, talking about a whole concept. As one person aptly put it, such sermons "have no point, but they are never pointless."

Meanwhile, back to my outline. I note a brief phrase or statement for however many points there are. Then I write a little something for a conclusion at the bottom of the second column—or on the back if need be.

That is the page I study from as I prepare for Sunday.

On a really good week, that page is formulated by Saturday afternoon. Most weeks it's finished late on Saturday night. Sometimes it's still coming together at four o'clock Sunday morning.

Now, that does not mean that I wait until four o'clock Sunday morning to work on my sermon. No way. Mentally I'm working on it all week, sometimes weeks ahead. The main points or general ideas may be formulated by Tuesday. By Wednesday noon my secretary presses me for something to go in the bulletin. She gets a title and a text, but not my points. I'm open, groping to the last minute for what God really wants me to say.

I have been known on rare occasions to change my mind between Wednesday and Sunday and go with an entirely different sermon from the title and text printed in the bulletin. Imagine that!

This outline procedure is the only way I do it.

My daughter does not do it this way. My sons do not do it this way. Maurice Berquist does not do it this way. I don't think you should do it this way. You should find a way—your own way—that makes sense to you and works for you.

That's good advice.

Our point is that being creative, being open to last-minute inspiration or speaking without notes does not mean that you are not writing or not outlining as you prepare the sermon.

People often ask, "Brother Berquist, do you ever write anything down?"

Yes, I do write things down as I think them out. Usually I "think" at the typewriter or write on yellow lined pads. You should see my office. Papers everywhere! I am always endeavoring to bring a little order. I even have files in a filing cabinet. But not everything is filed there. Like a typical right-brained person, my filing system is stacks—on the desk, on the bookshelves, on the floor.

But Gerald Marvel is a horse of another color! God invented chaos, but Gerald has perfected it! He carries his ideas around in a paper sack. And if you could poke around in his sack you would find an interesting array of the "stuff" sermons are made of.

Describing his sack, Gerald says:

> It may seem like a harebrained idea, but it works for me. I have made a sack out of two manila folders reinforced with binding tape. I keep stuff I really like in this sack—have for years. It's not in any particular order.
>
> In there I keep poetry that I like and am memorizing. There are newspaper clippings and notes I've made on things of particular interest to me that I think might find their way into a sermon someday.
>
> I am constantly making notes on all kinds of things. And I carry them with me. When, eventually, that material goes into a sermon, I keep the sermon outline and throw the notes away. The complete sermon is preserved on tape should I ever need to refer to it.

I carry in my sack a few sermon outlines I've preached before—ideas I have thought worthy of keeping around. Some of them I have preached on more than once.

In addition to what's in my sack, in my office I have stacks—by years—of sermon outlines. Every Monday morning, I take the sermon, clip it inside the morning worship folder, and with a heavy marker write on the outside the sermon title and the date. I keep them because every now and then someone will ask for a tape of a particular sermon. If they or I can recall the year, it's a fairly simple matter to run through that year's stack, find the sermon in question, and have the person who does our tape ministry send them a tape. I have tapes going back to 1973.

Actually, I am far more organized than most people may assume. I may not keep my closet the way my wife likes it, and I may not have files organized the way some preachers do. But I go back for years with my sermon outlines.

And I know what's in my sack.

One thing we want to underscore here is the amount of time and study that goes into sermon preparation. There is no single "best" approach to sermon development. Possibilities are as varied as there are people to design and deliver. But all sermons do have some features in common, and giving special attention to those will prove fruitful.

All sermons, for example, have three things in common structurally: *a beginning, a middle, and an end.* Each of those three aspects of the sermon deserve careful attention in planning what you are going to say and how you are going to say it.

1. Opening remarks set the tone.
Whether it is the first line in a magazine article, a book, a play, or a speech—the opening statement is important. That is also true for a sermon.

If all has gone well in the worship service, the congregation will have been led into a mood of anticipation and receptivity for the hearing of God's Word. The anthem has been sung, the music has ceased, and now all eyes are on the pastor as he or she steps forward to speak.

The first words spoken set the tone for whatever is to follow. Therefore careful thought should be given to what those words will be.

Will you begin with prayer? ... an immediate reading of the biblical text? ... a few informal words that relate in a personal way to the congregation? ... or something that has happened during the service?

Any of those are appropriate activities to precede the preaching event. But what then? What will be the opening sentence(s) to begin the sermon itself? That is the beginning that needs to be carefully planned.

In preaching as in life, "You never get a second chance to make a first impression." What we say at the outset establishes the mood and gives direction to the total piece.

2. A good beginning gets everyone on board.

Imagine that all the people sitting out there in the congregation have traffic lights in the middle of their foreheads, with the familiar colors: red, yellow, and green.

How many of those lights do you suppose are giving you a "green" signal?

"Yea, pastor, bring it on! Amen!"

"Preach it, sister!" "Right on!"

How many "yellow"?

"We're already running overtime. I hope he is brief today!"

How many "red"?

"Here comes another chapter of 'Guilt and Punishment.' Why did I ever promise Ethel I'd come with her today. I could be out on the links with Fred and George. I don't need this!"

Those, of course, are not all the thoughts running through those heads in front of you, but you get the idea. Many—not all, but many—of the minds out there are someplace else. Your first job is to rope them all and pull them into your corral.

Or, to shift metaphors, before you can take them anywhere, you've got to get them "tuned in" to your wave length.

You've got to get them to board the train.

As I see it, a good beginning does three things:

(a) A good beginning grabs attention.

What kinds of openings are attention getters?

A provocative question:
If someone offered you a guaranteed win on a Ten Million Dollar lottery ticket, would you take it?

An amazing statistic:
Here's one to chew on next time you bite into a Big Mac: A recent survey of 7,000 people in the USA and five other countries reports that more people recognize McDonald's golden arches than the cross of Christianity. An amazing 88 percent of those surveyed knew the golden arches, but only 54 percent could identify the cross.

A captivating story:
The story may be a dramatic retelling of the biblical event found in the sermon text. It may be a fictional or real-life incident (real-life is better!). It can be something from your personal life or something you recently read. Key words to characterize the story you choose are *relevant, recent, fresh, touching, provocative, even humorous* (some or all of those traits). Remember, too, that you captivate not only by the content of the story, but by the way you tell it.

Plan and rehearse your opening carefully.

Whatever "hook" you choose—statement, question, story—the idea is to *put your locomotive up front.* Get the train moving with everyone on board as you begin the journey.

(b) A good beginning introduces the main idea or theme of the sermon.

Introduction of the topic or theme may not happen in the first sentence. But somewhere in the opening segment—in that part of the sermon you consider to be "the beginning"—should be a clear indication of the subject, the theme, the main idea, the point you hope to make with the sermon. Like a tasty hors d'oeuvre, a good beginning whets the appetite of the audience for the rest of the meal (message) yet to come.

(c) A good beginning gives direction to the rest of the sermon.

Again, this direction may not be spelled out in the first sentence. But at some point within the introductory remarks, the congregation should get some idea of the approach you are taking and where you are going as you lead them in exploring the topic. Like a menu, it gives a hint of the courses to follow.

3. A good middle keeps everyone on board.

Once you have everyone with you, you are ready to present the "meat" of the sermon. It is time to move quickly into a clear presentation of your main point(s).

In stating your points, be plain.

This is no time for obscurity. A sermon should not be a guessing game for the congregation: "Let's try to figure out where in the world the pastor is going with this thing!"

God's prophets of old were straightforward and plain-spoken. And Jesus spoke in plain, simple terms that the common people heard gladly. We should do likewise.

That is not to say you can't have an element of surprise in a sermon now and then. Once in a great while you may want to keep the audience guessing until you make a particular revelation at the end. Even Jesus was deliberately obscure sometimes.

But I will tell you point blank that, as a rule, if the people in your audience don't have some idea where you are going, they won't follow you for long. There are too many other things for them to think about, like "What's cookin' for dinner?"

They have followed you on this hunt to chase rabbits, not to go snipe hunting!

So get your sermon organized in some logical way and give them some markers as you go along so they can tell where you are.

Use of words like *first, second, third* as markers always helps. But I try to avoid phrases like *my first main point, my second point,* and so on. Those seem overly obvious—predictable and monotonous. Other kinds of phrases are more subtle, but do the same thing:

- *"The first thing we notice is that … ."*
- *"Moving right along, here's another interesting aspect to this story."*
- *"Now we come to the "meat" of this passage."*
- *"Let's take a closer look at the heart of this story."*
- *"By now, you can guess where this story is headed."*
- *"In the light of what has happened so far, what do you suppose will be God's next move?"*

Another set of "markers" uses key words that all begin with the same letter—*Samson was strong, sexy, and stupid; finally sightless and spiritual.*

Or you can follow some logical movement though a passage of Scripture that presents within itself a clear path. From these titles, you can visualize possible paths a sermon might take: *Rahab and the Scarlet Cord* (Jericho's fall from Rahab's point of view); *Another Night with the Frogs* (Pharaoh ponders the plagues). The sequence of events in each story provides a natural flow of thought, a predictable outline.

You might ask, "How long should the middle be?"

That's an excellent question with an important answer: Just long enough to effectively make your point(s). The number of points will vary from sermon to sermon. Sometimes one, sometimes the "classic three," occasionally more.

Keep in mind that it is far better to have fewer points thoroughly discussed and well illustrated than to overload the sermon with concepts you don't have time in twenty-five minutes to develop adequately. Just running through a list is not preaching.

Beware also of the danger of getting carried away with too many illustrations. There is such a thing as too much of a good thing. Be selective.

People can only take in so much at one sitting. The old adage is true: *The mind can absorb only as much as the seat can endure.*

If you are watchful, you can tell when the audience is with you, and you can tell when they've "got it." When you see that happen, move to the conclusion whether or not you have covered all the material you had planned to use.

4. A good conclusion wraps it up.

Like a bow tied around a beautifully wrapped gift, the conclusion pulls all the elements of the sermon into one cohesive whole. Your final statements, perhaps embodied in a story, should be carefully chosen to deliver that "single effect" Poe talks about. This is where you "make the sale," so you want to be sure to leave ample time for people to respond. This is where, if you have done your job well, people will clearly see for themselves the answer to the question posed in the beginning: *What does God want people to think or do differently after they have heard the message?*

Like the introduction, the conclusion consists of several elements that each need consideration as you plan the sermon:

(a) Final statements or story.

This should be the most moving, inspiring, stirring part of the sermon, for it leads into the response. It is the last impression. Make it memorable.

(b) Appeal for a response.

People will not know how to respond to your sermon unless you tell them. You need to state clearly and specifically what you feel God wants them to do:

• make a decision to accept Christ.

• make a rededication of some part of their life for a specific purpose.

• pray for some specific need in their life.

• intercede in prayer for someone else.

• carry out an assignment during the next week that you will specify.

The list is endless. The point is that in your conclusion, you should state precisely their options for responding to the message.

(c) Invitation for response.

Open the altar and invite people to pray there or in their seats in response to what God has said to them through the message.

I close with a word of prayer and start a familiar hymn as I invite people to join me at the altar to pray. I like to move quickly from the last sentence of the sermon to the response, often starting the song without music (not difficult for me since I sing the same way I preach—without notes!). I dislike having people reaching for hymnals and turning pages. It breaks the mood. If they are under conviction, the fewer distractions the better.

Usually I am first to kneel at the altar to pray for the moving of God's Spirit upon the people to meet their various needs. I have found people less reluctant to come to the altar if somebody else is already there.

I have a point of concern here.

I acknowledge a growing trend to deemphasize coming to the altar in the belief that people are more comfortable making commitments at their seats. But, frankly, I am saddened by this move.

Certainly I believe that God can speak to people anywhere and that a decision made in the pew is no less sacred and binding than one made at the altar. But I continue to hold that the altar is a sacred place to meet God, and I feel strongly that we need to teach our people about the special role it has both in the worship experience and in their spiritual growth.

I believe, as the Bible says, that *"the altar sanctifies the gift"* (Matthew 23:19, KJV) and that whatever we place there—our lives, our money, our sickness, our broken relationships, our failures—God will use for our edification and God's glory. We rob our people of a real blessing if we fail to teach them that.

The Outline in Review

Richard Borden, in his book *Public Speaking as Listeners Like It,* captures the essence of what we have said here with an unforgettable outline that works for any kind of speech of any length—including sermons:

1. **Ho hum!**—Kindle a quick flame of spontaneous interest in your first sentence. START A FIRE!
2. **Why bring that up?**—BUILD A BRIDGE from the island of your listener's interests to the "mainland" of your topic. Until that bridge is built, you are not ready to begin the body of your speech.
3. **For instance**—GET DOWN TO CASES! The body of your speech must be keyed to one relentless audience demand, "For instance!" For every general assertion you make, give one or more examples. Resist the temptation to "put the idea in other words." What people want and respond to are not "other words," but examples (illustrations).
4. **So what?**—ASK FOR ACTION! The end of your speech, like your pencil, should have a point. Your conclusion must be more than a graceful leave-taking, more than a summary of main points, more than a reminder of your subject's general importance. It must answer questions like these: "Now what?" "Where do we go from here?" "What do you want us to do about what you have presented?"(Borden 3–15).

Thinking on Your Feet

So, the outline is finished. Sunday is here. The hour has come and you are on your feet to deliver the message you and God have worked on all week—for several weeks maybe. You are past the introduction and well into the middle. You're feeling pretty good about the way the message is going. Then comes the unexpected.

We've all had it happen.

While you are preaching—right in the middle of the sermon— like a bolt of lightning a new idea comes to you. Or perhaps you suddenly recall a pertinent fact or quote not in your outline. Whatever strikes, it is something you had not thought of as you were preparing the sermon.

It may come as a surprise to the novice preacher that sermon construction does not necessarily end when the outline is "put to bed" Saturday night. In fact, sermon editing is not over until the hymn of invitation is being sung. You need to have confidence that you can delete or incorporate as you speak.

So what do you do with this new idea that suddenly comes out of nowhere? Do you use it or stick with only what you have pre-pared?

It depends.

If you are confident of its accuracy and the illustration really fits—perhaps better than something else you had planned to use— by all means, pitch it in. If, on the other hand, it is a story or fact you have not been able to verify, resist the urge to use it until you have had opportunity to check it out.

Time is a factor, too. If you add in something new, you should be prepared to leave out something else.

And there is a flip side to this coin.

Many times in preaching, you will have researched and docu-mented a major point you are really proud of; but as you get to where it comes in, you suddenly realize, "I've already reached my audience. I don't need that." So, you leave it out.

Good move on your part!

A while back I was preaching somewhere in these United States, and I had based my whole sermon on a particular story I thought was tremendous. But when I got through preaching, I suddenly realized that I hadn't used the story at all. For some reason, as I stood before that particular audience and started sharing, the story just didn't fit.

The sermon was highly effective without it. We had a great service, but I had left out the main thing I had developed the message from.

It's still a good story. I used it another time.

Ideally, then, the dynamic of sermon construction goes on even during delivery, making adjustments for whatever God wants to do in the moment, and according to how the message is being received by the congregation.

Knowing When to Close

Developing a sensitivity for your audience is essential to good preaching.

That is one reason I feel it is important to preach without notes. Unencumbered by a written script, you are always taking your audience into account. You know when they are listening and when they are not. You know when they are ready to respond; and that moment of readiness, whenever it comes, should mark the climax—the end—of the sermon. You will have arrived.

Sad to say, I have listened to a great many sermons when the whole audience could have gotten up and walked out; and the speaker would not even have known it, because he was bent on preaching his sermon whether the people were with him or not.

If you are not watching your audience—if you don't know when you are not getting across—your people may not physically walk out on you, but they will walk out mentally. They will be doing everything in the world but listening to you. Yet you keep droning on. That, friend, is destructive.

You have preached your sermon in twenty minutes rather than the allotted thirty minutes, but you don't know you have reached the end of it.

Nothing is longer than going past the end.

I have watched it happen so many times—preachers ignore the obvious, determined to finish their outline regardless. But they're through. They are *through!* I am sitting there thinking, "That's all the airstrip you've got. Pull it down!" But they plow on, not knowing when to stop, because they are slaves to their outline.

A cardinal rule of selling, as any master salesman can tell you, is this: *after you've sold something, don't unsell it.*

Remember your ABC's: Always Be Closing!

If it takes only five minutes to get the sale made, quit.

Stop when you get the job done. After the nail is driven in, don't keep beating the wood.

*****

The important thing to remember as you prepare to preach is that your listeners are interested in only one thing: they just want to hear a clear, moving message from God. Getting that message takes a tremendous amount of reading, a tremendous amount of thinking, and a desperate amount of prayer and depending on the Holy Spirit.

It doesn't come easy.

We have all known times, more Sunday mornings than we would like to admit, when we have headed for church praying, "God, if you can do anything with this, you are a whole lot better than I."

A couple of hours later we go home humbled by the powerful way God came through, and all we can do is thank and praise God that the sermon was effective and people's needs were met.

Once again we stand in awe that our Father can and does use us.

Chapter 14

Expository Preaching

Some time ago I was in Israel with a professor from Anderson University's School of Theology. I asked him what he was teaching in seminary.

"Systematic theology," he replied.

"I don't believe in systematic theology," I said.

Yes, it was a bold statement; but since I am out of school and not being graded anymore, I can say what I think.

"Well, why not?" he responded.

"Because I believe in biblical theology."

"That's the same thing," he said.

"No, it is not the same thing," I countered, "because when you systematize theology, you make everything fit. You label yourself as either an Armenian or a Calvinist or whatever you are, and you take a position and follow it all the way through. The Bible doesn't do that."

I pressed on: "Actually scripture sometimes appears to be contradictory when in reality it is taking two poles and bringing them together. Systematic theology may be an aid to doctrinal study; but, if we are not careful, it can, from my perspective, reinforce our polarities rather than expand our understanding of Scripture."

Expository preaching—preaching centrally focused on God's Word—can help avoid that pitfall, not only for the preacher, but also for his or her parishioners.

What *Is* Expository Preaching?

Like so many contemporary "buzz words," *expository preaching* means whatever whoever is using the term wants it to mean. For our purposes here, we consider expository preaching to be a style of preaching that takes a section of Scripture—sometimes a whole book of the Bible—and moves through it in a way that exposes its meaning and relates it to life today.

As we all know, *expository* comes from the same root components as *exposition*—"a discourse explaining what is difficult to understand"—and *expose*—"to bring to light." The goal of expository preaching, then, is to bring light and meaning to scriptures that may be difficult to understand, and to help people move beyond superficial levels of understanding to deeper spiritual truths that often lie beneath the surface account of biblical events.

All the principles presented in previous chapters—in particular those *visual, verbal, visceral, vital, vicarious, verifiable, and victorious* qualities—come into play as we attempt to unlock the meaning of God's Word for our listeners.

While all expository preaching is Scripture oriented and Scripture centered—it can be done in many different ways. Some approaches, however, are more effective than others.

Many preachers, for example, build sermons that move consecutively through a book of the Bible. Series preaching can be an excellent technique for exposition. But we hope their teaching is not merely a verse-by-verse mechanical exercise. That can be a remarkably boring and unproductive enterprise. For in genuine expository preaching, not every verse is equal to every other verse.

In saying that, we in no way disavow that "*all* Scripture is given by God for reproof, correction," and so forth.

Certainly all verses are in the Bible for a purpose. But in preaching, some verses have more substance for elaboration than other verses. Saying that not all verses are equal for purposes of preaching does not devalue any of them as being a significant part of the inspired Word of God. But expository preaching does not require that something be "made" of every verse.

Jesus, our best example for expository preaching, quoted some verses from the Old Testament; but he did not quote every verse.

Paul quoted some verses, as did Matthew and others. But none of them recited a passage word for word, pausing after each verse to explain what it meant. Some verses need little or no explanation.

We have all heard preachers who try to spiritualize every verse of Scripture and every event, and in the process make fools of themselves by saying utterly ridiculous things.

When a verse doesn't have anything to say, don't make it say something it doesn't say.

"Now, we come to Verse 17. What does it mean?"

It may simply mean, "Hurry on to 18!"

I heard of one fellow who was preaching from the Bible. He started out in Genesis and went as far as he could. He was going on and on. He had gone for two hours and was still going when he said, "Now, we come to Moses. What shall we do with Moses?"

One man stood up and said, "He can have my place. I'm going home."

Sometimes, when you come to a certain verse in Scripture, it may be important in context, but not as important as other verses for understanding the main idea of the passage.

The point is that expository preaching is not a mechanical walk through a passage of scripture verse by verse. That kind of exercise has a definite place in Bible study. When people come for a Bible study, that is the kind of analysis they expect. There is a definite place for that in the overall teaching ministry of the church. But we ought to call it that—Bible study. It is not preaching.

We should also point out that expository preaching is different from topical preaching. I know some preachers decry and deplore topical preaching—selecting a topic and supporting it with Scripture. I don't share their disdain. Personally, I like topical preaching and think it has a place in a well-rounded preaching repertoire. The Bible itself contains many examples of topical preaching. Paul did it, and Matthew. Jesus did it. Others did, too. I would say that topical preaching is fine, so long as we do not violate Scripture. We all know that anyone can take a topic, find a text to suit it, and merely use that text as a springboard to get into his or her own ideas, never getting back to the Scripture.

No doubt we all have seen preachers use a text as a drunk man uses a lamppost: for support rather than illumination.

It is particularly troublesome to me to hear preachers take a text that gives one aspect of an issue and completely ignore or deny Scriptures that deal with the other side. I consider that a travesty of preaching and a betrayal of our call to be "rightly dividing the word of truth" (2 Timothy 2:15, KJV).

In my estimation, expository preaching, like all other styles of preaching, must meet Clyde Fant's definition, which we repeat here:

> Preaching is that form of verbal activity that moves between the historical revelation and the contemporary situation.

As I see it, we have no right to preach anything other than the Bible.

What I like best about expository preaching is that the outline for the message comes right out of the Bible passage. The Bible is central. The message is drawn directly from the Scripture and relates to the Scripture throughout.

But expository preaching stands on two legs. If our expository preaching is all one-sided in that we are only giving a commentary on Scripture, from my perspective, that is not preaching.

What people really need to know is that the Word of God has something to say about what is happening in their world right now—about their daily problems, about their kids, about issues of daily living.

Gerald Marvel makes a good observation on this point:

> If in your sermon all you do is take them into the world of the First Century and leave them there, you have done nothing more than take them on a trip back in time. Somewhere in your sermon you had better bring them back to what it means to their lives on Monday morning at work.

Expository preaching at its best does not divorce itself from life.

The Importance of Preaching the Whole Bible

A Latin phrase I learned during my seminary days has stuck with me and compelled me throughout my life to study the whole Bible and preach the whole Bible.

The words were these: *Scriptura, Scripturae, interpres.*

The meaning: "Scripture by Scripture is interpreted."

We cannot shed light on what we ourselves do not understand. The best way to understand what the Bible says and what it means is simply to keep reading the Bible—*the whole Bible.* The Bible explains itself far better than any commentary can. And what the Holy Spirit will reveal to *you* as you pray and study will be as valid as some revelation that has come to someone else.

Please understand, my intent here is not to belittle commentaries. A great deal of research and scholarship goes into them. Commentaries are fine. But I don't use them much. I have found it far more exciting to discover for myself the mysteries and truths of Scripture by studying the whole Bible and seeing the interconnectedness of all its parts.

When I find a puzzling passage, I stash it on the back burner of my mind someplace. Then, one day, when I am reading in another part of the Bible altogether, a word or a phrase will jump out at me; and suddenly the meaning of that obscure passage becomes crystal clear!

The excitement of those "a-ha moments" carries over into my preaching, because it is exhilarating and fun to share these new and helpful insights with others.

It can be that way for you, too.

Every year that I live I am more deeply convinced that time spent studying Scripture is profitable time.

I am a bookaholic, no question about it. I have a library lined with books, an attic lined with books, a garage lined with books, and hundreds more in storage—no other place for them. I give books away by the hundreds, and still I keep on accumulating them and reading them.

The other day for the hundredth time my wife moaned, "Honey, we've got no more place for books."

When we lived in Vancouver, Washington, I found a gigantic bookstore that would buy books. So I loaded four cartons of books into my car and took them over there to sell.

The obliging girl at the counter said, "Sure. We buy books."

She then started pulling books from my cartons and putting them in stacks. When she finished sorting, she said, "We'll buy these," gesturing toward one of the stacks. "The others," she said, "you can take back home. We can't sell them."

Being an inquisitive soul and a little wounded to think that some of my books were not good enough to sell, I said, "Well, what's wrong with them?"

She replied, "We just don't have a market for those."

Pressing for more information, I said, "What makes a market? I want to know what kind of books to bring you."

Then she said, "Well, I'll tell you. We don't buy any textbooks."

When she said that, I immediately thought about the millions of dollars spent every year in America on textbooks. As any college student can tell you, they are not cheap. I said to myself, what irony! As students, we bend our brains on these textbooks. We carry them around, having mortgaged the farm to buy them; and the truth is that even while they are still being printed, they are obsolete! Nothing is older than last year's science textbook. It's almost a joke.

Yesterday's cutting-edge knowledge is today carted off to the city dump, because the knowledge of this world passes away. But, in the words of a long-ago prophet, "the Word of our God stands forever" (Isaiah 40:8, NKJV).

In spite of the information explosion, *God's Word stands—unshaken and true!*

Every new discovery of science, medicine, psychology, archaeology, history, or literature in the past two thousand years has only served to verify what the Word of God has already said!

Yes, it pays to study the Bible. It is the one textbook that does not go out of date.

Consider the case of Norman Cousins, who cured himself of a rare disease that doctors diagnosed as hopeless. Of five hundred known cases on record, all had died.

Refusing to accept that prognosis, Cousins developed his own remedy—massive doses of Vitamin C and laughter. His doctors pooh-poohed the whole idea. But he found that twenty minutes of laughter could give him two hours' freedom from pain. Science supports his discovery, because we know that the mind creates endorphins, painkillers as effective as morphine in relieving pain.

In short, Cousins recovered from the illness, wrote an article for the *New England Journal of Medicine* and later a book about his experience called *Anatomy of an Illness.* His cure became major news in medical circles. He received thousands of inquiries from doctors about his unusual treatment and was invited to teach in the Cancer Section of a university in California, telling about the effect of emotions on the mind.

When I read *Anatomy of an Illness*, I said, "What do you know? The Bible proved true again!" A thousand years before Christ, Solomon said, "A merry heart does good / like medicine, / But a broken spirit dries the bones" (Proverbs 17:22, NKJV).

Norman Cousins was living proof of what I had been preaching for years. That scripture—like the rest of God's Word—is truth people need to hear.

When you preach the Bible, my friend, you not only explain the world we live in now; but you prepare people in advance to deal with problems of tomorrow. None of us knows what tomorrow holds, but God's Word gives us light and life for now and for the future.

Advantages of Expository Preaching

Because expository preaching is so closely tied to the Word of God, it poses many advantages.

1. Lessens the danger of lop-sided preaching.

Preaching expository messages levels out our preaching so that we don't get on a hobby horse and ride on only one track, presenting only one point of view. If we are students of the whole Bible, we will find that Scripture presents two positions on many things. Both positions are important to understand the whole truth of God's message.

2. Lessens the danger of warped theology.

When we preach the whole Bible, there is less danger of hanging a whole theological concept on only one verse or passage. The Bible itself says that "all Scripture is given by inspiration of God, and is profitable for doctrine, for reproof, for correction, for instruction in righteousness, that the man of God may be complete, thoroughly equipped for every good work" (2 Timothy 3:16–17, NKJV).

3. Lessens the danger of ignoring some parts of the Bible.

Certainly none of us understands all of Scripture, and we each find some parts more attractive than others. It is only natural that we tend to preach more often from those parts of the Bible we relate to more strongly; but if we are committed to expository preaching, we will, over time, cover the waterfront reasonably well.

Often when I am asked to speak in churches, I stay in pastors' homes. Many times I have had occasion to use their Bibles. I can always tell when a preacher is not preaching the whole Bible. Some sections of Scripture appear well-read and even worn—words underlined, notes in margins, dog-eared pages, edges darkened by finger oils. Generally those sections more often than not are the four Gospels, Psalms, and some of Paul's letters. But other pages covering large chunks of Scripture are pristine, untouched. On a few occasions, though portions of the Bible looked well used, I have even found some pages still stuck together, as they are sometimes when Bibles are new.

Preaching some of the Bible is, I suppose, better than preaching none of it—though I have run across a few cases of warped theology that made me wonder. Certainly, if large portions of Scripture are ignored, our exposition is apt to be one-sided and incomplete.

4. Heightens authority in the pulpit.

Because the main focus of expository preaching is the Word itself, we speak from a position of strength. The preacher never has more authority in the pulpit than when speaking directly from Scripture. Just holding the Bible has an impact. Even people who do not believe in the Bible still honor it.

5. Meets needs without preaching at people.

I have a rule I never violate. I do not preach *at* people. If I know somebody has a particular problem, or the church does, I do not preach at it in a sermon—for several reasons. In the first place, it's not fair. In the second place, it doesn't work. Third, that kind of preaching is in the flesh, not in the Spirit.

Once in a while in a revival meeting or a convention, somebody will come to me saying, "Brother Berquist, my husband (or my wife or my teenager) is coming to church tonight; and they really need to hear about this or that. So if you can work it into your sermon, please do."

I guarantee you, I will not come within a city block of that topic. I will deliberately avoid it, because when you are in the flesh doing that, it does more harm than good. You do not solve church problems or family problems that way!

But I have discovered that if you are going through Scripture in an expository preaching series, you don't miss anything. Every topic helpful to people—every kind of sin and every kind of situation—is covered. Yet, they know you are not preaching *at* them. It's there. The Scripture speaks; the Holy Spirit convicts. What more can you say? Needs are covered impartially without pointing fingers at anybody.

Sometimes, however, the Word of God will be so close and piercing that persons affected will think somebody has talked to you about them.

They will say, "Who told you about me?" or "You've been reading my mail!"

But if they know you are in a series or going through the Scripture, they can more readily accept the fact that it is God, not you, who is singling them out.

6. Enhances sermon preparation.

If you are preaching directly from the Word, often a natural outline for the sermon will come from the text itself. Also, much of what you will want to say comes from the Scripture itself. So you have a starting place in pulling the sermon together. If you are preaching without notes, being able to hang your points on the Scripture text makes it easier to remember what you plan to say.

*****

Enough said about what expository preaching is and is not. Now to the meat of the matter: how do we do it?

We can, I think, cover that topic best simply by walking through an expository sermon.

Expository Sample

Let me demonstrate how I put an expository sermon together.

Let's look, for example, at the first ten verses of Acts 28. I'll show you how the outline for the sermon comes right from the Bible passage, how we interpret what is happening, and how we move between *"the historical revelation"* (what the Bible says) and *"the contemporary situation"* (real-life situations to which listeners can relate).

1. Now when they had escaped, they then found out that the island was called Malta.

2. And the natives showed us unusual kindness; for they kindled a fire and made us all welcome, because of the rain that was falling and because of the cold.

3. But when Paul had gathered a bundle of sticks and laid them on the fire, a viper came out because of the heat, and fastened on his hand.

4. So when the natives saw the creature hanging from his hand, they said to one another, "No doubt this man is a murderer, whom, though he has escaped the sea, yet justice does not allow to live."

5. But he shook off the creature into the fire and suffered no harm.

6. However, they were expecting that he would swell up or suddenly fall down dead; but after they had looked for a long time and saw no harm come to him, they changed their minds and said that he was a god.

7. Now in that region there was an estate of the leading citizen of the island, whose name was Publius, who received us and entertained us courteously for three days.

8. And it happened that the father of Publius lay sick of a fever and dysentery. Paul went in to him and prayed, and he laid his hands on him and healed him.

9. So when this was done, the rest of those on the island who had diseases also came and were healed.

10. They also honored us in many ways; and when we departed, they provide such things as were necessary.

(Acts 28:1–10, NKJV)

First, what we have here is a good story.

That is a plus for preaching because people remember stories.

But beyond that, this story presents a situation all of us

encounter in life: how to deal with disaster. That is not a title for this sermon necessarily; it is just a theme found in the piece.

Paul certainly has the monopoly on disaster in this case. He was a prisoner to start with, held captive on a ship. He tried to warn them of disaster, but no one would listen. When at sea they were caught in the grip of a terrible storm for fourteen days; eventually even their food was thrown overboard to lighten the ship. When the ship ran aground, the soldiers wanted to kill all the prisoners; but the centurion in charge intervened and ordered everyone to abandon ship. Paul and the other prisoners swam ashore on pieces of wreckage. They washed up on the beach—cold, wet, hungry, and were met by kind natives. That is where our text begins.

As we said, there are many approaches to expository preaching. I'll show you the pattern that has worked best for me.

Step 1. *As the Bible is central to our preaching, I always begin with the text.*

Our purpose in preaching is to open—to shed light on—the Word of God so that it can speak to the hearts of our listeners. So I always start by reading the Bible passage.

I recommend that because I think, first of all, it gives you authority. It gives you credibility. It also allows your listeners to hear the complete text in context before you begin your discussion of it. Just in hearing the Word of God recited or read aloud to them—even without commentary—they will learn something about the Bible.

Step 2. *Having spoken the Bible, I then move immediately to the human situation.* I want the persons sitting before me to realize from the outset that it is not just Paul back here in the pages of the New Testament that we are talking about. So after reading the text, I would mention some disasters facing people today, to make a connection between my listeners and Paul

At this point, I do not go into any detailed discussion of contemporary disasters. I simply want to show that I know enough of what is happening to speak to those issues. I might simply name a few of the common crises of life people today may face in a given week: cancer, bankruptcy, divorce, losing a job, accidents of all kinds, death, teen pregnancy, adult pregnancy sometimes. I don't take a lot of time or make a major thing out of listing these crisis points, but I let my listeners know that here is where they can tune in. Somewhere in that list, I am going to pull many, if not all, of the audience on board.

In essence, I am saying to them: "It is *you*—the person in the pew—we are going to be talking about. *You*—and the problems *you* face. "Learning to survive the disasters of life" may be lessons we learn from the life of Paul, but the lessons apply directly to you."

Step 3. *Then I move back to the Bible story:*
Now, here is Paul—shipwrecked. It's bad enough to be a prisoner. On the ship they were going without food, so they were already hungry. Then he nearly drowns; has to swim ashore by clinging to wreckage from the ship. When he finally gets to shore, he finds that he has landed on "Alligator Island." The situation is bad.

Step 4. *Then I connect again to present-day parallels.*
Having replayed the major events, I then tag what is happening in the Bible story to reactions people today might have in similar situations. I might say something like this:
So Paul is in a mess.

The test of anyone's character is what happens in a crisis, isn't it? It isn't enough that your salvation is good on Easter Sunday morning when you are wearing new clothes and the sun is shining. How does it—and you—hold up when the bottom falls out of everything. Where do you go then?

Step 5. *With that thought in hand, we return to the Bible story:*
Well, what does Paul do? Now, we see what Paul is really made of. I'll tell you what I see in this Bible story. I see the "Portrait of an Overcomer."

I love this picture!

It may not tell us much about Paul's physical features; but I like the picture of Paul this passage paints, because it shows what makes a difference in people.

Let's take a look at it. You paint the picture in your mind's eye as we talk about it.

Step 6. *From this point, I will shift back and forth between the Bible story and the human element found in today's reality.*

With help from the natives, who prove to be friendlier than first anticipated, the survivors of the shipwreck build a fire. We see Paul out gathering wood.

There are two kinds of people in life: those who, when they get down, feel sorry for themselves; and those who say, there is still something to contribute. Isn't that true? So we notice that Paul here, shivering and wet from swimming ashore, is not just warming himself by the fire. He is gathering sticks.

Always there is a redemptive element in life if you are a contributing person. You may have lost everything, but you still have something to give. You are down, but you are not out. We can all paint pictures of that, can't we?

Don't you know people who are always on the receiving end? You go out to eat; they never pick up the check—some impediment in their reach! Always they are looking for help, but they never volunteer to help others. Right? But Paul is different. He is helping.

Now, notice in the story what happens when you do that. Let's see how it plays out in this picture of Paul.

He is gathering sticks to put on the fire. That is his nature. You are going to do what you naturally believe in doing, no matter where you are. If you are a taker, you will always be trying to take. If you are a giver, you will find a way to give.

But when you give, that does not mean you will be free from criticism, or that the world is going to understand. What happens to Paul when he starts putting sticks on the fire? He gets bit by a snake! Imagine that! Here he is trying to be helpful, and a viper—a snake or deadly insect of some kind—is lurking in the woodpile.

People are naive at this point. They want immediate response for doing good. They seem to say, "Well, I was cheerful for one day, for goodness sake." Or "I tithed this Sunday; how come I had a flat tire in the parking lot?"

I saw a book the other day titled *If God Loves Me, How Come I Can't Get My Locker Open?* That's one problem I haven't had to worry about for a long time. But you know how it goes. Life is like that. Bad things do happen to good people—even when they are doing good.

But what does Paul do? What do you do when you get hurt doing good? When you get criticized for trying to help? We've all been there. It has happened to all of us.

Well, take a note from Paul. If you are a giver, you can shake off a lot of things.

When I hear some preacher say, "In my last pastorate I got hurt," I always feel like saying, "Well, whoop-de-do! We get hurt all the time in this world. Think about it. We serve a Savior who was crucified. Don't be surprised to find that not the only cross in the world is the wooden one in front of your church. You will find crosses in your study. Many other crosses to bear in your ministry. But if you are rightly motivated, you can shake off the tribulations that beset you."

Paul's story is so true-to-life! That's what makes it interesting.

When Paul shakes off the viper unharmed, the same people who were saying he was a criminal getting the justice and punishment he deserved, suddenly change their minds. What is he now? He's a god!

If you live on the opinions of people, you are going to have a hard life. You will be depressed one day and overexalted the next. If you listen to people, you're in trouble.

Many stories illustrate that fact. The classic one is about the man who, with his son, was going to town leading a donkey. They walked—you know the story:

As they walked along, they passed a fellow who said, "Stupid people. Why don't you ride the donkey? Man, you're the oldest. You ought to get on."

So the man got on. But a little farther down the road, they met other travelers, who jeered as they went by: "Look at that guy. He's riding and making his little boy walk."

Shamed by the jeering, the man got off and put the son on the donkey. He walked.

Somebody else came along and said, "What a selfish son to let your old man walk while you with your young, strong limbs ride."

So they both got on the donkey.

But then people said, "What a cruel pair this is! Look at that poor donkey burdened by the weight of two people."

Finally, they both got off and carried the donkey!

See? Your nature cannot be dependent upon other people's reaction to you. Some days they are going to praise you; some days they are going to blame you. Endure it when they blame you, and don't take it too seriously when they praise you.

Step 7. *Driving home the main point.*

Thus we come to the final part of this outline, if I were preaching this sermon: *when our method is biblical, the message is biblical.*

After all these things have happened, the natives begin to realize that more than just a man is here. And Publius, the "head knocker" there, says, "By the way, my Daddy's sick. He's got dysentery. Would you come over and take a look at him?"

So Paul goes over and prays for the man, and God heals him.

The point is this: when you are behaving in a biblical way, you can expect biblical results.

Paul, apparently, does not formally preach to these people at all. Does he? The passage does not say that he does. But he does preach, nonetheless.

The best sermon any of us preach is what we are under fire.

Finally, after Publius's father has been healed, the entire heathen community change their viewpoint. The story says they bestow upon Paul many honors. When he departs, Paul says, "They loaded us with such things as were necessary."

*****

Now, I think any pastor reading this book could preach a sermon on that.

Couldn't you?

You are welcome to do it, because the notes are right there in your Bible.

This is, to my way of thinking, a reasonable example of how the Bible lends itself to expository preaching. We have not done historical violation. All the events actually happened, and that in itself generates interest. It is colorful.

Depending on the time you have and the amount of visualization you want to do, you can picture the rocky shore, the cold wind, the wet clothes, the glowing fire, the venomous viper. Don't get too vivid on the dysentery part!

You see Paul—coming into the scene drenched in salt-stained rags, shivering and cold—walking away at the end with garlands around his neck in victory.

It's a great sermon. All you do is simply take the Bible story and preach it.

Getting Meaning from Scripture

That kind of expository preaching can be cultivated. Here are a few tips about getting started—how you can get the text to speak to you—because the Scripture is full of opportunities for this kind of sermon.

1. Start with a familiar text.

Often the best method of Bible study is to begin with something you already know fairly well and look at it from a new light.

2. Pray for insight and wisdom.

The Bible says, "If any of you lacks wisdom, let him ask of God, who gives to all liberally and without reproach, and it will be given to him" (James 1:5, NKJV).

"Who gives to ALL...." That includes me.

And *you*!

We preachers all know that one of the reasons the Holy Spirit was sent to earth was to *"guide you into all truth."* Jesus said that. Yet how often do we approach sermon preparation by trying to pull together all the human wisdom we can find on a particular passage of Scripture before we have asked God to open the meaning for us? Shame on us for "expository preaching" that substitutes the wisdom of men for the wisdom of God.

3. Read the passage more than once—or twice.

As I preach and lecture around the country, people invariably ask, "Berquist, where did you get those far-out ideas for that passage of Scripture? We have never heard anything like that before."

I'll tell you my secret.

In my travels to do revivals, conferences, lectures, and what not, I spend a fair amount of time in motel rooms by myself. Often I use that time for Bible study. I pick out a particular passage of Scripture, and I read it over and over and over and over again—until it speaks to me.

Try it. You may come up with a few surprising ideas yourself!

4. Project yourself into the passage.

Take, for example, a text like the one about Paul that I gave you here. I had read that, I'm sure, many times in my life. But as I read it this time, I tried to put myself in Paul's place. The fact that I have been on the ocean and have known what it is to be cold and a stranger, helped me to identify with Paul.

I tried to get inside his skin, get inside his head, see the situation through his eyes.

My train of thought went something like this: Suddenly, for the first time, I saw him there by the fire, shivering and cold, and hunkered down; then looking around and saying, "Who's going to stoke the fire?" Well, when nobody else is looking for wood, you look for wood. If the fire's going out, make yourself useful. Gather some wood.

The more I thought about that, I said, "That's a great insight for pastors or laypeople.

If the fire is going out in your church, don't leave and run over to somebody else's place. Make yourself useful to help solve the problems.

People are always saying about church, "Did you get a blessing?" More appropriately we should say, "Did you *bring* a blessing? Do you give something?" I've had people like that in my church—people who bring something to it. God bless them!

Then from that point, my logic said, "So, you bring a blessing. But what happens when you do something good?"

I am old enough to know that whenever we do a good thing, we instinctively look for praise from somebody. You know how it goes: pin a rose on me. Well, people don't always pin a rose on you. Sometimes you get bit by the very first thing out of the bag. It is not unusual to get criticized for doing good.

I remember one time I drove down to a church to preach for the people there, at their invitation. I worked hard to prepare a sermon. That Sunday I got up early and drove about a hundred miles to get there; and I preached and God blessed. I thought He did, anyway. Whenever I am invited somewhere to preach, people usually give me something for car fare or mileage, sometimes an honorarium. At the very least, they usually try to pay my gas. But on this day I was leaving, and nobody had talked to me at all.

Finally a woman came and handed me an envelope. I waited till I got down the road a piece to open it and see what it was.

Inside was a note which said: "Probably the worst sermon I ever heard in my life. I am embarrassed for you, and I pray God will get you saved."

Talk about vipers!

Understand, I'm not paranoid about this point; but on that day I fully expected somebody to say something nice—at the very least to say, "We're glad you came." Well, before I got out of town, someone gave me a jar of jelly; so it wasn't a total loss.

But if you are looking for sympathy or appreciation, one is under *A* in the dictionary; the other is under *S*.

You are not always going to get praise. Sometimes you get attacks instead. But if you are mature in Christ, you can shake those off—take them in stride.

Well, I've gone from explaining to preaching. But I hope you are getting the idea of how to get some new light on a familiar passage.

5. Try out different viewpoints.
When I was writing a book on the twenty-third psalm, somebody said to me, "How long is the book going to be?"

I said, "About a hundred and fifty pages."

"You can talk one hundred and fifty pages on six verses?"

"Oh, yes," I said,. "and I won't have finished it then."

"How do you do it?"

"I just take something familiar and keep looking at it from a different viewpoint." Viewpoint is key. For whenever you change the viewpoint, you change the scenery.

You change the whole thing.

Looking at Scripture is not much different from taking a trip in a car.

Often in my travels, when I have to rent or borrow a car to drive some place, the people at the rental agency or the owners of the car will give me belaborous directions. "Start down this street," they

175

will say, "and go two blocks till you come to a service station on the corner. Turn right there and go four more blocks and turn left." They go on and on with infinite details. All the while, I am frantically marking everything so I don't forget—and, wonder of wonders, I get there fine.

But the problem is coming back, because on the return trip I am seeing everything from an entirely different viewpoint. That service station is no longer on the right. Where I turned left is now right. Everything looks different. It's a whole new world.

Similarly, if we can approach Scripture from a different angle, we get a whole new perspective.

When I was a pastor, I regularly made sick calls in the hospital. I loved to do it. But we had a fairly good-sized church of several hundred people, and I honestly did not know everybody that well. So more than once I would go in to see somebody whose name I knew, only to find myself standing by the bed looking down at an unfamiliar face thinking, "Do I know you?"

I knew the names—and this sounds terrible—but if you are used to seeing people wearing a suit and tie, standing up, and you go to the hospital to visit them, they don't look the same when they are lying down in white.

Scriptures, like people, look different when you see them from different angles. So look at the text you have chosen from the top down. Look at it backwards. Notice key words. Read it out loud, placing emphasis on different words in each sentence. Examine the verbs. Use your imagination to put yourself in the scene. What experiences have you had that are similar to what is happening in the text? Look up words you don't know the meaning of. Words often have more than one meaning. How does that affect your interpretation of the passage?

Of course, the whole time you are reading and reflecting on the text, you are praying that the Holy Spirit will unlock the meaning for you and help you make relevant connections to the people who will be hearing you speak.

That kind of study takes time. Don't rush through it.

My favorite illustration about Bible study is this:

We have a farmer out here who has a little acreage in—well, let's say Missouri.

He has a hundred acres. He's a very poor farmer—really poor—back in the hills somewhere. Lives in a small tumbledown shack, with another little house out back of that. You know the kind—crescent moon on the door. Lots of rocks in his fields. Impossible to work by hand, so he got a mule. He can't afford a tractor.

You ask him, "How's farming?"

He says, "Boy, it's rough. We're just barely making it."

"Well, how much land have you got?" you ask.

"A hundred acres, and I'm working like crazy. But I can't afford inside plumbing. Can't afford a car. Can't afford to send my kids to college. Things are rough. I'd like to have a bigger farm."

Well, one day he learns that the water table in this part of Missouri is only about twenty feet below the surface. So he drills a well down twenty feet and starts irrigating his farm. Now he doesn't wait for the rain to come. When the land is dry, he irrigates it and grows crops and makes money. Next thing you know, he has built a bigger house. And the little house out back is now inside the big house. He also bought a truck, and he is prospering.

So you say to him, "Well, you're looking better, doing better. How much are you farming?"

"A hundred acres."

A few years go by, and you meet this fellow again. You learn that he has a big house now. Five bedrooms and five bathrooms, all with Jacuzzis. He's driving a Jaguar. His kids all have sports cars, and his wife is driving a Lexus. His kids are in college, and he takes trips to Europe.

You say, "How much are you farming?"

"A hundred acres."

"On the same land?"

"Yeah." he says. "But we put down an oil well. Three thousand feet down, we got oil. So now we're making it fine."

Well, the trouble with our Bible study is that most of us live on the hard pan of the surface, and we hurry over that. We don't dig into it. We don't let our imaginations play with it. We don't let the Spirit of God lead us in it.

We want "instant sermons," like instant potatoes. Consequently, the spiritual food we dish up for our congregations on Sunday morning tastes about as flat. We hurry around looking for quick fixes, copying anything we can get. Meanwhile, we are starving to death and our people are starving to death—all within the Promised Land of the Word of God.

Isn't that true?

I have learned that Bible study takes discipline and diligence, my friend. And the deeper you dig, the richer it gets.

We have great wealth at our fingertips in God's Word. Our prayer as we study should be, "God, don't let me sit here and complain that I don't have the resources. I am sitting on top of an infinite supply."

I promise you this, if you will do what I am suggesting—take the Bible and start reading it with your imagination—you will find that you have more than enough insight there to be original and new.

You have had it all the time. It's just a matter of putting down the well.

Chapter 15

The Art of Illustration

A young pastor once said to me, "I'm only twenty-nine; I feel a little unprepared."

Charles Spurgeon was about sixteen when he started preaching. At twenty-two, as pastor of the London Tabernacle, he was preaching to ten thousand people; and his sermons were being wired across the Atlantic each Monday morning.

To the "Thirty Something" and under: never be labeled or intimidated by your youth or inexperience. Jesus was only thirty when he began his ministry. The important factor here is not years, but the importance of the calling you have.

Spurgeon's life gives testimony to that fact.

For a time he lived with his grandparents in a huge manse, or parsonage as we call it. Their house, though large, was dark and gloomy because England had at that time what was called a "window tax." Houses were taxed not on size, but on the number of windows, much as taxes today might be based on the number of bathrooms or other amenities in a home. But the window tax was unusual in that people, to avoid paying the tax, would board up their windows. Spurgeon's grandparents were no exception. They sacrificed light to avoid taxes.

Imagine the dismal environment that created for Spurgeon to grow up in, for there was no electricity in those days; and lamps were scarce, expensive to operate, and smoky. Spurgeon's experiences in that darkened house may well have inspired him to say later: "God, help me to put more windows in my sermons."

I like that analogy.

Illustrations, pastor, are truly windows in your sermons

As you surely know, at least a fourth of our English words come from Latin. Not many people want to study Latin these days since technically it is classified as a "dead language." But the truth is, we all speak Latin every day, because so many words we use in daily conversation are Latin based, and *illustration* is one of them.

Lustrare, from which *illustration* comes, is a Latin verb. *Lustro* means "to throw light on." Thus we use illustrations to "throw light on" the message.

Notice an important distinction here: illustrations are not the message, but rather the light that makes the message visible and understandable to people.

As preachers, we are called upon to *illustrate* the gospel—*to shed light* on the gospel. But I have to tell you emphatically, friends—and at this point I find myself a little rancorous and angry—as preachers, we are not very skilled at illustration.

In my travels I listen to a lot of preachers. And many times my prayer as I listen is this: "Oh, God, help this preacher open some windows on this thing; it's getting stuffy." "Help him throw some light on this subject; it's dark." "Help her to illustrate this concept."

Sad as it seems, I have listened sometimes to forty-five minutes of preaching without one illustration of any kind. Oh, truth was there. And it was documented with Scripture and with argument and with everything else—but there was no illumination, no light. So, I sat there trying to illustrate the point of the sermon to myself. How does this thing apply in life? How can I use it? How can I make it palatable and useful to other people? It was good mental exercise, so I didn't waste the time. But all the while I wanted to say to the speaker: "Hey, you've got a great idea. Why don't you light it up a little bit? Why don't you put some life into it?"

Reminds me of a supposedly true story about an Anderson camp meeting many years ago. It was in the days before Warner Auditorium, when meetings were held in the old wooden tabernacle and funeral parlor fans provided the only air-conditioning. A few people may still remember Sister Cotton, a dear black saint, who always dressed in white and often sat on the platform during the services.

One hot summer's afternoon, the speaker waxed long and tedious. And in the heat, after the noon meal, little wonder that heads were nodding, including Sister Cotton's. But the speaker, impervious to the fact that his audience was drifting mentally, was droning on and on.

Suddenly Sister Cotton, jerked awake, stood to her feet and shouted, "Come on, brother, put some juice in it!"

For our purposes here, *juice* and *light* mean the same thing!

Opening the Windows

How can we become more confident about opening the windows and putting light into our sermons? These concepts about light offer valuable clues.

1. Light is invisible.

We cannot see light. All we can see is what light falls on. Light is odorless, colorless, invisible. It does not call attention to itself.

In illustrating, this concept is perhaps the most important. A story that grows bigger than the message, is no longer an illustration. When a story is so vivid that people remember nothing else, its value as an illustration is lost.

A good illustration, like light, does not call attention to itself.

Using illustrations is like using gestures. Gestures, in fact, are a form of illustration. And the same rules apply. When people only remember how the speaker continually waved his or her arms about, that gesturing was not effective because it called attention to itself.

All speakers have mannerisms to some degree, which we hope are not distracting. But if they become so dominant that listeners grow preoccupied with them rather than with the message, that spells disaster.

Likewise, when an illustration becomes dominant, the point is lost.

The illustration that hits the point and backs off in a burst of light is great. But if you make that the focal point of the entire sermon, you can obscure the point and ruin the whole thing. Occasionally I have done that—made the illustration virtually all there was in the sermon. I have learned from those mistakes.

We have all experienced the frustration of people remembering a story we once told but not the point being made. While we cannot control what people remember, we can be more careful to build strong connections between illustrations we use and the points they are to illuminate. An effective illustration will always have a natural or logical tie-in to the message. Without that, a good story is just a good story, but totally ineffective as an illustration. If people don't get the point, the story has not illustrated anything.

I confess that once in a while I have told a story that didn't illustrate anything. I suspect we all have. All of us have at least one wonderful story we love to tell because it always gets a big reaction from the audience. It has nothing whatever to do with the message, but it's interesting and it keeps folks awake.

Come to think of it, that may not be all that bad!

But those occasions should be rare. And it had better be some story!

People expect sermons to have a theme or a main point. If you bring in some off-the-wall story or go off on a tangent, they may laugh at your joke or whatever, but internally they grow impatient. People who come to hear a message from God are not interested in time fillers.

Another way we detract from the effectiveness of illustrations is to preface them with statements that call attention to them.

Saying, "Let me now illustrate this point with a story," robs the story of any surprise element. It blunts the edge. If you are going to throw light on the message, let the story throw the light. You don't have to call attention to light, you know. When you go into a darkened room, you throw the switch, and the light reveals. You don't announce to everyone, "We will now turn on the light."

No, you just turn the light on. The light speaks for itself.

2. Light reveals.

Light is essential to sight. If there were no light, what would we see? Nothing. In the dark nothing is visible

The simplest way to think of an effective illustration is this: "I am going to throw light on this subject." The subject can be true and significant; but if you don't shine light on it, nobody will see it. As they used to say, "If you are winking at your girlfriend in the dark, you are the only one who knows it."

Light reveals color and form. Ideas take shape in people's minds when light is turned on them.

When you illustrate something, you first must have a truth. So the first question I ask about any Scripture I have chosen to preach on is this: What truth is there? What basic principle or concept do I want to teach or emphasize in the message?

The abstract truth I see in the story I told of Paul by the fire is that we are largely responsible for what shape our life takes. That is the concept I want to bring out. But standing behind the pulpit—or even beside the pulpit—and merely stating that truth is not enough to assure that the people will understand what I mean. Even if they comprehend the words, they are not likely to grasp their full meaning or how the concept applies to them personally. Even less likely is their remembering it without further illumination.

Listen to yourself. Use your most pious, preacher-like voice with resonant, authoritative tones and measured emphasis on the key words:

"You are responsible for the shape your life takes."

It sounds impressive. The statement is certainly true: we each make the mold into which life is poured. And it is appropriate to state that point clearly and emphatically. *Then* start illustrating.

Follow that abstract statement with one or more examples of the concept played out in analogies or images people can visualize and relate to. We might, for example, say something like this:

Let's suppose you are making a pan of jello. You make it in the shape of a heart or in the shape of a circle or whatever. The tin determines the shape of the final product.

In the wilderness at the foot of Mount Sinai, Aaron, you recall, said, "I put the gold in the fire and out came this calf." But he eliminated some steps there, because first he had made a form in which to pour the gold.

You pattern makers or tool makers, know that is true. Everything from your car to your egg beater is made that way. Somebody makes a form, a mold, and from that is made a casting, and so forth. But you make the form.

I heard a story about a woman whose husband liked to go fishing. Worst of all, he liked to fish on Sunday. For years she nagged at him about going fishing instead of going to church. Finally, one morning as she was preparing to go to the holy place to worship the

Lord and he was starting off with his rod and reel headed for the lake, she just exploded and said, "You know, nobody but a worthless, spineless, ambitionless person would spend his time fishing!"

He said, "Well, that may be true; but just remember, Jesus chose fishermen for his disciples."

And she shot back: "Two wrongs don't make a right!"

Well, she had already determined how she felt about fishermen and about her husband, and facts are not going to change anything about her opinion. The concrete is poured in the shape of her choosing. Her mind is set. And her life—and the lives of those around her—will be affected by that mind-set.

Three illustrations—an easy-to-visualize example of a jello mold shaping the outcome, a biblical example, and a contemporary situation—breathe life into the abstract concept and give people specific situations they can project themselves into.

Again, the light itself is not the important thing, but what it reveals about a truth.

3. Light reveals color and character.

What color would everything be if there were no light? Totally black. No color.

Let's imagine that I have on a blue sweater. You have on a red one. It is amazing that when light shines on a color, the color is partly reflected and partly absorbed. Black absorbs all the light; the rest of the colors reflect the light in varying degrees. The more ways you can let light play on things, the more colors you see.

Adding a touch of color to illustrations brings them to life in a dramatic way. So when you are preaching, take every opportunity to give color to things. As we said earlier, don't be satisfied just to say, "A boy ran down the street."

Think details. What kind of boy? A "red-headed boy"!

Immediately he comes alive in your mind.

The Psalmist David came alive for me like that one day when I heard a preacher say that David was a red-head. I didn't know that. Why, I had always thought he was a blonde Swede, like me! But now I see him out there getting freckles in the sun, looking after his sheep. Adding that touch of color made it a little more real to see the shepherd boy there on the hillside.

Adding color doesn't change what a thing is, but it enables people to see it more vividly; makes it seem real.

Sharpening Descriptive Skills

So how do we give color to things?

"Use more adjectives," is a common answer. And that is one way. But a word of caution here: piling on a string of adjectives is not the best way to do it. With adjectives you can rather quickly get too much of a good thing.

Occasionally I meet someone who has been to a preaching seminar where participants were told to be descriptive. Problem is, now the poor preacher is still describing a thing long after his listeners have lost interest in it.

Gerald Marvel tells of something he read years ago by Harry Emerson Fosdick on colorful language. Fosdick is trying to bring home the idea of Christ as the central focus of a person's life. Here is the way he does it:

> Christ becomes the dominant purpose of a man's life. It runs through every part of his life as a thread runs through a necklace and gives the smallest bead a place and a meaning of value.

He packages the whole concept in that one colorful image! Then he adds: *"Without it, life's happenings are as scattered as beads on a bedroom floor."*

That is a sermon right there. Then, shifting to another image, he adds another dimension: *"Every little wave on the beach has the throb of the mighty ocean."* Both images are ones most people can identify with. And that is the key to metaphoric preaching.

Pictorial analogies like those are classic. Fosdic was truly a prince of preachers, an artist with words. We can learn a great deal from studying the phraseology of skilled speakers like him. Here is his secret: powerful speech is terse, condensed, to the point. Through discipline and practice, unnecessary words are pruned away. The remainder then are thoughtfully arranged to have the most dramatic effect.

Once you have in mind an image you want to use, ask yourself these questions: Could any words be added to make it better? Or would the focus be sharper if some words were cut? In Fosdick's statements about the necklace, for example, anything we might add would, as I see it, take away from the overall effect. And I don't see where we could cut any words and not diminish the meaning. He says just enough and not too much.

I know some preachers who would not stop where he does. They would elaborate:

> Now, you have all seen a necklace—a pearl necklace or a sapphire necklace or a plastic necklace or what not. Well, you know, everybody has got a necklace in their head there. The rich folks have got the pearl necklaces, and the rest of us have got the plastic ones. We've all got a necklace.

Elaboration is easy to do. But for the point Fosdick is making, is all that extra verbiage necessary? Does it really add anything? And, interestingly, he could have said *string of beads*; but *string of beads* doesn't capture the same mental image or feeling as *necklace,* does it? Oh, in a different culture it might; but the point is that frugality of words almost always carries more punch. You want to say just enough, for example, to project that picture of David, the red-headed shepherd boy. You need not belabor the image by saying, "He was probably about five feet seven with broad shoulders and suntanned complexion." Just get some color in and get going.

Remember: adjectives are good when they add flavor to what you are describing; but when you have enough salt on the potatoes, adding more ruins them.

If you really want to make your preaching better, try this exercise: Take a sermon you have written down or recorded and *cut out all the deadwood*—every word you can omit without diminishing the main idea.

For some of us, that will be a lot of chopping!

But take heart, once you catch onto the idea that "less is more"—meaning that fewer words generally pack more wallop than more words—you will enjoy the challenge of becoming less wordy and more precise.

Remember this key to vivid description: specific nouns and strong verbs.

Adjectives and other descriptive phrases can be effective; but when you get carried away and go on and on with descriptors, you dilute the effect with every one you add.

Contemporizing the Bible Story

I've been asked: How do you add color to a Bible story and still be verifiable?

One way is to contemporize the story.

Once when Gerald Marvel was preaching on Abraham's leaving Chaldea, he said that Lot "wanted to go back to Ur with the Neon lights and the French fries." In other words, he took something five thousand years old and brought it right down to Main Street, USA. He contemporized it.

That was back in the early sixties, and he remembers debating whether or not to say it that way. As it turned out, contemporizing the story gave it special appeal to the youth. That one phrase brought the Bible down off the shelf and presented it as "life in the streets." And nothing detracted from the truth of the matter by giving it a contemporary twist.

Using Objects to Illustrate

One time I was the evangelist for a meeting in Southern California, and I was preaching about the power of God. Walking over to the tabernacle that night, I found a piece of wire lying on the street—just ordinary house wiring wire about a foot long, beat up and dirty. I bent it double and put it in my pocket.

When I got up to preach, I said, "I want to show you a marvelous invention."

Then I held up that wire and said:

> This thing can fry eggs and heat a house, curl your hair and iron your clothes, bring music into your life, and many other wonderful things. Take note. Because it is a channel through which the power goes, you have all these wonders of modern science at your disposal. Likewise, if you become a channel for God's power, you can do all kinds of wonderful things.

Anything can become a memorable illustration. Often people tell me they remember a point I made years ago in a sermon using

At the Sea of Galilee

Rena holding Bob, Gerald holding Jerry,
and Lori in the center

In Jamaica

The young pastor:
Gerald Marvel, 1969

With Harley-Davison

In South India

Gerald and Rena in Moscow

The family, Christmas 1993

as an illustration the Sears and Roebuck catalog. Sears no longer has a catalog. But back in the days when it was Sears and Roebuck, the catalog had their motto on the cover: "Satisfaction Guaranteed or Your Money Back."

"That," I said, "is what we are all after: satisfaction or your money back. Sounds like a great deal."

Then, flipping through the catalog index, I said, "Satisfaction guaranteed. Well, what do we need for satisfaction? Let's see if they've got any peace."

Scanning down the list:

"Hum-m-m … pantyhose … pipe … no peace there. Let's try love—to have satisfaction, you gotta have love. Love … love … hum-m-m … lace … lariats … lawn mowers … locks … no luck. Do you suppose they carry joy? Not the soap for dishes! Real joy."

And so the search continued for "satisfaction guaranteed." But, alas, we could not find in the catalog where real satisfaction was guaranteed. That had to come from a different Book. And you can guess where we went from there.

Carry an object with you into the pulpit and use it to illustrate a point in the sermon. The visual stimulation holds attention and gives your listeners something concrete and relevant on which to hang the concept you want them to understand and remember.

Using Drama to Illustrate

Adding an element of drama throws light on a sermon topic in a memorable way.

Gerald's wife, Rena, for years taught a class in the sanctuary. And twice in that class she went through the Bible. Each trip through took about two years. On the second round she said, "Gerald, I'll do it; but to go Sunday after Sunday after Sunday, there has to be something different the second time through, because some who went through the first time are still there. How can I break up the journey and add a new dimension to it?"

They struck on the idea of first-person portrayals to introduce key individuals as they appear in the Bible chronology. When Moses left the scene, for example, and Joshua came on, she featured an interview with the new lead character. Gerald promised to help and for a year was a featured performer, appearing in costume and beard—whatever their costume department would concoct.

The same dramatic technique also works for sermons done in first person. But that kind of presentation demands a good deal more time and effort than it takes to prepare an ordinary sermon. To be effective, first-person portrayals have to be conversational and believable—that means being expressive and fluent. You do not get up there and stammer around in a monotonous, deadpan voice: "Uh … well … as you know … uh … I was in born in Egypt. "No way! It takes in-depth research and much rehearsal to pull off that kind of characterization. But when you do, it's a sermon people never forget!

Some of the most effective first-person presentations I have seen simply dramatize Scripture verbatim. A few years ago when Dan McCraw was worship leader for the CBH Bible Conference at Montreat, North Carolina, he did a dramatic recitation of the entire book of Colossians that was spellbinding. But he was hesitant about doing the piece when he arrived at the conference center.

He said to the woman coordinating the program, "I want to do this, but I'm not sure it will work."

She said, "Well, you are in prison when you are writing this—in bonds."

And he said, "Yeah, but I don't have any handcuffs or anything like that to suggest a prison cell."

So she scouted around and found somewhere in that auditorium a piece of ordinary chain. And Dan wrapped it around his wrists and stood with his hands in front of him while he spoke, with this chain on all the time, and gestured with both hands bound together. It was powerful. I'll never forget it.

Even the simplest of props, you see, can make an indelible impression in the mind of your listeners. Not only does it hold their attention, but it gives them a peg on which to hang what you are saying—attaching the point of the sermon to their memory with a visual image they cannot forget.

So if you don't have a drama department to equip you, be creative. Use whatever is at hand. Something very simple can create a compelling image.

Many sermons, however, can benefit from dramatic touches without being full-blown dramatic performances. Gerald often incorporates elements of drama into his sermons. One memorable illustration he used when preaching on "The Pure in Heart" was taken from the King Arthur legend. Sir Lancelot speaks:

> My good blade [*pantomimes drawing his sword*] can carve the cask of men. / My sturdy lance thrusteth sure. / My strength is as the strength of ten, / Because my heart is pure. [*Softly repeats last phrase*] My heart is pure.

The combination of poetic imagery with dramatic movement at just the right place creates a powerful effect. It is the kind of thing not generally done with manuscript preaching. But when it is done, even children and youth are with you.

Using Visualization to Illustrate

I want to emphasize an important point here about drama. We certainly cannot—nor would we want to—act out every sermon. But we need to learn how to interject those dramatic elements into every sermon. Everybody remembers drama largely because of its visual impact. And we can learn to do that *verbally.*

If you walk out in first-century attire, obviously people are going to remember that. But our challenge is to paint that same picture just as vividly and dramatically with words.

The goal is to create a verbal picture so colorful and clear that people can see it through their imagination in the same detail as a physical re-enactment before their eyes.

People will see the picture if you paint it vividly enough. The key is to appeal to the pictorial ability of people's minds. Remember, the mind thinks in pictures. We think in images. Everyone has the ability to imagine. So effective preaching stimulates *image*ination.

If you are, for example, preaching on Bartimaeus, ask your people, "How does a blind man think?"

> He thinks by feel; he doesn't think in images. He has never seen; therefore he has no mental storehouse of pictures. Up until that moment with Jesus, Bartimaeus has lived in a world of bleakness … blackness … blankness … blindness. His demanding cries have stopped the Lord. And there he stands in the silence of the moment

with the people pressing in, leaning forward in hushed expectancy—the only sound is a little whisper of the air between him and Christ. Bartimaeus standing in bleak ... black ... blank ... blindness. Then the word is spoken—and the explosion of color comes upon him!"

When you tell that story with that kind of detail, people will see those colors. They will have visualized the bleak, black, blank blindness that preceded the explosion. And then when it comes—they will experience vicariously the Bartimaeus miracle in a way they will never forget. The empathy stimulated by those mental images will trigger a depth of understanding in your listeners that no amount of factual explaining could ever achieve. Visualization is powerful!

How Much Illustration Is Enough?

Is it possible to overillustrate? If so, how do you know when to cut back?

There is a danger here.

If you are fortunate to come up with a number of illustrations on a particular theme, you might be tempted to unload the whole wagon in one sermon. We have all been guilty of that. But when we overload a sermon with illustrations, it diminishes the effectiveness. For one thing, using too many illustrations makes the sermon unnecessarily long. After a time people get physically and mentally tired and begin to tune us out.

A barrage of many different visual images also tends to confuse rather than illuminate.

Yet another problem with using too many illustrations is rushing through them, for sake of time, giving each one only superficial treatment. Ideally, we should take one or two of the very best ones and develop them in sufficient detail to allow listeners to visualize and internalize the story. Internalization drives the point home forcefully.

For an illustration to be effective, the visual images have to soak in so that the listeners become personally involved—both intellectually and emotionally—in the story. Creating a vicarious experience and leading it to an effective conclusion takes time.

The secret, then, to effective illustrating when you have a number of illustrations to choose from is to evaluate which one says it best—not which one is the most clever ... or the most amusing ... or the most entertaining, but which one *best* drives home the point.

If you can do it with one illustration or two, that is enough. Fosdick did it with a string of beads and the image of waves backed by the mighty ocean. Two illustrations did the job for him. While there is no rule about the ideal number of illustrations to use in a sermon, going on endlessly just because you have stories to tell will only wear people out.

Occasionally I hear preachers who labor their point so much my mind is saying, "I got that. Move on. I'm not dense. You have made your point. Let's go."

Remember, light is invisible. What it reveals is the important thing. When your point is revealed, you need not keep on revealing it over and over.

In bowling, if you hit a strike on the first ball you don't get another ball. You don't need another ball. In that case, you don't say, "Well, look, I paid for five balls and I intend to use all five!" Likewise in sermon delivery. You may have an arsenal of illustrations to hammer home the point you want to make, but stay tuned in to your audience. You can tell when most of them have got the point. Don't keep shooting at them after you have hit the target.

Some of the most powerful preaching occurs when you are confined to a time limit. And you have experienced that, I'm sure. You know you have only a given amount of time to say what you have to say. So you sort through all you have prepared and select only the essentials—the pithy points and the one illustration that flashes the light—and you are done. That is effective preaching.

In sermon delivery, it is not so much a matter of the minutes involved, but the fact that people have only so much attention span. Yes, I know that D. S. Warner and many others of the old-time preachers back at the turn of the century preached for three and four hours. But this is the decade of the nineties. We are speaking these days to generations of people who grew up, not by flickering firelight, but by the flickering light of television sets geared to seven-and-a-half-minute cycles with commercial breaks.

It is the age of instant. So if you can say it with less, say it with less.

Gerald Marvel has both a verbal and a visual illustration of the value of pruning.

Some time ago our church honored all its adults reared in a Church of God minister's home, as well as the ordained pastors in our church. There are ten of us.

I wrote a script for a set of slides I put together to introduce all these ministers to the congregation. We are fortunate in our church to have Doug Hamilton, a visual aids expert who agreed to synchronize my slide program with the dissolver to go along with my script.

He sat down in my study and said, "Now, Pastor, read me a description on one of your pictures."

So I did.

"Cut it in half."

"Cut it in half? Do you know how long I pored over this manuscript?"

"Cut it in half! Thirteen minutes max—that's the time you have to do this sort of thing.

"I was thinking more like twenty-five," I said.

"Thirteen max."

So, for the next two hours we went through there, cutting everything that wasn't absolutely essential. It was painful. We cut an awful lot of good stuff. Interesting stuff.

Finally we got through the thing. More than half of everything I had created went out.

Even then he said, "It's still too long, but we'll make it work because it's your voice and we'll keep it moving."

It finished out at seventeen minutes.

"Four minutes too long," he said; "but we'll make it because they have not heard your voice on recording before."

Half of everything I had done was in the waste can—disappointing to me because I had invested so much time and had worked so hard on it. But seeing the finished product, I had to admit, you wouldn't have wanted to say any more.

*****

Using illustrations requires discipline and judgement. It requires learning to be selective, to pare down many times, to choose only the best. It takes a little creativity, time, and rehearsal to be effective. But the rewards are worth the investment.

So open the windows and let the light in! Your congregation will bless you for it.

Finding Illustrations

Often I hear the question: "Where do you find illustrations?"

"What books or mail-order resources do you look to for ideas?" preachers ask.

Well, frankly, I don't use prepackaged collections of illustrations. Those books have always disappointed me. Much of what is there seems hackneyed—stories repeated over and over in sermons and newsletters—or dated, having little appeal to life in the nineties.

I like illustrations that are original and fresh, parables that grow out of my personal life and the lives of people around me. I also get many ideas from reading books and magazines in many fields, both current and historic in content.

Reading as a Source of Illustrations

Avid reading in many fields provides an excellent source of illustrations.

Clyde Fant suggests that every preacher should continually be reading at least six books. I lose track of exactly how many I am into at any given time, but it is surely three times that many at various levels. Wherever I am at the moment, I habitually pick up a book and randomly scan a paragraph or even a few sentences. Again and again, I am amazed at how even plunging into the middle of something can trigger a new idea.

Understand, the purpose of reading is not to steal someone else's ideas. We read to create in our own mind a stimulating environment for new ideas. Consequently, the wider the range we read in, the better it is for fostering creativity. I read business and trade magazines as well as books in psychology, science, and medicine. Certainly I don't take all my illustrations from there, but I have found those fields rich in parallels for Bible truths.

If you aspire to breathe new life into your sermons, be inquisitive. Find some time every week, if not every day, to read. Almost anything you read has the potential for enlightening the gospel. As you train your mind to be open to the possibilities, you will find yourself making more and more "real life" connections between Scripture and what you read in newspapers, magazines, and books.

Using Personal Experiences as Illustrations

When I was growing up, I was told by experts in the field of preaching: "Don't be personal." Eventually, I came to know that those "experts" were wrong.

"You can't be personal," they said, "because you should deal with the gospel."

They implied that an example from my personal life would be worldly and would somehow contaminate the gospel.

Look, even the gospel in its purest form was clothed in flesh. The gospel still has to be clothed in flesh for people to understand it. And my experiences qualify as proper "clothing" because I am flesh. About twenty pounds too much of it, but I am flesh. I am a person. I know what it is to try to live out the gospel in real life, and maybe—just maybe—my struggles with it, and my victories, will help someone else.

So today, it doesn't matter to me what the "experts" think about using personal experiences in preaching. What happens to me when I share something personal and what happens to the people who hear me and relate to what I am saying and respond to God because of it—that is what matters.

No preacher I know is more personal in his sermons than Gerald Marvel. I listened to him week after week when we lived in Vancouver and were in town, and I loved it. I feel as if I know all about his home town (Moore, Oklahoma), his grandmother, his brother Sharrill, and his brother Joe. I know about his school days and much of what happened to him when he was growing up. I know a good deal about things he is interested in and dreams he has for the future.

But here is the important thing—this is the key: I never get the feeling that he is telling us, "Hey, look at me. I'm so great."

Why is that? Because the Gerald Marvel he presents is not always perfect. He is not afraid to tell about his embarrassments, his problems, his vulnerabilities. And you needn't be afraid to share yours. People relate to that. If you can be honest enough to let people see the human side of you, they will identify with the gospel message as it relates to your personal experience—and theirs.

People today are hungry for the personal touch. Society is becoming more and more impersonal. When we make the message personal, we touch people at a point of their deepest need. Experiences from your life—or the lives of other people—can open the door of hearts to receive the gospel, because the gospel itself is personal. God saves people on a personal basis. One at a time.

Being Real in Illustrations

Throughout this book we have asked in wonder and amazement, "Why does God in wisdom choose us—imperfect earthen vessels—to carry the gospel."

The answer is not complicated really: God uses us because people will respond to us. Human beings relate to human beings. And the more human we make our preaching, the more people will understand it, relate to it, and respond to it with positive action.

That is why I am disturbed to hear so much preaching that is not human. It is so abstract and, many times, so academic that it simply does not come close to where people live. It never puts on overalls and gets dirt under its fingernails.

People want to know about life. What they loved about Jesus, the reason he was so powerful, was that he was not like the rabbis or doctors of the law—the Sadducees and the Pharisees, who were always splitting hairs over doctrine and theology. Jesus talked about birds … seeds … crops … fishing … sheep … vineyards—things people lived with every day of their lives.

We cannot improve on Jesus' preaching. But we can try to emulate him.

While those other preachers—the Bible scholars of his day—

were off in their musty libraries getting the "truth of God," the Truth passed them by. Jesus was so human they didn't recognize him. I am convinced that God purposely put his son in the grubby little nowhere town of Nazareth for thirty years—where he could study life!

Study the Scriptures, yes. But also study life. People loved to hear Jesus because they could understand him. Nobody could understand a Pharisee, because he was so high above everybody else. Even when a Pharisee walked down the street, he was ringing a bell to keep people away from him.

Listen, many times pastors—sometimes unknowingly, sometimes intentionally—assume a kind of "pastoral tone" when they speak in the pulpit. That, to me, is just like the Pharisee ringing his bell. But the bell in this case signifies, "Time to go to sleep!" That "phoney" voice with its stilted inflections is simply not human. And humans don't relate to it.

Who you are—how you live every day and how you present yourself before your people in the pulpit—is your strongest sermon illustration. Be human. Be real.

Making Illustration a Way of Life

Gerald Marvel is one of the best illustrators preaching today. He is a student of words and metaphoric speech, his foundation for verbal prowess. But even more important, he is a student of human beings and the human condition; and what he learns there finds its way into his sermons every week. Here are some of his suggestions for better illustrating:

My advice for anyone wanting to become a better illustrator of sermons is simply this: Learn to think illustration ... learn to hear illustration ... learn to see illustration. Be illustration. Start building your file, your repertoire of stories and bits of information—whether you house them in well-documented, color-coded, and cross-referenced files or carry them around in a paper sack like mine. Illustrations are all around you. Jewels for the asking.

The source is people all around you. Once you tap into their lives—their knowledge and experiences are like an artesian well that never runs dry.

Pick up the phone when you're working on a sermon. I do it all the time. If I want to use an illustration about the physical body, some function I don't understand, I simply call one of the many nurses in our church. Shirley Short, for example, is an expert in physiology. You have them in your church, too. Talk to them.

Once I wanted to use the words of an old World War II song. I doubted that anybody would remember it. Nevertheless, I stepped into my wife's Sunday school class the next Sunday and asked, "Anybody remember that old song, 'There's a Star Spangled Banner Waving Somewhere'?"

"Why, sure, we remember that."

Voila, I had the illustration I wanted. It's as simple as that.

All day long illustrations bombard us. Some of us see them, but for many preachers, great illustrations slip by unnoticed. It used to bother me that Berk could see more illustrations than I could. Why couldn't I see them? Because I had not yet learned to be constantly thinking illustration. Dynamically visual preachers are continually thinking about potential sermons, so that living and illustrating become synonymous.

Now, as I go through every week, ideas for sermons are always "cooking on the back burner," and I am always on the alert for appropriate illustrations for them.

Drawing upon your people for illustrations

Where do sermon illustrations come from? The best ones are all around you—like jewels begging to be picked up. As Gerald says:

You never know what you are going to uncover in a person's life. That's what makes people so fascinating.

Learn to get people to talk to you—even people you think would like to chew you up and spit you out in little pieces. Talk to them. Ask them things about their lives.

Take people to lunch. Don't always be sitting around waiting for somebody to take you.

Hear me on that. I get so tired of preachers always thinking they have to be taken out. Take your people to lunch. It isn't hard to do. Just walk up to someone or call them up and say, "I want to take you to lunch!"

Then over hamburgers at the Totem Pole—or whatever the local fast-food hangout is in your area—ask them about their lives. What you learn will amaze you and may, one day, find its way into a sermon.

Real-life stories to enrich any sermon are residing in the hearts and minds of the people in your church and in your community. Their stories are yours for the asking. And when you flash those gems from the pulpit on Sunday morning, people stay awake. You will have captured their attention with a name they know and a story or bit of information they didn't know. You can have them on the edge of their seats, eager to get to church to hear what new thing you learned during the week—about them or someone they know.

Gerald once concluded a sermon with the story about his friend Harold Harrison, who fancied pigeons. One day Harrison told him that all pigeon stock is usually imported from Brussels, Belgium.

> "Brussels," Harrison point out, "is the pigeon capital of the world."
>
> "Oh?" Marvel countered off-handedly. "I thought the courthouse in Norman, Oklahoma, was!"
>
> Ignoring the humor, Harrison went on to tell how risky the pigeon business was.
>
> "In 1960," he said, "a pair of pigeons cost between five and seven hundred dollars—a lot of money back then. And you could easily lose your investment by careless treatment during their quarantine period when the shipment arrived in the United States."
>
> "How's that?"
>
> "Well," Harrison said, "they either get sick and die of pneumonia, or the caretakers leave the cages open and the birds fly home."
>
> "Then," Gerald said, "it hit me like a thunderbolt, and I turned to Harrison and said, 'Those birds are going to fly back to Brussels, Belgium? You're telling me that?' "
>
> Harrison pressed on. "They're going to fly up over Manhattan Island, do their customary 360 degrees..."
>
> "And," Gerald finished the sentence, "they are going to start out across the Atlantic Ocean."
>
> "They're going to burn all the glucose out of their system," Harrison affirmed.
>
> "But," he said, "when that little bird hits the water in death, he was on course for home."

Needless to say, Gerald got a lot of mileage out of that powerful and beautiful illustration in future sermons. And on one occasion he was visiting in a home about three months after using the story, and a little boy there said, "Pastor, tell me about that bird again—when it was flying home."

Talk about relevance! When you shed light on a passage of Scripture with a real-life illustration you picked up just days before from someone in the congregation or a neighbor down the street, God's Word comes alive for people! They listen because what you are telling them is interesting ... relevant ... fresh.

But another dynamic is at work here. Unless you get to know your people on a personal level, how can you know what kinds of sermons to pitch to them week after week? How do you know what they will relate to? what they are interested in? what they need to hear? Sad to say, many preachers are poor pitchers because they don't know their batters. Consequently, their preaching is "hit or miss"—too many "curve balls," with none of them crossing the plate.

Yes, I know the Holy Spirit can work through almost any sermon to touch a heart or change a life. But the Spirit works best when the preacher, like a seasoned farmer, prepares the soil and adds a little fertilizer for the seed of God's Word to take root in. Part of that "soil preparation" comes about through well-chosen illustrations.

Gerald Marvel's sermons are filled with those kinds of illustrations. And he will tell you that the time spent with his parishioners in the process of gathering information and stories has enriched his life and made him a better preacher—and a better pastor. For in the process, he has built valuable relationships with the people he has been called to serve.

Years ago a missionary went out to serve in some foreign field. And he was there for a time. But no matter what he did, it didn't fly. The people were unresponsive. Finally the missions board sent a replacement, but that missionary fared no better.

After a few years, they sent another replacement. And it wasn't long till this man started sending back reports of people being saved ... a church being built ... people rallying around him—even in this heathen territory.

When they asked him the secret of his success, he said, "It's very simple. When I came here, I said to these people: 'I know some things you don't know, and you know some things I don't know. So if you will tell me what you know, I will tell you what I know.' "

And even though they may have been a primitive tribe, they had many things to teach him—language, customs, culture, stories, traditions, feelings—all of that. And he was wise enough to sit humbly and listen—to them.

As a consequence, they could teach him.

And then he was given an opportunity to teach them—about Jesus.

One of the great advantages of this approach to garnering illustrations is that all of us are sitting in the midst of people who would love to contribute to our lives. Conceivably, even your worst enemies—if you have any—if you go to them and let them know you need them, could become your friends. And your sermons will be the richer for it. This is one of the great secrets not only of preaching, but of successful pastoring.

*****

Every day, illustrations are all around us. It's a matter of training ourselves to tune in and pick them up. Jesus spoke of people who have eyes, but see not; and ears, but hear not. The world is full of wonders. But a blind man cannot describe a sunset; nor a deaf man, a symphony. If your ears are closed and your eyes are closed, you miss much that could bring light into your sermons.

The quest for illuminating illustrations, thus, begins with a daily prayer:

> Father, open my mind and heart this day to the heartbeat of life around me. Help me see and hear and feel the needs around me. And open my spiritual eyes to see vital connections between your Word and those needs—like manna from heaven or a handful of stars.
>
> Give me light, Father, to bring help and hope and instruction to these people whom you have called me to serve. Amen.

Chapter 17

Preaching without Notes

If I could give you one gift to enhance your preaching ministry, it would be to preach without notes. For helping you experience the freedom of preaching without notes would be a valuable gift not only for you, but also for the people who hear you.

I say that because I have often been asked to talk about this aspect of preaching; and each time I do, one or more persons who take it seriously get in touch with me later to say, "I tried it; and I want you to know, Brother Berquist, it has made a big difference in my life and in my acceptability as a preacher."

Nothing is more demanding, or more rewarding, than the ministry of preaching. And the most demanding and the most rewarding style of preaching, as I see it, is preaching without notes.

Let me tell you how I happened to come to preach without notes.

When I finally finished college (after cramming four years into six!), I embarked on a full-time career of evangelism. I started out following the pattern of all the evangelists I had seen or heard before. I bought a black notebook, about 5½-by-8½ inch in size. It was convenient (about the size of a Bible) and black (it looked like a Bible). Then I got some outlines, which I carried into the pulpit in the black notebook and used to preach.

As it happened, fairly early in my career I was invited to preach at a meeting in North Apollo, Pennsylvania. W. C. Wood was pastor there. And on Tuesday of the first week of the revival, Brother Wood said, "Would you like to go to Pittsburgh with me?"

Well, I was young and single and eager to go anyplace. I had never been to Pittsburgh, and I had nothing else to do.

He said, "We will have lunch there at the church, and we'll hear a man preach."

So we went to the Presbyterian Church in Pittsburgh. And there, to my surprise, were about a thousand businessmen gathered in the church for a luncheon. I think the lunch cost a dollar each, which tells something about the time period. And it was a nice meal.

When we had finished eating, a man walked out on the platform. I can see him now—nondescript-looking, not large, wearing a dark suit. He stood for a moment looking out over the crowd. Then he began to speak:

Today I want to take you on a journey. We are standing outside the Circus Maximus in Rome. We follow the crowd through one of the great archways marking the entrance, where we are swept along by the river of people flowing into this great arena and, finally, find ourselves sitting on stone seats with thousands of people.

At the far end of the arena, on the western end, sits the Emperor—seated there so the sun will not blind his eyes in the afternoon. And we watch with interest as sword swallowers and dancers, lancers and jugglers perform on the arena's floor.

As we watch, an electric air of excitement suddenly pulsates through the crowd, as if something is about to happen.

All eyes turn toward the end of the arena; the gazes fasten on some heavy oak doors. Guards approach the doors and open them. Out walk a small group of people—several men and women. They are dressed simply, but they walk with an air of dignity though their hands are tied. They move with the guards to the front of the Emperor's booth, where some words are spoken to them. Then trumpets sound to draw the attention of the crowd as a question is put to these simple people:

"Will you burn incense here in front of the Emperor?"

Breathless, the crowd waits for the answer.

There is silence.

The people are then led to the center of the arena. And, while the crowd watches, a booming voice cries out:

"These have denied faith in the Emperor, and they will die."

Then to the little band of captives, he shouts: "One last appeal: Will you bow before the Emperor of Rome?"

This time their answer is a song. They begin to sing a hymn:

If we live with Him, we will die with Him.
If we suffer with Him, we shall reign with Him;
We cannot deny our Lord.

Moments later the massive oak doors swing open once again. Lions that have been starved for days are unleashed. They pounce upon the prisoners, and we watch in amazement and horror as the brave little party is reduced to a pile of bloody rags and fragments of bones. The crowd leaves.

But in the air, the song still floats:

> If we live with Him, we shall die with Him.
> If we suffer with Him, we shall reign with Him.
> We cannot deny our Lord.

Friends, as I listened to that man speak, I looked around at the thousand pairs of eyes fastened on that preacher in his black suit. He held our minds and our hearts in the palm of his hand as he began to talk in a simple and direct way about what it means to suffer for Christ, so that we can reign with him. Twenty minutes later —I couldn't have told you if it was twenty minutes … a day … or a lifetime—for I was transported to immortal, eternal truth, and walked out of there speechless and deeply moved.

Finally, when I regained my speech, I said to Brother Wood, "I never saw a man preach like that before, but that's the way to do it."

That's the way to do it, because he spoke without any distraction to my heart—and not to my heart only, but to a thousand businessmen who crowded a luncheon in the middle of a busy day.

As we drove home, I made a vow to myself: "I don't know how he did it, but that's the way it's done. And I will learn how to do it."

I did not know at the time that Clarence McCartney was a world-famous preacher. He had not at that time written the book *Preaching without Notes,* but that way of preaching was his trademark. I heard him only one time, yet I can repeat his sermon almost verbatim even to this day—almost fifty years later. That is powerful preaching!

Back in North Apollo that night, for the first time I left my black notebook in the room.

I gave my text and preached. And from that time to this, I have preached without notes. And at every opportunity, I encourage others to try it, because I believe it is the most effective way to preach.

Why Preach without Notes?

Before moving into the mechanics of preaching without notes, let me make a few general comments.

1. First and foremost, preaching without notes is not preaching without preparation.

I have met people who said, "I tried it, and my people couldn't stand it." Well, if you mean by preaching without notes that you simply get up and open your mouth and ask God to fill it, I don't wonder that your people are appalled at the results.

God does fill your mouth with words to say when you preach without notes but he follows a particular sequence in that filling. It goes something like this:

I fill your heart;
I fill your brain;
then I fill your mouth.

Without the first two fillings, the last filling is highly unfulfilling!

People preaching without notes generally appear relaxed, even casual. If you hear Gerald Marvel preach, for example, your first impression is that he just walks out there and takes a text ... stands there looking at you for a moment ... then says, "Now, back in Oklahoma ..." and starts preaching.

Very shortly you find yourself saying, "I wish I could do that."

But suppose you could go behind the scenes to the four o'clock Sunday morning hour when he is alone with God, or look in on the many hours prior to that when he—like anyone else who preaches effectively without notes—is probing and planning, thinking, studying, digging, rehearsing, and all the rest that goes into it.

Suddenly you would realize that the whole business of art is to make it look artless. The finest art is art that conceals art, and the most masterful skill is one that is honed until it looks easy and natural.

The first misconception I want to clear up is that preaching without notes is an easy way to preach.

Not so.

All effective preaching—with or without notes—is hard work!

But it is much easier to read from a manuscript. With a manuscript, once you have thought up or copied down the content and rehearsed reading it, you're home. The fact that you may look like a kiwi bird, bobbing up and down, or a news reporter reading from cue cards is another issue. Preaching without notes requires a different kind of preparation and rehearsal and mind-set during delivery.

Unfortunately, any sermon—delivered with or without notes—that is hastily prepared and reaches only a shallow part of your own life will probably reach only the shallow part of somebody else's life.

It's hard to start a fire if your own wood's wet.

It's hard to ring someone else's bell when the clapper is missing from yours.

It's hard to inspire somebody else when you are not inspired yourself.

And it's hard to make a permanent part of someone else's life something you can't remember for twenty minutes when you are standing in front of them.

If those were your toes I just stepped on there, it's okay to say, "Ouch!"

Believe me, I am not trying to vilify you or make you feel bad. I just want you to know that preaching without notes is not the easiest way to do it. But it is, I think, the most productive.

2. Preaching without notes does wonders for your simplicity.
You are less likely to make sermons overly complicated if you have to make them easy for you to recall.

Simplicity, however, does not mean shallowness. In fact, wisdom is simple. If you want people to remember what you say, you need to make it memorable. And is it not true that the most memorable statements—the most quotable quotes—are the simplest?

3. Preaching without notes allows a greater degree of eye contact with the audience.
Any skilled speaker will tell you that eye contact is a highly important part of communication. In fact, eye contact is one of the most powerful tools a speaker has to gain and command attention. If you don't look at people, you break that contact and greatly

weaken the overall effectiveness of your delivery.

I have known preachers who, I will guarantee you, were so out of touch with their congregations that they hardly knew anyone was out there when they were preaching. They looked at the ceiling all the time they preached or at their notes all the time. You could walk out and get a cup of coffee, and they would never know it! They were just bent on getting through the sermon whether the people were with them or not.

When I am preaching, I have to know people are with me. I watch everybody. If they sneeze, I see them. If they wiggle, I see them. If they write notes, I see them. And it upsets me, because I want them to listen. What I am saying to them is important.

On occasion I have even called people to task for not paying attention. I remember a trio of teenagers I reprimanded one time in Daytona—Gary Garmon, Greg Sempsrott, and Brian Hogan. Right in the middle of my sermon, I just stopped preaching and said, "You three boys in the back, you need to settle down and straighten up." Never had to call them down again. Interestingly enough, all three of those fellows are in the ministry today, trying to get teenagers to listen to them!

It is important to maintain eye contact, even when using a manuscript. Audiences simply will not stay with you, if you are looking up, down, off to the side—everywhere except at them.

I recall a quartet that sang at our church one Sunday night. Good singers ... sang a song from the hymnal that we all knew by heart. I had sung the song since I was seven, and most of them surely had sung it since they were children. They knew the words as well as I did. In fact, the song was so familiar that I even knew both the melody and the bass part (no small feat for someone who sings without notes!). Yet, as familiar as that song was, every one of those men held a hymnal in his hand; and ever so often every one of them looked down at the book.

And I kept saying to myself, "Cut it out, fellows. You know that song! Why are you penalizing your performance and the song's effectiveness by such an unnecessary distraction as looking down at the words?"

Well, the answer is obvious: they looked down simply because they had the book.

Likewise, preachers often stand in the pulpit, bobbing their heads up and down—like courting geese—looking at their manuscript, simply because the script is there! It becomes a crutch. If the script weren't there, they might be surprised to discover that they really don't need it.

Once freed up to make and maintain eye contact with the audience, speakers find communication happening on a higher level.

4. Preaching without notes liberates you to modify what you are saying according to the response you are getting.

It is possible to preach well with a manuscript, but you can relate to your audience better without one. If you can get by at all preaching without notes, you will find it's like getting wings to soar, for you then have freedom to watch people and respond to them.

If you are watching your audience as you preach, you can tell when you are not getting across; and you can change your approach. But if you are not looking at people—if you are focused instead on following your script—you miss that.

Also, with a manuscript, you feel less inclined to make on-the-spot changes in the sermon. You are more prone to think, "If I leave this out, it will hurt the message." Actually, it would probably help it. I leave things out all the time, usually for the better. And I insert things occasionally that I didn't know I knew. Sometimes it's good; sometimes it isn't. But at least I am free to do that, and I think that's an advantage.

My emphasis at this point is on something central to the whole act of preaching: *we are not talking just about speech-making here. We are talking about allowing God's Spirit to work with us and to keep us flexible.*

I admit to being almost fanatical about flexibility; but I have observed that whenever people predict how God is going to act, he usually moves in a different way.

Similarly, when you and I set up a rigorous method or routine of how God is going to work, and we don't trust God to work in the moment, we sometimes miss what he wants to do. It is more than a matter of trusting your own mind. Certainly it is important to do that, but it is even more important to trust the Spirit.

But I must hasten to point out that the opposite extreme view is equally bad. I have met preachers who say, "I don't have to do much about sermon preparation; I just trust God."

You know what the Bible says about trusting God—in this passage, for example:

> Consider the lilies how they grow: they neither toil nor spin;
> and yet I say to you, even Solomon in all his glory
> was not arrayed like one of these.
> If then God so clothes the grass, which today is in the field
> and tomorrow is thrown into the oven, how much more
> will He clothe you, O, you of little faith?
>
> (Luke 12:27–28, NKJV)

Obviously God will provide basic needs, clothing included; but you still have to put your clothes on in the morning. When you get under the shower, you may say, "Well, Holy Spirit, no need to take thought of what I should wear...." Well, you may not take thought, but somebody will before the day is over. And you will have a rough life if you walk out on the street like that. You may not get arrested—because they can't get anything on you! But you will demonstrate the fact that even though God has promised to clothe you, you still have to do something about it.

The same is true about clothing your mind. God will give to you—and later bring to your remembrance—the things that ought to be there, but God will involve you in the process. Your study, your preparation—even your fears and sense of dependency—are an act of faith.

If you are not always running a little scared, you are not really running very much.

You may say, "Well, Berquist, you have been preaching for half a century, off and on. Are you still nervous when you get up to preach?"

Yes. I am. I am not nervous about preaching—I mean just getting up in front of a crowd. You get used to that. Television camera, radio microphone, or whatever—that doesn't bother me. But I am apprehensive and on edge that God will be able to speak through me to say what needs to be said.

The tension I feel comes from standing between God and the people, prepared, but ready in an instant to deviate from that plan if

I get a clue from God or the people that something other than what I have prearranged is what God wants to do in that moment.

5. Preaching without notes requires learning to trust your mind.

Your brain is a very sensitive part of your anatomy. Treat it like an idiot, and it will live up to your expectations. When you tell yourself, "I can't remember all this," your mind will not remember it.

But making a statement like that is nonsense! Of course, you can remember "all this." You thought of it once, why can you not think of it twice? If you can create a sermon out of a vacuum, why can you not recreate it on your feet in the pulpit? If your brain can tell your hand to write it, why can your brain not tell your mouth to speak it?

"But, writing and speaking are two different things," someone will say.

Yes, they are different to some extent; but the same principle applies to both. The more you trust your mind to work, the more it will work. The more you develop skill in speaking without notes, the better you can do it. Relying on your mind to remember things sharpens its ability to do just that.

Certainly I am not perfect when it comes to remembering. I forget things. I know I forget directions, because they are not that important to me, I guess. But sermons and stories, scriptures, poems—things like that, I can remember.

Some people say, "I can't remember names or faces."

Friend, I guarantee you, if you were to loan somebody a thousand dollars, you would remember that person's name and face, phone number and fingerprints! And you would remember when they were supposed to repay you. You would not forget a detail.

Listen, you have a treasure more precious than a thousand dollars in the gospel. And when you feel it is important to master the Scriptures, speak out of the overflow of your heart, and train yourself to do it in the most unrestricted manner possible—you will find it immensely rewarding. You can learn to speak effectively without notes if you want to badly enough.

If you abandon yourself to your memory, your memory will work. If you don't, you will go on the same way you always have.

If you have not been brave enough previously to trust your memory to deliver a message without notes, I hope the suggestions we make here will give you enough confidence to try it soon.

Your people will say, "Wow! What happened to you?"

For both you and they will find that the same message—the same ideas you had before—suddenly have become more interesting, more relevant, more memorable.

6. And, finally, preaching without notes gives you a sense of authority.

In communication, the way a person presents information has a a great effect on building trust and confidence—believability.

Perception is about seventy-five percent of what effective communication is about. It is not what you are that gets taken into account; it is what you are perceived as being. And the aura of added confidence that comes from preaching without notes helps you to be perceived as one who knows—someone people can have confidence in.

Suppose you were in the market for a car. You spot a 1988 Corvette sitting on the recycle lot, and you step over for a closer look. There it sits all shiny and nice, and you say to the approaching salesperson, "I'm interested in this car."

As expected, the salesperson says, "Okay. I'd like to sell you this car."

Then suppose the salesperson starts reading to you a sales pitch from a stock sheet:

"This is a 1988 Corvette ... uh ... (looking down at the brochure). It is equipped with ... uh ... (looking down) power steering and uh ... (looking down) cruise control. It's got custom upholstery ... (looking it up) ... yes ... custom upholstery. It has ... uh (looking down) a V-8 engine that runs on ... (scanning the sheet) uh ... premium fuel...."

Would you be likely to buy that car or any other vehicle from that salesperson?

Probably not.

Any salesperson worth their salt, knows the product. They know it by heart—all aspects of it—so that he can present it with confidence to any prospective buyer who comes along.

Well, friend, what you and I are "selling" from the pulpits of our churches is of far greater importance to the present and future well-being of our "customers" than the purchase of a car. Our presentation deserves at least the effort a car salesperson puts into the study and mastery of the material to make a sale.

That said, let's talk about how to do it.

How to Get Started

The key to preaching without notes is this: your memory is activated as you trust your memory. If you don't trust it, it won't work.

But here is the good news: the more you preach without notes, the easier it gets.

Gerald Marvel testifies that he made a conscious decision to preach without notes before he was out of college. And his daughter, Lori, early on made that same decision. As Gerald tells it, Lori's first preaching experience came about this way.

> I know you can learn to preach without notes, because I have. Even my daughter has preached without notes from the time she delivered her first sermon.
>
> When my children were growing up, I often took them individually out for breakfast. One morning when Lori was a senior in high school, we were having breakfast together, and I said, "Soon you'll be going to college. Have you had any idea about what you are going to major in?
>
> "No," she said, "I really don't know. I know what I would do if I were a man."
>
> And I said, "What would you do if you were a man?"
>
> "I'd be a preacher. "
>
> "Well, what has being a man got to do with it?"
>
> "They are just more accepted," she said.
>
> "No," I said, "if you feel God calling you to be a preacher, you go ahead."
>
> And she said, "Do you really mean it, Dad? Do you really mean it?"
>
> "Yeah. I really mean it. If you feel God calling you, you do it."
>
> That seemed to unleash her a little bit.
>
> Sometime after that, before she got into college, I had to make a trip to New Bethlehem, Pennsylvania, to hold a revival. I didn't have a preacher to fill the pulpit in my absence, so I went to Lori

and said, "Are you still feeling called to the ministry?"

"Yeah."

"Well, Lori," I said, "I'm going to be gone to New Bethlehem. You're on. You're going to preach."

"But, Dad, I have never preached."

I said, "You pray about it tonight."

And she said, "Dad, I haven't even been to college."

And I said, "You pray about it. If you are going to be a preacher, you are going to preach."

Next day she had a meeting with me.

"I'll preach," she said, "if I can preach the way I want to preach. I don't want to use notes, Dad."

"That's your business, not mine," I said.

"I don't want you telling me what to preach. I have my sermon."

Then she added, "When you leave, would you give me the key to the church, so I can slip down there all by myself, and just get the feel of what it's like to preach in that church."

I packed my bag, gave her the key to the church, and left.

Sunday afternoon, I called long distance to see how things went. My wife, Rena, said there wasn't time to tell everything by phone, but she told me this much: "Lori was just a little tiny thing up there on the platform. She got up and said, "I'm delivering the sermon today"; read the text; walked out into the middle of the chancel, wearing a lavaliere mike; and delivered the sermon. She preached out of her heart, had the congregation stand, and opened the altar. People came and prayed, and people were crying."

From that moment on, my daughter has been wanting to preach, preach, preach.

She has asked me about preaching without notes. "How do you do it, Dad?"

My answer to her is the same I would give anyone.

"You just do it! If you are not willing to fail, you'll never do it.

"You didn't learn how to ride a bike the first time you got on it. You might have made a few feet. You didn't learn how to swim the first time you got in the water. You might have flounced around and got a few gasps of air, but you didn't swim. The first time you sat down behind a typewriter, you didn't learn how to type. In fact, you didn't even learn how to walk the first time you got on your feet.

"You have to be willing to fail. You must be willing to say, 'Here goes nothing, but it's what I want to do.' "

The first step, then—and it is the hardest—is sincerely desiring to preach without notes and *daring to try*. It's being willing to step out there on faith—daring to trust your memory. It's believing that the Holy Spirit can and will bring to your remembrance what you, with God's help, have prepared to say.

Once committed to do it, be thorough in preparation. Start with a simple message—one you know you can remember. Don't try to uncap some deep theological, intricate issue.

Start with a subject so simple you may be tempted to say, "That's not even a sermon."

Gerald once delivered a highly effective message about the woman who anointed Jesus with spikenard just before his death. It came to him in a flash of inspiration at the last minute—literally. He was waiting in a pastor's study before the service in which he was to speak. He had wrestled with his text for more than a week, but was not satisfied with what he had prepared. Suddenly his eyes focused on a small alabaster box in the pastor's bookcase, and these words came to him: "She gave the BEST she had ... to the BEST she knew ... the BEST way she knew how." That simple outline became his sermon.

A simple statement like that—one that flows right out of the Bible text—gives you the skeleton for the sermon. All you have to do then is fill in the blanks.

Preparation for the message proceeds in much the same way as if you were preparing a written manuscript:

- prayerfully seeking a topic
- prayerfully studying the Bible text
- garnering illustrations
- deciding on the sequence of points and illustrations in the body of the message
- planning an attention-getting beginning
- planning an effective closing and response.

If you plan to speak without notes, my advice is that you not write out the sermon in manuscript form. I will concede that, especially in the beginning, if writing some or all of it out helps you mentally give attention to descriptive details or steps in a process or important facts, you can certainly do that. And you can use what you have written for study. If you have a photographic memory, you might even remember points by their location on the page. But I do not recommend that you memorize your sermon verbatim.

Some preachers, I know, speak without notes by memorizing a written manuscript. And certainly that kind of delivery is far more effective than reading from a prepared script. But that is not the kind of preaching without notes we are advocating here. Memorizing a prewritten text still, in most cases, does not allow for a delivery that is fresh and spontaneous. Nor does it keep channels open for the Holy Spirit to work as freely during the presentation. A speaker preoccupied with remembering a memorized text will likely be less open to a change in direction the Spirit might take at some point during the message.

And, frankly, for many speakers, trying to recall verbatim a memorized script only heightens tension and anxiety because they are more afraid than ever of forgetting.

Far better is the method recommended by speech instructors for extemporaneous speaking: develop a simple outline—with key words that are easy to remember—and then rehearse your speech from that outline. That way, you become confident of the content of the sermon, but are not locked into an exact wording.

You may, of course, memorize parts of the sermon if you wish: the scripture text, lines of poetry or direct quotes, your opening sentence, or any other statement you want to be sure to say a certain way. That kind of memorization can be effective. The overall effect will still be spontaneous, not as if you were reciting the entire message by rote. And by not memorizing everything, you still leave room for spontaneity and the moving of the Spirit.

You may also read excerpts from written material as a part of the sermon. But that kind of thing is best kept to a minimum. Most of the time it is better to "tell" rather than "read" long passages. Telling holds interest better than reading.

Tips for Remembering

Most people who speak without notes develop some system for remembering key words from their outline. Ideas can be related or connected in many ways.

One interesting device for recall is the acronym—a word or phrase created by the initial letters of words representing points in the message. For example, a sermon titled "Add **VIGOR** to Your Life" might have as its main points *V*itality, *I*ntentionality, *G*odliness, *O*rder, *R*esponsiveness—or any other words you might choose beginning with letters to spell vigor.

Another popular system is using alliteration—identifying main points with key words that begin with the same letter, such as *desire, difficulty, determination,* and so forth. We used that technique earlier in this book to list seven characteristics of effective preaching—all beginning with the letter *V: Visual, Verbal, Visceral, Verifiable, Vital, Vicarious, Victorious.*

Alliteration is fun to do, but let me insert a word of caution. I personally enjoy the mental gymnastics of thinking up word associations that begin with the same letter. But I do not do it all the time, because it becomes a pattern. As a technique in general, it's not bad. But that kind of alliteration can get wearisome if it is used for every sermon, especially if ideas are forced into words that don't necessarily fit.

Besides that, I find that it is really better to connect ideas as they flow naturally out of a story or a circumstance or a situation.

Sensuous Preaching as an Aid to Memory

As you prepare your sermon, the more specific, detailed, colorful, and related your ideas are, the easier they will be to remember. And the easier it is for you to remember, the easier it will be for your listeners to remember. The more vivid the message is in your own mind, the more vivid it will be in their minds. That is the objective.

Now before you get all excited thinking that this section is X-rated, let me explain that *sensuous* is a sanctified word that simply means "related to the senses"—not to be confused with *sensual,* which is something else altogether!

The wonderful truth is that there is not just one gate, but many, through which information comes into the brain.

> We have a sense of sight,
> a sense of smell,

a sense of touch,
a sense of hearing,
a sense of taste—
and each of these is a door into the mind.

Educational research has proved that the more faculties that are involved in perception, the more are involved in recollection and the longer the retention.

Dedication of children is
a vital pastoral ministry

First Church Vancouver celebrates
24 years with Pastor and Mrs. Marvel

For example, if you ever smell a certain fragrance related to a particular event, you never forget it. By the same token, if you ever tasted a particular food in a certain situation and later taste it again, you will feel the whole experience coming back.

Several years ago a man was injured in a wreck and part of his brain was exposed. As doctors began working to restore him, they touched part of his brain with an electrode of some kind; and he said, "I smell the flowers." He could see and smell the flowers at his grandmother's funeral. And each time they activated that part of his brain, that scene flashed before him.

Well, that is true of all experiences of life. Everything is recorded in our mind, so that if we enhance ideas and information with these things—sights, sounds, odors, tastes, and tactile objects we can mentally touch—they are easier to recall.

Exercise your power of verbal expression. With determination, diligence, and practice, learn to describe things. Follow John Denton's example: as you are driving down the street, describe out loud to yourself in minute detail everything you see. Make words your friends. Work at developing a vivid vocabulary, and practice using it in everyday conversation. Becoming a better conversationalist will help you become a better preacher—a communicator who can connect with an audience on a more personal level.

Vivid, colorful pictures make a sermon easier to visualize and remember. And, making it easier for you to remember also makes it easier for your listeners to "see" and "hear" and "taste" and "smell" and "touch—and, consequently, to understand and remember.

If, for example, your outline flows from Scripture—as we illustrated earlier in the chapter on expository preaching—whenever in the future your listeners reread that scripture, they will remember the points you made relating to it.

Relatedness and vividness are all-important to this matter of preaching without notes.

Remembering Ideas in Sequence

Gerald Marvel developed a memory system by copying the ancient Greeks, whose famous orators all spoke without notes. This is the way they did it.

All Greek orators had a home. And so do you. Close your eyes. Call to memory your house. You know every room by heart. You are not likely to forget those rooms, are you? Well, copy the Greeks. Try hanging the various parts of your outline in the rooms of your house.

Greek homes, for example, had an entrance court or a foyer. Introductory remarks would be appropriately placed there, mentally. The first concept or main point could go on the table in the eating area. Another idea would go in the sleeping quarters—put that idea to sleep on the bed. Moving to their library or study, the Greeks might put several thoughts there, around on the shelves or wherever they kept their scrolls. Their conclusion would go out on the patio. Then, when they stood to speak, they simply made a mental journey through their house. Connecting their thoughts to familiar objects in their home made it easy to remember the points and the order of presenting them.

In a preaching seminar at Mid-America Bible College, Gerald Marvel shared with pastors and would-be pastors some other ways he remembers sermon points:

In my "Blue Book," where I keep notes on what I think are excellent sermon ideas, I have listed twenty-one concepts of what I call *one another*. If I ever do preach that sermon, it will be different from anything I've done before. Let me show you how I would go about remembering a long list like that for a sermon without notes.

First, let me point out that if I were to do this sermon, I would not say to my church: "Today I am going to discuss twenty-one references from the New Testament using one another."

No way. They would all be asleep in a minute!

I would have twenty-one in mind, but would tune the people in by another route. I would start off by saying something like this:

"We are the body of Christ. We have a responsibility to one another, and we have to be open with one another. Let's think for a moment about this word *one another.*"

Then I'd tell a little about one another as it appears in the New Testament. And from there I'd go into the many ways our lives are involved with one another today. In a twenty-five minute sermon, I might not cover all twenty-one of them; but I would do a lot of them.

And here is how I would remember them.

In preparing the sermon, I would list—mentally or on paper—the twenty-one "one anothers," with a mental picture of something I would associate with each one. For example:

1. Love one another. I would probably envision a heart with a Cupid's arrow through it.

2. Admonish one another. I would mentally picture a parent correcting a child.

3. Edify one another. I would mentally picture a building—a great edifice.

And so on down the line, using pictures as a tool for memory. When I have all the separate images in mind, I might then arrange or group them into one large mental picture—the heart sitting on top of the building, for example, with the parent admonishing the child down on the steps at the entrance to the building. The more exaggerated and grotesque the mental image, the better you will remember it. Try it.

Another favorite device of mine is one many of you can relate to. Did you ride a bus to school, going over the same route for a number of years? Do you still remember that bus route?

Well, next time you want to preach without notes, put your thoughts at the stops along that bus route. It makes a wonderful framework.

I was riding the school bus back in 1941. I can't tell you how many times—when trying to remember a number of things in a sermon—I've hung ideas on that old bus route. Why not? I'm a sentimentalist anyway. I enjoy remembering good times in my life; so when I'm preaching, I like the idea of riding on the bus with Crado Miller again. It adds an undercurrent of excitement for me in my preaching to see us riding down Sunny Lane Road, then stopping at the Luckett's place to pick up the Marvel boys and the Sullivans, who live across the road. Then we head on down to where we got stuck one time and on down to the Robinson School and on across, coming back by Cal Anderson's store. Then it's back down to the Clothier School House and on to Sunny Lane Road again, passing under the viaduct and finally going back into town on Highway 77. And I put my thoughts there. It's a ready-made frame work that's fun for me to use. Try it using your old bus route.

Or, if you didn't ride a school bus, did you have a paper route? Do you still remember your customers' houses? Use that. Practice when you have to go to the store sometime, and you don't want to write down the ten things you need to get. Hang them on your paper route. Put the items on the front porch of every house where you used to throw papers.

Or use the itinerary from a trip you enjoyed.

You already have a framework tucked away in your mind, if you will just use it.

Another thing I do that any preacher can do is to associate different parts of my sermon with certain places in the congregation — the front pew, the back row, the balcony, the left-hand section, the right-hand section, the center section. That keeps me moving as I preach and looking at different segments of the congregation. It's simple. And it works. You can do it, too.

Helpful mnemonic devices—such as those Gerald mentioned — appear in publications like *The Memory Book*, by Jerry Lucas and Harry Lorayne. Many such books are currently on the market, and while they do not address public speaking as such, they do offer lots of tricks for remembering that can be applied to preaching without notes.

The Outline as a Memory Tool

A carefully planned, but simple outline is an aid to memory.

The key is to keep the outline simple. A half-dozen words may be all you need to remember your main points and the illustrations that go with them. Or you may flesh it out a little more, depending upon the complexity of the message and whether or not you feel that you need to include facts, statistics, quotes, transition phrases, beginning and closing sentences, and so on for study as you prepare.

Recall Gerald Marvel's outlining technique: one sheet of paper divided into two columns. While he is preaching, he says the outline is like a road map. He does not carry it with him to the pulpit; but in his mind, he can see the written outline in detail as he moves through the message. He knows when he is in the opening section, when he is coming into the first main point, and the next. In his mind's eye, he can see the transition sentence at the bottom of the first column, leading into the next main point, and so on.

As was mentioned earlier, in preparing to preach without notes, rehearsing from an outline is better than trying to memorize a manuscript. The outline is much easier to remember.

Rehearsal as an Aid to Memory

When you first begin to preach without notes, going over the sermon several times before you present it to the congregation is important. Practice builds confidence.

Gerald Marvel's daughter, Lori, was instinctively right in wanting to "get the feel" of moving around and speaking from the platform in the church before delivering the sermon. Letting go of the pulpit is a major step in experiencing a new kind of freedom in preaching and a closer level of communication with the people. The more "at home" you feel on the platform, the more your mind can focus on what you want to say.

And practice at home before a mirror is also helpful as you plan to step from behind the pulpit to deliver the message. Thinking ahead about how you will stand and possible gestures—and viewing yourself in a full-length mirror as you do them—will help you choose movements that look comfortable and natural for you. Practicing a range of gestures and movements until they feel and look natural will also build confidence and help you be more relaxed in your delivery of the message.

Knowing that you don't look awkward standing out there "naked," so to speak, without the pulpit to hide behind, takes away much of the apprehension of speaking without notes. If you are confident and relaxed about the way you look, all your energy and concentration can go into delivery of the message.

Gestures and movement, by the way, can also aid recall. We have a kinetic memory—the body almost subconsciously remembers rehearsed movements. Try attaching ideas or words to specific gestures or movement to various places where you might stand on the platform. Then later, during the sermon, moving to that pre-arranged place or making that rehearsed gesture will trigger memory of the idea or words associated with it.

Another way to build confidence and aid memory is to be continually rehearsing potential sermon material. When I read or hear a good story that has potential for sermon illustration, I repeat it as often as I can in conversations with family and friends. That's a great way to test drive new material to see how it goes over with people. Whenever you tell the story always include as much detail as possible. Note people's reactions. If it is a humorous story, do they laugh in the right places? Experiment with expression and timing.

The more you repeat a story, the better you get at telling it and the more confident you become. More important, you make that story part of your mental treasury of illustrations, ready for use at a moment's notice in various sermons as occasions arise.

Jot down quotes, facts, or particular statements for Sunday's sermon on three-by-five cards or note paper and carry them in your pocket or purse. As you go about your weekly duties and calls, pull them out and read over them while you are sitting at traffic lights, waiting for food in restaurants, or walking up the steps to the fourth floor of the hospital. Use those normally wasted moments to set those ideas more firmly in your mind

Dealing with Forgetting

Finally, let's talk about the big fear in everyone's mind: "What if I forget?"

Well, suppose that when you are up preaching you do forget something. So what?

Suppose that the first time you preach without notes you speak only fourteen minutes rather than your customary twenty-five or thirty minutes. Don't be concerned. Your people will be saying, "That's the greatest message we've ever heard!"

Shorter may be better.

And back in your study when reviewing your outline to see how you did, don't berate yourself when you discover that you left out a whole section. Maybe the Holy Spirit is more involved than you think!

Don't kick yourself for it. If you left something out, lift it from your outline and say, "That thing might work somewhere else." Hang onto it. You may find that it really fits better into another sermon later on.

You may say, "But, I only got in one of my three points."

Look at it this way: maybe you can take two more Sundays to cover the other two points.

But let's play out that worst scenario. Suppose during the sermon your mind goes completely blank. It has happened to me. Right in the middle of a sentence, I can't remember someone's name or the last line of the poem or what comes next.

At times like that, I've found the audience relieved and delighted to discover that I am only human after all. I simply confess that whatever it was just "fell off the edge of my mind," quoting the wisdom of my friend Jonathan Weir at age five. Or I make some quip like, "Of all the things I've lost, I hate losing my mind the most!" We have a good laugh at my expense and move on to the next point.

Another "out" if you lose your train of thought is simply to go back to the Scripture, pick up another idea from there, and move on.

If even that doesn't work and you are totally blank, simply bring the message to a close. Tell the people that the altar is open, that

God is there to meet their needs, and invite them to come and pray. You might want to be the first to kneel there as further incentive for them to come.

I generally do that anyway—kneel at the altar after my sermon while the hymn is being sung—to place whatever I have said, be it much or little, on the altar as an offering to God and pray for the moving of the Spirit on the people. Often I have found that my being there has made the altar more inviting for others to come.

Be encouraged by this thought:

Only you and God—and possibly your spouse if you shared with him or her ahead of time—know what you had planned to say. Delivering God's message is not a test in memory recall. You should be concerned about only one thing: getting a message across. And your sermon is a vehicle—a means to an end, not the end in itself.

Try to relax. Worry less about remembering word for word or point for point what you had planned and rehearsed. Focus instead on the needs of the people in front of you in relation to your topic, and speak from your heart about how God can meet those needs. You may find yourself saying things—powerful things!—that were never on your outline or in your notes.

You may experience that magic moment when God's Word and God's messenger are lifted by the power of God's Spirit to connect with the people at a level beyond anything you could ever achieve in your own ingenuity.

Trust the Spirit to speak through you. He will.

And don't be concerned if your first sermons without notes lack the depth of material that you—or someone else you have heard— might deliver from a manuscript. Eventually you can achieve the same depth in preaching without notes as from a manuscript. It just takes time, determination, patience with yourself, and practice.

In the meantime, remember, our primary objective is to express, not impress.

Trust me on this: once you deliver one sermon without notes, you will be less fearful of forgetting. And, as we said earlier, the more you stand and deliver without notes, the easier it becomes to remember what you want to say. Your mind becomes acclimated to remembering, and you find that you really can trust the Spirit to help you remember and to put words into your mouth as you are preaching. Depth will come as you diligently prepare, then relax and trust God to be with you "in the moment" and to speak to the people through you.

Epilogue

Late in life, I learned some axioms in the ministry that I like to pass along. One of them is this: *If you want your boat to come to shore, help somebody else's boat to get there.* Another way of coming at that same idea, from the flip side, is a quote from Abraham Lincoln: "You cannot keep a man down in a ditch, without remaining there with him."

I say those two things in the same paragraph because in my youth I unconsciously learned the skill of the "put down." And over time I found out that it was neither a holy nor a productive skill. Much more to be coveted is the ability to uplift and encourage. The person who stops to help another is twice blessed, for the rewards are both immediate and long-term.

I can tell you honestly that Gerald and I have taken great delight in leading several conferences around the country to share some of what we have learned about preaching. We really looked forward to sharing. Not because we needed something else to do—both of us were overcommitted and left many other things undone to do these things. But we looked forward to those encounters because we believe in the ministry of preaching. We are eager to share whatever we have learned in the school of life to help others of you become the best you can be in the ministry.

What Gerald often said in our conferences goes for both of us: "It is our prayer and our hope that not only will you learn all we have to teach you, but that you will far exceed anything we have done and be used of God in a greater way."

We are that concerned about the work of the church. And if what we have learned has helped you in some small way, we are glad.

Of course, whenever you give the best you have, you always get more in return than you gave. We ourselves have learned from the many participants who shared with us in the various conferences. Your questions forced us to think about things we normally might not have thought about. Your ideas have stretched our own. We thank you for that.

In the ministry, particularly in your local area, the more you can support, encourage, and edify people, the more you will be edified.

Proverbs says, "He that waters shall himself be watered."

That is to say, you cannot nourish someone else's life without nourishing your own. I was touched by the story Gerald told of a man whose life was like a desert, crying out for a few drops of recognition and acceptance and listening. Dear friends, there is no town so small, no church so small, that there are not at least a dozen people crying out for somebody to listen to them.

The Art of Listening

In these pages, we have said much about preaching as a calling —and it is that—and as a skill—and it is that. And I would certainly encourage you to excel in speaking to the best of your ability. But there is a skill even more highly regarded and more lavishly prized than the skill of preaching, and that is the skill of listening.

As Gerald shared about listening to an old soldier whose heart was full of memories and his mind full of pain, I want to tell you that if I know anything about people, when Gerald left, that man was walking about a foot off the ground. And when Gerald returned to listen to him again, that man probably thought, "Pastor Marvel is the greatest preacher I ever heard." Yet all Gerald said was, "Tell me about your experiences in the war."

I truly believe that most of the hurts of your people could be healed if you could just learn to listen. Not only will you understand more, but you will also help more.

A while back I was in a church that had invited a funeral director to speak to the Sunday morning Sunday school class. I've been in dead classes before, but they don't always have a funeral director attend. This fellow, however, inserted a certain amount of life into the situation as he talked about grief and grieving.

The story was simple as he told it.

A young couple was very active in civic affairs. They lived in a suburban area near a fairly large town. The young man was aggressive and up-and-coming in business.

One night when their children were young, they hired a sitter to care for the kids while they went into town. While the parents were gone, the sitter decided to drive the kids up to the ice cream stand in town. Between the house and town the road crossed a section of railroad track. There was no marker there. And, as it would happen, on their way back home, a train hit the car.

While the parents were in town having dinner or attending some civic function, their children were both killed.

When they came home to find this sorrow, they were cast into the worst kind of grief and despair. For a few days, the town rallied around them because, of course, it was a major disaster. At the funeral a bigger crowd gathered than the funeral chapel could accommodate. But as soon as the service was over, nobody came around to talk to them. Not a soul.

The people said to each other, "I don't know what to say to them. What do you say to people in a situation like that? How do you talk to them?"

Thus, not knowing what to say, they avoided them.

Whenever anyone crossed their path in the course of ordinary work, they avoided the subject of the children because they didn't know what to say. So, day by day, these two parents grew more and more isolated. Finally, the man, almost as a direct result of his grief, developed cancer, and he was dying, even though still in his youth.

A journalist who heard about the man's illness said, "Well, I don't know what to say, but I'm going to go out and see him. And I want him to try to express on tape what he feels."

He sat down beside the bed and asked the man a question: "No one knew what to say to you. We still don't know what to say. But could you tell us what you feel having gone through this terrible tragedy?"

The man on the bed started talking. And, according to the story, as I got it from this doctor, the tape in the recorder ran out, and the man kept on talking. He talked for eight hours without stopping. Then, the next day he got physically stronger. Soon the cancer went into remission. He got well.

The ministry of healing is listening first to the call of God:

I have chosen you before you were born. You do not understand it; you cannot explain it. But I am God, and I have called you. And I will put my words in your mouth. You shall not be afraid of their faces—their acceptance or their rejection—for I have called you.

And I am asking you to do for them what I do for you. To be a listening ear in the time of trouble. To be a shoulder to cry on in times of sorrow. I have asked you to be one who builds up, an encourager. And I will encourage you.

I cannot think of a higher or holier calling in all this world.

Many stories are told that are classics in the ministry. One that has deeply moved me across the years is an old story I am sure you have heard and probably told.

A missionary in China was struggling to make ends meet. It was not an easy place. Finances were so bad it seemed impossible for the missionary to stay on.

About that time, an executive of a major United States oil company visited him and said, "You have a good education and a great mind. You know the language. But you are not making it as a preacher. People are not responding to you. But I can offer you a job any time with our company. We will pay you $50,000 a year."

In that day $50,000 was like $250,000 now.

And the missionary said, "No, I cannot take it."

The oil executive said, "Would you do it for $75,000?"

He said, "No, I cannot take it."

"For $100,000, would you?"

He said, "No ... no ... no."

Finally the business man said, "How much do you want? What salary is enough for you?"

The missionary said, "Oh, my friend, the first figure you gave was far more than I ever expected to earn in my whole lifetime. Money is not the problem."

"What is the problem?"

"The money is fantastic. But ... the job isn't big enough."

Think about that. We are in a big work—you and I. And it is our prayer—Gerald's and mine—that the ideas we have shared in various preaching seminars and in this book have helped you realize that we not only have a big job, we have a big God—who has made big promises, who has big power, who has big plans. And God calls us to the task.

The job is big enough. And we can be equal to the task, if God has called us. God knows more than we know what is in us and what we are capable of doing in God's name.

Every time you preach with the anointing of God's Spirit, every time you witness with victory, every time you endure without any visible signs of victory, remember this: We are workers together with God, and in that we will rejoice!

Acknowledgements

Anderson Camp Meeting, 1954, was a red-letter event for one teenager from Drexel, North Carolina. Besides being my first trip to Anderson, Indiana, for the International Convention of the Church of God, it was also the first time I heard Maurice Berquist speak. It would not be the last. The entire Drexel delegation fell in love with "Berk"; and over the years he and his wife, Berny, visited Drexel many times and became close family friends.

But for me—like Gerald Marvel and so many others whose lives Berk touched—Maurice Berquist was more than friend. He was a surrogate brother, hero, model, teacher, spiritual guide, mentor, advocate. Berk profoundly influenced my spiritual development through the years.

Berk gave all of us confidence to stretch beyond our "comfort zones"—both intellectually and spiritually. He unlocked the mysteries of the Bible in ways that were fascinating and fun—the depth of his faith as infectious as his humor. He made us believe that with God's help we could do wondrous things—miraculous things!

But Berk's most significant gift to me was the realization that this astute teacher was still very much "the student." Through the years, it was both inspiring and challenging to know that this tremendous Bible scholar was himself still zealously probing, searching, questioning, stretching the boundaries of his own intellect and creativity—to better understand God. And the motive of that understanding was always to help people—to help them get a better grasp on the power and the promises of God for them.

It has been a privilege to finish this project Berk started before his last trek to India. Having previously edited several of his published works, I felt at home with his material. In fact, I could almost imagine his peering over my shoulder from time to time to chuckle and smile approvingly on the way a particular section was turning out.

A Handful of Stars is, for me, a way of extending Berk's ministry—his great love of preaching and his giftedness as a teacher—so that other generations may yet come under the influence of his great mind and heart.

Completing this book is also my way of saying, "Thank you, Berk, for honoring so faithfully God's call upon your life and for making a difference in our lives and in the church."

I am indebted to the following people whose interest in and support of the project made it such an enjoyable task:

Berny Berquist for her enthusiastic encouragement from start to finish, generously granting access to Berk's personal papers, books, tapes, and photographs.

Gerald and Rena Marvel for their warm approval of the project and their gracious assistance with information and photographs.

Forrest Robinson and Johnny Creasong for providing copies of the audiotapes of the preaching seminar Maurice Berquist and Gerald Marvel conducted at Mid-America Bible College in May of 1990, from which came much of the material used in the book.

Edna McCall, a retired executive secretary and my mother-in-law, for countless hours spent transcribing seminar and sermon tapes. Completing the project in the time allotted would have been impossible without her diligent assistance.

Helen Clarke, for transcribing the tape of the Memorial Service for Maurice Berquist celebrated on February 16, 1993, in Wichita, Kansas.

Dan Harman and the editorial staff of Warner Press for their encouragement and creative help in the publishing process.

My mother, Minnie Belle Cooper, and especially my husband, Don McCall, for their steadfast encouragement and patience during my many months of "hermithood" with cassette tapes and the computer.

You, the readers, who complete the creative cycle. May the ideas we have gleaned from Maurice Berquist and Gerald Marvel enable you to breathe new life into your congregations through the ministry of preaching.

By purchasing *A Handful of Stars* you have also made a contribution in Berk's name to support missions in Russia. Getting the gospel into Russia was a cause dear to Berk's heart, since he helped establish the radio ministry to Russia while serving as Secretary-Treasurer for the Mass Communications Board. Consequently, proceeds from this book will be shared by the Missionary Board and CBH radio ministries for Russian projects.

—Maxine McCall

Bibliography

Augsburger, David. *Caring Enough to Hear and Be Heard.* Ventura, Calif: Regal Books, 1982.

Bartlett, John. *Familiar Quotations.* Fourteenth edition. Boston: Little, Brown and Company, 1968.

Borden, Richard C. *Public Speaking as Listeners Like It!* New York: Harper and Brothers, 1935.

Bresee, W. Floyd. "Illustrations in Preaching," *Ministry,* September, 1984, 17–20, 30.

Brueggemann, Walter. *Finally Comes the Poet: Daring Speech for Proclamation.* Philadelphia: Fortress Press, 1989.

Buechner, Frederick. *Telling the Truth.* New York: Harper and Row, 1977.

Buzan, Tony. *Using Both Sides of Your Brain.* New York: E. P. Dutton, Inc, 1983.

Cousins, Norman. *Anatomy of an Illness as Perceived by the Patient: Reflections on Healing and Regeneration.* Scranton, Pa: W. W. Norton & Co, 1979.

Dallimore, Arnold. *Spurgeon.* Chicago: Moody Press, 1984.

Elwood, Maren. *Characters Make Your Story.* Cambridge: Riverside Press, 1942.

Fant, Clyde E. *Preaching for Today.* New York: Harper and Row, 1975.

Flesch, Rudolf. *The Art of Plain Talk.* New York: Harper and Brothers, 1946.

Freeman, Harold. *Variety in Biblical Preaching: Innovative Techniques and Fresh Ideas.* Word Publishers, 1987.

Hall, John. *God's Word through Preaching.* Grand Rapids: Baker Book House, 1979.

Keck, L. Robert. *The Spirit of Synergy: God's Power and You.* Third printing. Nashville: Abingdon, 1980.

Lorayne, Harry and Jerry Lucas. *The Memory Book.* New York: Hippocrene Books, 1989.

McCartney, Clarence E. *Preaching without Notes.* New York: Abingdon-Cokesbury Press, 1946.

McLuhan, Marshall. *Understanding Media.* New York: McGraw-Hill, 1964.

Samples, Bob. *The Metaphoric Mind: A Celebration of Creative Consciousness.* New York: Addison-Wesley Publishing Company, Inc, 1976.

Sandman, Peter M., David M. Rubin, and David B. Sachsman. *Media: An Introductory Analysis of American Mass Communications.* Englewood Cliffs, NJ: Prentice-Hall Inc, 1972.

Sheldon, Charles M. *In His Steps.* New York: Grossett & Dunlap, 1969.

Turnball, Ralph G. *A History of Preaching.* Grand Rapids: Baker Book House, 1974.

Von Oech, Roger. *A Whack on the Side of the Head: How to Unlock Your Mind for Innovation.* New York: Warner Books, Inc, 1983.